1981 MY GAY AMERICAN ROAD TRIP

"This book documents a remarkable journey through gay male life in the early 1980s, when the post-Stonewall fervor for building community institutions made it the heyday of gay bars, restaurants, sports associations (who knew Houston had 55 gay bowling teams in 1981?), strip clubs, and easy hookups, just before AIDS cast a shadow over everything. Doyle's journal is especially valuable because he takes us beyond the coasts to highlight the vibrant gay scenes in large cities and small towns across the South and West, including New Orleans, Houston, Dallas, Phoenix, Denver, Kansas City, and, yes, LA and San Francisco, too. From close encounters with Grace Jones and Diana Ross to even closer encounters with the men he met along the way, this book is full of insights and vivid sketches of people and places in those pre-AIDS days."

George Chauncey
DeWitt Clinton Professor of History, Columbia University
Gay New York: Gender, Urban Culture, and the Making of the Gay Male World, 1890-1940

"In *1981—My Gay American Road Trip*, JD Doyle offers a vision in the first-person of what life looked like for many men traversing the gay recesses of post-Stonewall, pre-AIDS America: free, joyous, and full of possibility, even amidst persistent stigma. Doyle's road trip journals and accompanying commentary represent an important firsthand account of a period in gay American history that is too often overlooked."

Eric Cervini, PhD
The Deviant's War: The Homosexual vs. the United States of America

---

"Through both words and images, this book offers a window into a lost era of gay cruise bars, restaurants, and bookstores—a time when a handsome young gay man with a mustache could travel across the country and find a cornucopia of gay guesthouses, shops, cultural events waiting for him in every city. And as 'new meat' in town, he often didn't even need to book a hotel room. It also gives insight into the equally lost world of local gay journalism. This was when scores of newspapers served local communities and were beginning to organize nationally. It reminded me of Alan Helms' *Young Man from the Provinces: A Gay Life Before Stonewall.*

David K Johnson
The Lavender Scare: The Cold War Persecution of Gays and Lesbians in the Federal Government and *Buying Gay*

"JD Doyle, producer of the radio show and website *Queer Music Heritage*, peoples' historian and archivist extraordinaire, presents the diary of his 1981 road trip, south, west, and north, age 34, across 24 states and 180 bars. The fabulous photos and valuable text document just before the year AIDS hit, creating a chasm between a modern liberatory era and a nightmare time. Recording visits with fellow liberationists, friends, and family, Doyle documents a moment in his and our history. Thanks, JD!"

Jonathan Ned Katz
The Daring Life and Dangerous Times of Eve Adams and *Gay American History*

"JD Doyle's road trip book is unique and valuable. His journal records his experiences as a sexually active gay man in the 1970s and early 1980s in many cities in the USA, including smaller ones. As a memoir, the writing is personal but it is also journalistic and reflects a way of being that ended with the arrival of AIDS and the Internet. Think of this as a fun-loving and adventuresome history book."

Allen Young
The Gay Report, Out of the Closets: Voices of Gay Liberation, and *Lavender Culture* (all co-authored with Karla Jay)

1981

MY
GAY AMERICAN
ROAD TRIP

A SLICE OF OUR PRE-AIDS CULTURE

JD DOYLE

A QMH Press book from New Texture

Copyright © 2023 JD Doyle; all rights reserved

Photographs and archival materials supplied by the JD Doyle Archives except where noted.

Edited by Jay Arora

Cover portrait by Scott Swoveland (detail)

Designed by Wyatt Doyle

NewTexture.com

 @NewTexture   @ThisIsNewTexture

 facebook.com/jd.doyle   @JDDoyleArchives

Booksellers: *1981—My Gay American Road Trip* is available through Ingram Book Company

ISBN 978-1-943444-41-0

First softcover edition: June 2023

Also available in hardcover

Printed in the United States of America

10 9 8 7 6 5 4 3 2 1

CONTENTS

Foreword *by Hugh Ryan* 7
My Introduction—Pre-Norfolk 11
Norfolk 23
Beginning the Trip 53
Atlanta 57
New Orleans 67
Baton Rouge 73
Houston 79
Houston…and there's a love story 99
Dallas 119
Albuquerque / Tucson / Phoenix / Las Vegas 143
San Diego 163
Los Angeles 173
San Francisco 189
San Francisco, Part 2 211
Salt Lake City / Denver 231
Omaha / Kansas City / Oklahoma City 243
Texas, Part 2 253
Memphis / Columbus 259
Hometown and Rochester 265
Philadelphia 271
Norfolk 283
Epilogue 289
Notes 305

Foreword *by Hugh Ryan*

I'VE ALWAYS loved the diaries of others, an early indicator of my passion for history, or perhaps just a symptom of my nosy nature. As a kid, I was fascinated by the idea that we might all perceive the world uniquely; that my "blue" and your "blue" could be entirely different colors; that we can never truly be certain what is happening in someone else's head – all those stupid/profound ideas that interest mostly toddlers, philosophers, and stoners. And, of course, historians, like myself and the incomparable chronicler whose history you are about to read: JD Doyle.

Me? I started collecting diaries in my mid-twenties. I found my first in a basement rummage sale in Ireland. It was the notebook of a schoolboy from the 1890s, filled with French grammar exercises, an essay on the Sino-Japanese war, and dozens of hand-drawn illustrations—a diagram of how to build a battery, a map of "Palestine in the year of our Lord," an anatomical heart. The thick, coarse paper had survived a century largely unscathed, but the thin, red leather binding flaked away like dandruff in my hands.

I was hooked.

Of course, I kept an eye out for queer diaries. Of course, I almost never found them. There was a boy from the 1920s who filled the pages of a skinny composition book with notes about his dandy outfits and the wild escapades of his chums, who once dared him to wear a half-dead flower in the buttonhole of his school uniform—*and he did!* Was that queer? Unknowable. But it was unusual behavior for the time, and it tripped my gaydar, that indefinable and unreliable spidey-sense. Most of the time, that's all I found of queer history in these journals—hints and possibilities.

A diary like the one you're about to read would have been my holy grail: undeniably queer, and focused on documenting the queer world. JD Doyle is a historian by nature, by which I mean an explorer of the unknown and a keeper of its records. His *Queer Music Heritage* site is an incredible resource, as I discovered while writing *When Brooklyn Was Queer*—when I needed an image of the famous Brooklyn drag star, Jean Malin, JD had preserved the only copy I could find. And unlike some who hoard our history like dragons on a treasure mound, JD has worked tirelessly to share what he has saved.

That impulse, to record and present the true history of LGBTQ people, is the spirit that animates *1981—My Gay American Road Trip*. In the pages of this book, JD glowingly records a wide swath of a world that is in danger of being forgotten today: the post-Stonewall, pre-AIDS gay male network of bars, newspapers, clubs (and the fabulous music *in* those clubs), cruising sites, conferences, bowling leagues, restaurants, shops, streets, and more. But this is no dry cataloguing. Instead, it is a felt journey through these spaces, and what they meant to one young gay man as he traveled across America exploring adult gay selfhood.

The year of JD's trip, 1981, is a bright dividing line slashed across our history, as the first diagnosed AIDS cases changed what it meant to be gay in America. JD reports to us from the edge of a precipice, giving us life, community, and even a love story, all in the invisible prodrome of devastation.

Today, you can find out, queer role models in places where they would have been unimaginable a few decades ago: leading

Foreword by Hugh Ryan

superhero movies, billionaire corporations, and Cabinet-level government departments. With so much gained, it is impossible for young people to understand what was lost, and what value it had. The separate spaces. The secret spaces. Spaces that did not *allow* or *embrace* gay people, but were instead made for us. Made by us. These are the places JD Doyle takes us on his journey.

Prepare to be initiated.

The Stonewall Uprising was 1969; the first named cases of AIDS were in 1981. Trapped between the closet and the casket, this ephemeral fairy bubble existed for twelve precious years. Now, thanks to JD, you can see it for yourself, through his eyes—the closest we may ever get to knowing what "blue" looks like to someone else.

Hugh Ryan is the author of When Brooklyn Was Queer *and* The Women's House of Detention.

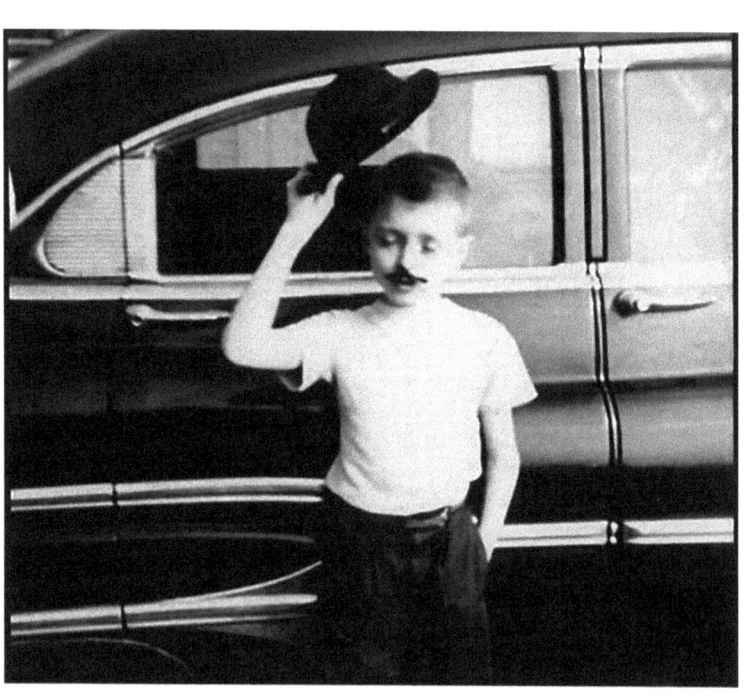

My Introduction—Pre-Norfolk

ACTOR Danny Kaye once said, "To travel is to take a journey into yourself." This was very much true, as I was getting way outside of the box of my experiences, both physical and emotional. The bulk of this book comes from a journal kept over an almost 5-month cross-country trip from April to August of 1981.

This was all about forty years ago, and it now takes on a different light. I am now an active gay historian, so I am very conscious of the place in history of what I wrote. I am a gay man commenting on a time of our culture just before AIDS hit us. This is a slice of that time, the last days of the "candy store." And I call it that because we were now a dozen years past Stonewall and more and more able to feel free to pursue being out of the closet politically and sexually. And then AIDS stopped us.

But I think I should give you a bit of my coming out story to set the stage. I want to start about twenty-eight years earlier.

I was born in 1947, and grew up in a rural area near the small town of Salem, Ohio and went to a country school. I didn't have neighborhood kids to play with, as there were just not any near enough, so my first years were a bit solitary. My dad had built the house at the edge of my grandfather's farm. I remember granddad had an outhouse, and our bathroom was indoors. It was very country, with corn fields and the like.

I remember a particular incident that seems a bit telling, with an innocent glimpse into my future. One day, when I was in the first grade, I asked my teacher, Mrs. Mountz, "Which eye do you use to wink at a girl, and which eye do you use to wink at a boy?" She must have thought that was the most adorable thing so, instead of answering, she said, "Well, I don't know, let's go ask the principal." So, off we went to his office. I still remember exactly where each of us stood as I repeated the question. This was rural Ohio, around 1953, so imagine all the possibilities. He looked at me for a moment, and then just said, "Use whichever eye feels natural."

Now, I'm not saying this necessarily meant I was a future queer, but that the memory was riveted into my memory all this time must mean something. Another memory also sticks out: I was in the sixth grade at Buckeye Elementary School in Salem, Ohio, a small town of 12,000. This was a conservative time in a conservative state. The year was 1959. Eisenhower was in his second term. The Edsel was still the attention-getting new car. On State Street (our Main Street), the two focal points were the Woolworth Five and Dime and the State Theatre, only three doors apart. A few blocks up on Lincoln Avenue was the junior high, and a number of blocks further, the relatively new high school, the only one in town. We were a pleasant dot in the country, 25 miles from the nearest city, Youngstown (where I would go to college).

It was a normal school day. I was at the end of a hallway near a classroom door. A bunch of the rougher boys were carousing around a few feet away and one of them called out, "You, queer!" Now, it wasn't directed at me, but it left a definite impression—I can still recall that scene in my mind all these decades later. I didn't think, at least at the time, that the boy's words had a "gay" connotation—but they could have, as I was quite naive. Regardless, his words stood out in my mind. I secretly knew I was in that group they despised, even if I didn't quite know what that meant.

As I said, this was a conservative time—I have no memory of hearing *faggot* or any of the other homo-associated terms during high school. It was outside of the consciousness of that place

My Introduction—Pre-Norfolk

As a young teen, in about the most butch photo I could find.

and time. That doesn't mean I skated through—I was still a misfit and was picked on. Being picked on seemed easier in those days though, at least in my schools. Of course, there were bullies, but kids (as far as I knew) weren't stuffed into lockers, didn't have their books knocked out of their hands, didn't get "swirlies" in the restroom toilets, etc. I endured, hung with the other eggheads, had many more friends who were girls than boys, and avoided sports at any cost.

Though I remember one time I could not avoid playing touch football in the yard behind the school. This was still grade school. The ball was dropped by someone on the other team and,

High school and college senior photos; no more Brylcreem.

by some fluke, I stopped it. I immediately threw it to the closest member of "my" team, one of the bullies named Jay. I remember his look of disgust because I did not know (or care) that the play was already automatically over. That also sticks in my memory.[1]

Here's one more early memory. I remembered it as I had recently read an article about repressed childhood memories, and it made me think of one. I was maybe five and my parents took me to the Canfield Fair. This was a decent annual small-town event in rural Canfield, Ohio, population 7000. So, this was about 1953.

I had wandered a little away from them, but they were still in sight, maybe 50 feet away. A man—maybe 20-25, a bit heavy—started talking with me and was telling me he wasn't sure where his car was parked, and did I want to help him look for it? I remember I wasn't scared, but he kind of creeped me out. I said no. Good decision. But why did this stick in my subconscious mind? Did it trigger some "gay" connotation my mind had not yet formed?

I was a nerdy and very introverted kid in high school. Being

My Introduction—Pre-Norfolk

President of the French Club was about my only extracurricular activity, and that was about ten girls and me. In the misogynist Sixties, they all felt a male should be President, so I won. I ran against a girl and we each voted for each other. In researching this book, I checked my high school yearbook and was shocked to find the French Club had about forty members. That must have been just on paper, as I surely do not remember more than about ten ever showing up for meetings. And, geez, I had forgotten I was also in the Slide Rule Club. Total nerd. (By the mid-1970s pocket calculators had made slide rules a memory.)

Also, in 1964, as a junior in high school, I bought my first Barbra Streisand recording, *The Third Album*. And very shortly after, the other three albums released by her by that year. This was many years before I had I the context to process what this might mean, but looking back, I think it meant I was gay. I also had teen idols, like Bobby Vee and especially Rick Nelson—though again, I had not formulated in my mind that these were really gay crushes.

I went to all the sports games, but just to be sociable, and hang out with my best friend Kenny and with the few friends I had. I did not give a damn about sports and still don't.

Queer was still a predominantly negative term. Homophobes did not care if there were "well-behaved" gays and lesbians—and forget the rest of the alphabet, that was way beyond them. We were sick, amoral, or criminal. We were all *queer*. Their hatred didn't differentiate.

I couldn't wait to graduate and escape with the rest of the class of '65. Still repressed about being gay, it took me a long time to process it all. After all, I was a shy boy in a time with no role models, way before the internet. I didn't know anyone who was gay. I would have many more years left in the closet.

Moving on, for college I chose a five-year curriculum in Chemical Engineering at nearby Youngstown State University, well known for its academic excellence. And I did well, though reflecting on it, the courses were hard enough that I had very little time for socializing, and no car to use to do any. I stayed at a dorm in the YMCA, where we all had single rooms. And, yes, there would later be the easy jokes about it being *fun to stay at the YMCA*.

I can remember hearing only one gay story from those years. I think I was in my last year (making it 1970) and there was a brief time when several rooms were rented to non-university students. These were guys none of us knew at all. Late one night my friend Glen, who had the room across from me, knocked loudly at my door, "JD, JD, wake up!" I answered the door in my white jockey shorts. Of course, that attire was quite common in a men's dorm.

Glen started to relate what had happened. Another friend, from quite a way down the hall, had just been propositioned by one of the transient guys. The guy had asked Paul if he wanted a blowjob. And Paul calmly just said no and that was about all there was to it. Of course, the story spread like wildfire. But as Glen was telling me about it, I started to get an erection, which in tight jockey shorts would be difficult to hide, so I quickly had to sit down. I don't know if he noticed, but again, it was an event etched in my mind.

Upon graduation I took an engineering job at Kodak, in Rochester, NY. That was kind of a depressed year for job offers, with almost everyone in my class (of about 25 Chem-Es) getting three offers. My other two were in Akron, Ohio and Midland, Michigan. Akron was much too close to home and Midland too isolated, so Kodak seemed like a good choice—and yet, I certainly had wished for a warmer climate.

It was a good job. This was before digital photography had drastically affected that industry, and I was in the Photo Chemicals division. We made the solutions used to process film and paper, generally a mixing and packaging operation rather than one of chemical reactions. I did well, bought a house in the suburbs after a year or so, and was all settled in. Of course, all my friends were straight, and were mostly from work. During all this time I like to say that I was "processing" being gay, and I was fairly naïve about it. I dated women very little, never had sex with a woman, and am still therefore a Gold Star Gay. (*Platinum* Gays are those who have never had sex with a woman *and* were born by cesarean section.)

Lake Ontario, Rochester; July 1970

In 1970, I unfortunately had to join the National Guard. The draft was still on and my number, 295, was the last one called. It was either the Guard or Viet Nam, and I knew I was allergic to rice paddies. So, I spent six long years putting up with military bullshit, with monthly meetings and two weeks in the summer at Camp Drum, in Watertown. I hated every second. I was assigned as the company armorer. Can you imagine me knowing how to assemble and disassemble an M-16 rifle?

I remember a couple vacation trips I took during the early 1970s, to Los Angeles and Provincetown. And I remember being aware of gay people I saw, such as the guys holding hands on the beach, etc. But I did not know what to do about those observances and was too afraid to venture any closer. Additionally, these were the years when there were no gay role models. The only people I could identify on TV as being gay were Liberace, Paul Lynde, and Truman Capote. I sure did not identify with them, which made my processing more difficult. Obviously, this was many decades before the internet, and, at times, being in the closet felt more like solitary confinement.

Again, from the closet, I remember my joking defense mechanism whenever anyone would ask if I was dating any women: I was saving myself for Linda Ronstadt.

Around the spring of 1976 I had gotten up the courage to buy a copy of *In Touch* magazine, and I knew I was buying *Blueboy* magazine in 1977. (I have since researched the magazines and recognized which issues I had bought from the covers.)

I got involved with a group very into record collecting. One did a volunteer oldies radio show at the local high school station (WGMC) in Greece, NY called the Friday Night of Gold. Many of us hung out during the broadcast and would go for pizza afterwards. That radio host, Ron Stein, and his wife Jackie became life-long friends (and will show up later in the book).

But by the mid-'70s I was fairly addicted to collecting records, a hobby that would serve me well for several decades. And that in a way sets up the story of my first time.

I was 29. While I knew I was gay, I didn't know any gay people, nor had I ever had a gay experience. My 30th birthday was only weeks away, and I had promised myself I would take care of this omission before I reached 30. I had planned a weekend trip to Toronto, half on the pretext of attending a record collectors' flea market. I enjoyed looking at old records and was an avid collector, but I also knew that attending this particular show would place me in the heart of a large and trendy city without worry that I might run into someone I knew. Looking back on it, the whole thing seems a lot more premeditated than I'm sure it did then, but I do think my actions were more than just a subconscious move to put myself in a position where something might happen.

I did the three-hour drive to Toronto on a Saturday afternoon, checked into my hotel, ate dinner, and then was ready to walk up and down Younge Street to look at all the interesting shops.

A few months earlier I had discovered *The Advocate* at a local newspaper stand. I had even got up the nerve to carry one or two copies up to the register and, feigning nonchalance, tried to convince the cashier that to buy a gay magazine was the most natural thing in the world. Of course, not a word was said by me or the cashier, who could not have cared less. At any rate, I wanted to see more gay literature (translation: pornography) which wasn't available at the stores near where I lived.

So I happened onto a magazine store just a few blocks from the hotel—it probably had some innocuous name, maybe just Magazines—and I went in. The shop was very clean and well-lit and certainly not a dive. I casually wandered over to the section that stocked *Blueboy*, *In Touch*, and *Mandate* magazines and started browsing. After a little while I noticed a nice-looking young man beside me, also looking at a magazine. He was also occasionally looking at me. Now, I had already figured out what eye contact was, and this was definitely it.

After a few minutes he put back the magazine and casually made his way toward the door, glancing back once or twice. Since I didn't need to be hit over the head with a brick, I also put back the magazine I had been pretending to read and casually (sort of) wandered to the door.

He was only a few feet down the street and had paused, waiting for me to catch up. I didn't until the words came out of my mouth have any idea what I was going to say to him. He said, "Hi," and I said, "Would you like some company?" He said he did, so off we walked to my hotel. I was pleased with myself that at least I had not used any of those famed clichés such as *"Do you know where such-and-such street is?"*

By the time we got to the hotel, we both had first names. His was Scott. In the hotel room I thought I had better tell (warn) him that I had never done this before. He seemed actually pleased. Later I learned that I too was a first for him, his first

American.

He was very gentle and considerate, and one thing very quickly led to another. I remember that the TV was on in the background, and this was the night of the Miss America Pageant, September 11, 1977. I thought it was somehow ironic that my first gay sexual experience would be in front of Miss America.

Scott stayed the whole night, and I knew that I was very fortunate that my first time was with someone who cared enough to make it a beautiful experience.[2]

So, I had achieved my mission of having sex with a man before my 30th birthday. People may think, geez, this was *old*, and I agree.

By 1978, I had two more sexual experiences. One was with a guy, David D., whose personal ad I found in *The Advocate*. He had his own issues dealing with being gay, which I understood only later may have involved some internalized homophobia. I know he had a group of gay friends (he had shown me photos), but he would not introduce me to them. I had gotten the feeling that he thought he was somehow protecting me. At this point I sure did not want any protection. I knew I needed more contact with more people, not for sex but social contacts. Sadly, that did not happen.

And I had one more or less random tricking contact. I was browsing in the record department of a JM Fields store. (This was a discount department store chain that went out of business in the late 1970s.) I was just looking at the record albums and not really paying attention when a nice-looking young guy came up to me and asked, "Do you know where the restrooms are?" I said I did not, and he replied, "Well, I do."

Whoa! That was a surprise, but I quickly rallied and told him I wasn't going to do anything in a restroom, and after a moment or so of conversation said we could go to my home. He followed me in his car, and I remember in the bedroom he stood next to the bed with his pants and underwear pushed down to his knees with a full erection, waiting. I told him he would need to get undressed. And I don't remember much more about it, except that we did not exchange names.

During 1978, I clearly remember meeting two gay guys visiting from Buffalo. They were shopping at my friend Ron's record store on Monroe Avenue called Play It Again, Sam. I hung out there almost every Saturday, and one day Ron called me and said I should get down there to meet these two guys, as they were avid record collectors and, like me, were fans of Girl Group music. I went and we all hit it off, so I invited them to my house to see my record room and collection, and after that I brought them back to where they were staying near Ron's store.

We decided to go with one of their friends to a nearby bar. By that time, we had shared enough that we all knew we were gay. This was one of my first chances to interact with other gay guys, the first time to meet with more than one at a time. And the bar they took me to was, of course, a gay bar: the Avenue Pub on Monroe Avenue, which is still in business. That bar has a nice neighborhood feel to it and though we were there in the afternoon, I liked it. Several years later I would revisit this bar during my cross-country trip.

Escape from Rochester

By mid-1978 I had worked for Kodak for eight years—a good job at a good company. I was respected as an engineer in my division and was doing well, and I thought Rochester was a nice city. However, I hated the climate, and the winter of 1977/78 had been among the most brutal on record.

Usually, if there are a few inches of snow on your driveway, you shovel it yourself. However, I had to call for a plow 14 times after the snow got to be 2-3 feet deep and I needed to get my car out to go to work. The idea of leaving your car parked outside of your warm garage at the end of the driveway so you can get out was ridiculous, so I needed to make a decision. I began looking for another job and contacted a headhunter agency. Ultimately, I accepted an offer from Virginia Chemicals, located in Portsmouth, across a river from Norfolk, and I moved there that September.

I want to make comment that this chapter, being named "Pre-Norfolk," marks a huge change in my life as if everything was either before or after coming out. I think it goes even further beyond that; I was not *myself* until I was out and interacting with other gay and lesbian people. Not being yourself impacts your social and emotional growth as a person, delaying it probably ten or fifteen years. I was not fully comfortable as a teen or college kid because I did not know how to act in the ways that society considered "normal." Those years where we were supposed to grow, we were hiding in the closet.

Endnotes

1   From my article published in *Spectrum*, July 23, 2020.

2   I wrote this story for *Our Own Community Press*, Norfolk, February 1980: https://houstonlgbthistory.org/jd-book-links.html

ONE

Norfolk

Coming Out Shifts Into High Gear

It was not consciously in my head that I would move to Norfolk and immediately come out, but that is exactly what happened. After having been there for a week, I called the Gay Hot Line sponsored by the gay and lesbian group that met at what would become known as "the church." That group was the Unitarian Universalist Gay Community (UUGC) and they did everything.[1]

Established in 1976, their activities grew to include operating the gay hotline, providing speakers for colleges and community forums, issuing a newspaper, and other general social/educational activities. The group also organized several conferences held at a local university. One, the 4th Tidewater Lesbian & Gay Conference (July 1980) featured about 50 workshops and eight keynote speakers, including Harry Hay, Mel Boozer, Lucia Valesca, Sylvia Witts-Vitale, Meryl Friedman, and Michael Collins. There was also a concert by Therese Edell. It was quite a sophisticated project, put together by a very talented group of people. The church gave them full autonomy, essentially leaving the group alone while very generously allotting space for meetings and a quite large room for newspaper production.

The person I reached on that brave first phone call was Dennis Buckland, and he gave me the specifics of their meetings, inviting me to stop by. Many have described their "first contact" as when they drove around the block a dozen times before finding the nerve to actually stop, at a meeting or bar. I only drove around the block once before I parked the car. The group consisted of both men and women, and I was amazed at how welcoming everyone was. I bonded with several of them quickly. Dennis would become a very close friend, and I remain in touch with others to this day.

Before I was in the group very long, I started volunteering to help with the newspaper, *Our Own Community Press*. This included typing up articles, writing them, doing hand lettering, the layout work, etc. Obviously, this was pre-computer and word processing. There were no publishing programs available, and no spell-check. Articles had to be typed by hand in the exact column width desired for the final layout. Headlines were done by hand, one letter at a time, using a product called Chartpak Letters, still sold today. This is a method of transferring lettering onto paper by rubbing the letter from the sheet, in the desired font and size. Very tedious work!

While newspaper work was new to me, I soon discovered I had an aptitude for doing the layout, and it wasn't long before I was in charge of that. In a volunteer group like that, if someone wants to do something and can do it, they generally are gladly given that role. As in most volunteer groups, most of the labor was done by a small group of people. There was a dedicated core who managed the writing, editing, typing, layout, distribution, advertising soliciting, photography, etc.

Coming Out to Parents

Shortly after having come out in Norfolk, I was comfortable enough with myself to come out to my family in Ohio. As we were over 400 miles apart and they certainly would not be dropping in on me, there was no real necessity to do so. But nevertheless, it felt important to me. As I rarely went home to visit I did so by writing a letter. After they got it, they called me on the phone right away. They both were on the line and said they

Our Own staff (clockwise from left) Jim Early, Susan Strattner, Lynn Johnson, Fred Osgood, JD, and Robin Wagner.

loved me, and my being gay made no difference to them. After that, Dad would <u>never</u> bring it up in conversation, though Mom would. She would call me up to make inquiries such as, "Did you hear that Rock Hudson had AIDS?" In 2006 they met my partner Jeff when we came to visit, and that went well; he totally charmed them.

While it "made no difference" to them…they requested "just don't tell the relatives." Mom was born in Belgium, so those relatives were not really in contact, but Dad had five brothers, all married, so there were lots of cousins. My parents and I always got along, and why not? I was a model child. But actually, there was no reason to tell the relatives; my life was somewhere else. So I followed their wishes and I never did. I guess both parents told my brother, Mike. He is ten years younger, and accordingly we were never really close in those years.

When I moved away to Rochester, my little brother was 13, so

JD, Dad, Mom, Mike; around 1988

was not much a part of my life. These days he loves to get links to articles about me. And tells me about bragging about whatever awards I get, so that's nice. And as for the cousins, and their kids? Mostly I've never met their kids, and cannot keep their names straight. Hey, I moved away 51 years ago. And now many are on Facebook, and I have an easily found (very gay) presence there.

Back to my involvement with the newspaper. (I want to detail this part of Norfolk gay life, as it has never really been captured, and the historian in me says I need to do this.) I had already been volunteering for the newspaper for almost a year. In the late summer of 1979, Editor Jim Early announced that he intended to step down, having filled that role for several years. There were few people qualified to step into his shoes, and even fewer who wanted to. So, although I was already spending about 20 hours a month doing the layout (volunteers did all the work), I reluctantly agreed to be the Editor. This was one of the best decisions of my life, as my involvement with *Our Own* was one of the proudest accomplishments of my life. I guess you could tell this by my writing so much about it.

Norfolk

My first issue as Editor was the October 1979 issue, which provided coverage of the first March on Washington for Lesbian & Gay Rights.[2] With Norfolk being only a three-hour drive from DC, many of our members were attending, probably 30-40. I was also one of the people covering the event for the paper, keeping notes on different parts of the weekend, and taking lots of photos. (Which I still have, gathered in a scrapbook and shown on my website.)

For the edition of the paper after the March, we filled a full page with a collage of photos from it, and I included a photo of myself in the collage.[3] This was a conscious step in my coming out process. No one was identified in the photos, and it was unlikely anyone at work would ever see it. But this was overcoming the fear or hesitation to have my photo in a public newspaper.

It was another step in owning my identity.

The coverage of the March on Washington was certainly one of the highlights of my term as Editor, which lasted less than a year. Another occurrence that stands out was a small controversy involving one of the bar owners.

Our newspaper was distributed in all the gay bars in the city, which is where the vast majority of people would obtain the paper each month. We were running in the November 1979 issue a small story about local policemen threatening to enforce the State's ABC liquor laws. Those laws included the authority to suspend the license of any establishment that had been determined to be a meeting place for homosexuals (along with a laundry list of other unsavory groups). The law was seldom enforced, but the police were flexing their muscle and had the ABC laws on their side.

Businessman Dick LeDonne owned two of the more popular bars, including the Oar House. Although, ironically, he was the one who gave us the story to begin with, he had changed his mind. He now felt that reporting on police harassment would be bad publicity. He came close to threatening that if we covered that story, he would not allow us to place the paper in his bars for distribution. I'm pleased that instead of caving to that veiled demand, I instead wrote a half-page editorial, detailing for the whole community to read, the issues and his intent to stifle our coverage. The result was that distribution continued uninterrupted.[4]

Separatism Issues

Another issue I dealt with during my time as Editor was separatism, which was present in our community (and across the country) in the late '70s. This is something very seldom heard about today. There were many lesbians who would have nothing to do with gay men, in any context. When you considered some of our group's projects, both local and national, this would sometimes bring its own difficulties in trying to accommodate various viewpoints.

For example, it was common then for separatists to use spell-

Rally ahead of the March on Washington, 1979
(Photo by Larry Butler)

ings like *womyn*, *womon*, and *womin* to avoid a male connection, and to make a statement. One way we handled this was to dedicate the two center pages (that would fold out together) as "Lesbians, Front & Center." These pages were produced solely by women. I like to think that I personally dealt with the various challenges quite well, and I credit this background to being a strong influence on my later activism work.

Another of the paper's projects during my time there was an employer survey regarding job protection and workplace discrimination policies. It was sent to probably more than 50 of the local employers, and the paper reported the results. This was in terms of course as to which companies had any policies at all, and which did not even respond. Remember that this was early 1980. I do not remember if it was my idea, but I was listed as project coordinator, so probably. Workplace protection for gays and lesbians was hardly being discussed at all. So even though the number of responses we received was a low percentage of those sent out, I would like to think that for even those who did not reply it was a lesson in awareness of issues they should consider.[5]

The presence of discrimination was ever important in our daily lives. So, in each monthly issue of the newspaper, there was a section, usually on the second page near the masthead giving the names of who helped with that issue. In those days of no job protection, very few people agreed to having their full name listed, including me. So, you might see a statement like: *This issue was put together with the help of Dennis, Fred, Jayr, Carol, Susan, Del, Donna, Doug, Janelle, Steve, Garland, Jim, Scott, JD, Carl, etc.* ... First names only. My name, first name only, initially appeared in the November 1978 issue.

Another event the paper covered was the showing of the movie *Cruising*. This was a very controversial movie. At the time there had not been very many mainstream movies dealing with gay people, and this one depicted a *homicidal* gay character. Movies up to that time did not have any balance in the way gays and lesbians were shown, and happy and well-adjusted characters were not present at all. The characters were all sick or criminal or both. So this movie was picketed in many cities, and our group was among those doing the picketing in Norfolk. This was naturally a cover story for *Our Own*, with my article on it.[6]

The BIG Controversy

Okay, it's time to mention the BIG controversy that occurred when I was Editor, and in fact started in the very last issue I headed, March of 1980. I included in that issue about a half page of cartoons, that had appeared in the *National Lampoon*, which were concerning gay people, and I titled that section as follows: "How Our 'Friends' at the *National Lampoon* See Us." I distinctly remember doing the layout and asking the other person who happened to be present, Fred, his opinion if he thought the cartoons were offensive, or words to that effect. Fred was a longtime member of the group, and, I believe, a founding member. My reason for printing them was not for humor, but to in a way report how another publication viewed gay people. He said he didn't think so. Little did we know.

Among the distribution points for the newspaper were the library branches of the City of Virginia Beach, neighboring Norfolk. Someone saw a copy of that issue there and complained to the Library Board. The Board decided that the paper be removed from the Library system. The ACLU believed this to be a freedom of speech or a censorship issue, and on our behalf a lawsuit was issued.

This became big news in a big hurry, and there were town council meetings called, and finally a city referendum and it made headlines in the local city paper (*The Virginian Pilot*) and soon in many mainstream newspapers across the country. Various aspects of the controversy were featured on television on the news on several occasions. All of this lasted for almost a year. Oh yeah, the particular cartoon that caused the furor showed in two panels a small boy who in the first panel was sucking his thumb. In the second panel he had pulled his hand out of his mouth, and the end of his thumb looked like a penis.[7]

I can remember a few months later helping with the layout. We did a whole page collage of the headlines from various city and gay newspapers concerning the lawsuit. This was a big ongoing story. I believe the issue was finally resolved with the suit being dropped, and the policy established for a reference copy of *Our Own* being available at the libraries only by requesting them at a desk.

The big victory of all of this was the tremendous amount of publicity it generated, and that it made many people in the Tidewater area, gay and straight, aware that we existed. As the saying goes, we could not have bought this kind of publicity. So, in a way, my biggest single contribution to the gay movement then was running in the newspaper a cartoon of a little boy sucking his thumb.

The End of My Term

I mentioned earlier that in many volunteer groups, it ended up with very few people doing all of the work. This was the situation here as well. Despite pleas at our weekly gatherings for help (writing, typing, etc.) very little materialized. I was working about 80 hours a month on the newspaper, doing probably 90% of the work, in addition to my regular job and attempts at a social life. I burnt out. I could no longer carry that load. I felt the only way to re-energize our group would be for me to resign dramatically. I prepared a statement to be read by my friend Del at a regular Friday night meeting, at which I would not attend.[8]

My approach worked, at least for that time, as it panicked the group into realizing they needed to take drastic actions to re-group the way the work was done. I recall that three people were selected to be the new Editors. I was not resentful or concerned about the conception that the group had abused me by in effect forcing me to do that much work. And I loved the paper and was dedicated to it, but I needed a break. I was only Editor for six months, and in my memory, it sure seemed like much longer. That is likely because I was already volunteering heavily for almost a year prior to stepping up to be Editor.

I stayed away for I think two or three months and then came back and very guardedly agreed to give assistance. For example, in July of 1980 the group held the 4th Tidewater Lesbian & Gay Conference, and I took on the project of doing the layout for the conference program (12 newspaper-size pages). And though this was unofficial, I hosted a fundraiser at my townhouse to help raise money for that conference. Well, we could surely not have a showing of *The Other Side of Aspen*[9] at the church! Seems like about 15 attended.

I continued this arms-length relationship with the newspaper until the next spring, at which time when I left for my cross-country trip.

One thing I credit to working on *Our Own* is my sense of community. An Editor has the responsibility to cover the entire gay & lesbian community. Again this was way too early for the BT of LGBT to be part of the equation. Without patting myself on the back (okay, maybe a little) I have been told a number of times that my approach to my websites, and maybe in particular my *Queer Music Heritage* programming was very inclusive. This was not in just covering many musical genres. I worked especially hard honoring Women's Music and that by Transgender artists. I was having fun and was not even thinking of it being any extra effort.

I hope providing this much depth into my involvement with *Our Own Community Press* will explain not only my ability to use my experience as entrée into various newspaper offices across the country but also my avid interest in doing so.

Poetry

Oh, yeah, during my year of working on the newspaper I wrote some very amateur poetry, which the paper graciously published, mostly dealing with coming out and my new relationships. I am including these to show another side of my personality.

Here are three…

a familiar refrain

you were there again
last night, I saw you
but then,
I've seen you many times before,
there, or at one of the other bars,
yes, I noticed you long ago,
leaning up against the rail,
or dancing,
with one of your circle of friends
(other unattainables),
I even know your name,
but I don't speak,

nor, of course do you,
and so it goes,
the scene replayed once more

the light from the hall

the light from the hall
sneaks through the
half open door
not noticing
just you and I
standing
in the shadows
near the dresser

and you unbutton
my shirt
and I yours
so slowly
as we touch
and enfold
the night

the presence

it was, I suppose
a perfect evening—
with dinner
at your apartment
and wine
and the stereo—
and one thing,
as expected,
led to another,
and it was
very good,
although at times
a little crowded—
with you, and me
and your lover,
who was out of town

My Life in Norfolk, Other Than the Newspaper

And I was soaking up gay culture, learning about gay books and devouring them. This was a time of an explosion of books by gay and lesbian authors into the new world of bookstores devoted to sell them.

Before a gay market could emerge, distribution channels had to open. In the 1950s and 1960s there were challenges. Obscenity laws created great barriers, and it wasn't until 1967 (via a court case) that it was even possible to send an openly gay magazine through the mail. This victory also meant that companies could send out catalogs advertising gay books. This was important, as traditional bookstores would not be selling books for the gay market. One of the first gay bookstores was the Oscar Wilde Memorial Bookshop, founded in NYC by Craig Rodwell in 1967.

It took several years for the market to appear, and in the late 1970s the books themselves showed up. For a lot of LGBT people this was the first time the literature was even available. Like my friends, I had spent my life not being able to read about my gay world, to learn my culture's history. I felt like I had to read everything I could, in all categories. I could not get enough.[10]

Gay Art

During my time in Norfolk I also became more aware of gay art, in that one of the members of the UUGC group was Jack Whitlow. Jack was quite talented in the area of erotic pencil and charcoal drawings. We became friends and over time I collected about a dozen of his drawings, one even of me. (No, I'm not going to share it.) But I enjoyed posing for his photographs several times. I always visited him when on vacation back to Norfolk. He died in 2015. I have set up a gallery of his work on one of my websites.[11]

NYC Trip

In 1980 I took a short trip to NYC to visit Michael Collins, whom I had met the previous July at the Tidewater Lesbian & Gay Conference during which he was a keynote speaker. Michael was coordinator of Affirmation: United Methodists for Lesbian & Gay Concerns. We had hit it off and I visited him and his roommate Tim Gay, who lived in Greenwich Village. It was interesting staying in December in a quite cold apartment (with their cats who would not leave you alone). It happened that during my stay John Lennon was murdered, and we talked about joining the many thousands who were gathering for the observances. Due to the sheer volume of people participating, that would have meant probably walking thirty-some blocks in below freezing temperatures, so we stayed home.

Norfolk Bars

I am going to include a bit of history here, as I think it is worth capturing.

During my three years in Norfolk (September 1978 to September 1981) I visited just about all the bars. Of the six men's bars, my favorite by far was the Nickelodeon, 118 W City Hall Avenue, and it was only open for the first year that I lived there. It was owned by Steve Brown, who was a member of the UUGC, and very supportive of the group. His was the first business to advertise in the fledgling newspaper (*Our Own Community Press*), in November 1977, when they began having paid ads. Steve was a faithful advertiser, often with full page ads. On nights that the UUGC met, Tuesdays, many of us would go directly from the meeting to the "Nickel" to socialize, with their ten cent beers.

For a dash of history for that club, Steve's family had owned the previous business in that location, a bar/restaurant named the Tuxedo Lounge. By at least 1977 it was the Nickelodeon, and as I generally went with a gang of friends. I always loved it. The city was doing urban renewal and had designated that block for total demolition, which they fought for a while, but that could not be avoided.

After it closed, I wrote an article for *Our Own* entitled, "If This Is Tuesday, I Must Be At the Nickel," which is how many of us felt. Steve's bar, as I wrote, "always represented the right blend for a bar—somewhere between cruising and socializing, with more emphasis on the latter, but enough of the former." The bar had been one of Norfolk's oldest gay bars. Only the Cue and the Continental had been open longer. And its closing was preceded by the urban renewal closings of two other downtown bars, Mickey's and The Ritz.

Like many old city bars, it was long, narrow, and definitely not fancy. I am fortunate to have the photo of it included here. I fondly remember the t-shirts and wooden nickel tokens that were passed out. There was a long-running ad for the bar with a drawing of a young man leaning against an old jukebox. I somehow conned Steve into posing like the guy in the drawing, so we could superimpose him into his ad. He was a good sport about it.[12]

The closing party was a two-night affair, and I know I went for the last night (probably both), and after 2 AM the doors were locked, and you could not re-enter. It got fairly wild. I mostly remember standing up in a booth with my friend Donna, just watching the...shenanigans. I believe people were having sex in

the back area, but I did not go back to verify.

While I loved this bar the most (probably because it was more of a social outlet for me) I only took home three guys from there. One of them though, Wayne A., was one of the best-looking men with whom I've spent the night in my life (well, for my tastes). And it was one of those experiences where you want to stop him during sex and ask, "Wait! how are you doing that!"

I mentioned that Mickey's and (next door) The Ritz on Brooke Avenue downtown had either already closed by the time I got there, or I just didn't hear about them enough to go. They were owned by Tony Pritchard. He next opened Norfolk's first gay disco, The Cue, on 46th & Killam Streets. That bar got some attention by hosting the *Blueboy* Man of the Year Norfolk Regional Contest in August 1980, and in June that year I wrote a favorable article about their Sunday buffet dinners, a terrific value. In some of their ads they billed themselves as a "show bar," meaning drag shows. I do not really remember the bar and my notes indicate I only met one trick there.

Tony Pritchard's other main bar, also a disco, was The Late Show (111 11th St). It was a large club with a very large dance floor, and I remember it well. With later hours, it was technically

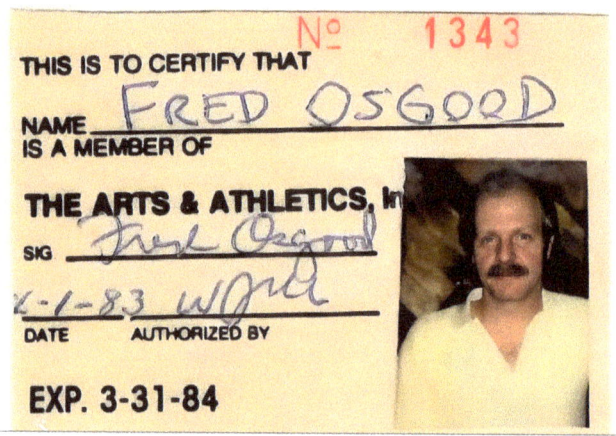

As a private club, The Late Show did not advertise, but here's a membership card. **(Courtesy Fred Osgood)**

a private club and there were photo membership cards, which got you out of waiting in line at the door. I must have gone there often, as I met 12 guys there (not on the same night, of course). As a private club, it was likely later in the evening and people may have been more ready to pick a partner for the night.

One memory of The Late Show I have is from October 1979. I was there talking with a group of friends, and in the background, I could hear the opening of the then-new "No More Tears (Enough Is Enough)" by Barbra Streisand and Donna Summer. It has a long, slow intro that lasts about a minute 45 seconds, and I could just, under the song that was already playing, hear the DJ layering it in. I looked at my friend across from me, and could tell he heard it too, and *(poof!)* we dashed for the dance floor, without a word to each other or our friends.

In November 1978, Pritchard opened The Paddock on 125 W Plume Street, downtown, not far from the Nickelodeon, which was still open for another year. This was a leather/Western bar, and the ads billed it that way. It had been a restaurant and had a good corner location, and the minimal décor worked well as

Norfolk

that style of bar. It wasn't really my cup of tea as I only met two guys there.

One was Sammy Williams, from the touring company of *A Chorus Line*. He had won a Featured Actor Tony Award for his work in the Broadway run. I recognized him and requested an

The Paddock

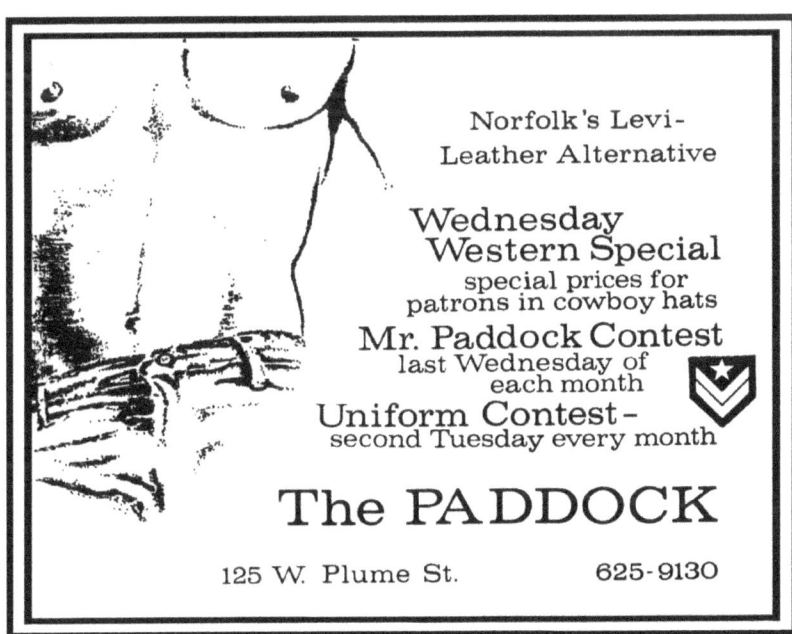

Norfolk's Levi-Leather Alternative

Wednesday Western Special
special prices for patrons in cowboy hats

Mr. Paddock Contest
last Wednesday of each month

Uniform Contest –
second Tuesday every month

The PADDOCK

125 W. Plume St.   625-9130

interview, which we recorded a day or so later. In the interview he went into fascinating detail regarding the play and actors and the motivations of his character, and aspects of his own life that contributed to what he brought to the role. It ended up being a two-page interview, complete with the photos I took of him, and was a piece of journalism that was among my best. The interview was in his hotel room and afterward we, er, played around a bit.[13]

A club that had a rocky existence regarding the gay community was The Nutcracker, a disco at 846 E. Little Creek Road, so quite a distance from all of the other bars. Owned by Mark & Loretta Gross, they were only open from September 1978 to August 1979. I think the community was never clear on whether or not they really wanted gay customers. I rarely went there, and never met anyone at that club.

Another club where I wasn't even looking for action was Shirley's, a women's restaurant and bar. It opened in November 1978, and I remember lots of good breakfasts there.

The last bar for this section was one of the best, the Oar House, at 4107 Colley Avenue, and fairly close to The Cue. It opened in January 1979, and according to the ads for the first six months, the hosts were "Steve Brown, Dick LeDonne, and Bob Summers." I do not know the backstory, but Steve was apparently forced out, leaving ownership to the other two. At any rate, it was a good looking bar, really a restaurant/disco, nicely done with lots of paneling, and decent lighting. It was much more brightly lit than the other clubs, perhaps as it was also a restaurant. I am not sure how late they served meals and of course later at night it was all disco. I remember dancing there quite a bit, and…gosh…I picked up 23 tricks during my time in Norfolk.

And of course, I have music memories of that club: Dan Hartman's "Relight My Fire," Bonnie Pointer's "Heaven Must Have Sent You" and "I Can't Help Myself," T-Connection's "At Midnight," which mixed very nicely into "The Boss," by Diana Ross, and I adored a couple by Viola Wills, "If You Could Read My Mind" and "Gonna Get Along Without You Now."

Naturally, like most of the other dance bars there were drag

shows at the Oar House. I know our local version of Diana Ross performed there. She now goes by Diana *Rhoss*, and *Our Own* did a large cover photo and interview with her.[14] I helped arrange the photo shoot and group coordinator Jayr Ellis did the interview. I remember her arriving the afternoon of the shoot, looking stunning.

Those were most of the bars available. I had been to almost all, except for Mickey's, and The Continental, which were downtown and not really where I wanted to go. And there was one private club, The Ghent Society, which I gather was fairly exclusive. I think the membership fee was $40 (about $130 in today's dollars). I never was very curious about it.[15]

Okay, after telling you how many tricks I met in these different bars I will add that I met 16 guys whom I went home with at the UUGC meetings. Eight of those were in my first six months there. I was the new face in town for a little while. I guess I should mention, as the historian that I already was back then, the way I am remembering the precise numbers is that I kept a list of all my encounters.

My Coming Out Song

However uneven our experiences were with The Nutcracker, I can credit it with an important memory. A while back I was asked if I had a coming out song. This is the song I thought of, and it involved socializing with my new friends. They took me to The Nutcracker. This would have been late in 1978. I remember exactly where we were sitting when my friend Bob Halcums asked me to dance. He knew I was still tentative about my coming out process and wasn't sure I was ready to dance my first dance with a man. But when I recognized the song, I knew it was time…to dance to Linda Clifford's "If My Friends Could See Me Now."

The First Time I Heard Gay Music

My social life in Norfolk was definitely centered on the newspaper and the bars, but I want to relate an important non-newspaper event orchestrated by the UUGC that happened in September 1979. It was indeed important to me.

A concert was held to benefit the hotline, and the group brought down from Philadelphia very-gay singer/songwriter Tom Wilson (he later went by Tom Wilson Weinberg). Our unofficial

John Whyte and Tom Wilson Weinberg
(Photo by Bill Davis)

organizational leader, Jayr Ellis, thought it would be a great idea to get local gay businesspeople involved, so he persuaded a furniture store owner to house Tom and his partner John Whyte while they were in Norfolk for the concert. At the very last minute the furniture guy backed out, and Jayr asked if I could put them up. I had ample room in my townhouse, so I picked them up at the airport. I was very honored to do so.

That evening was their concert, at the UU hall, and I loved it. Tom sang material mostly from his album, *Gay Name Game*, and the material was very gay indeed. Here's where the title of this section comes in. LGBT people today may not understand but remember this was 1979.

Until Tom's concert, I HAD NEVER HEARD MUSIC THAT SPOKE TO ME. I mean, this was early in our history's music, and I had only been out of the closet for a year. You could not hear lyrically gay music on the radio (as if you can even do that often today). This was music for which I did not have to switch the pronouns in my head to make them seem real.

This was *our* music. This concert may have launched my love of our music and, in a way, my future radio show, *Queer Music Heritage*. I interviewed Tom more than once during my 15-year run of the show, and we have stayed in contact all these years. On the previous page is a photo of Tom and his partner John, while they performed a spoken-word piece, "1:00 AM," from the album *Gay Name Game*.[16]

And, regarding my QMH show, one of my driving forces was to showcase the music of LGBT artists never heard on regular radio, whether by a new artist or a pioneer. It was always important for me to play lyrically gay music. If an artist sent me a CD that contained one lyrically gay song, well that was very likely the one I would pick to play. Our voices needed to be heard, not just by others but also by ourselves.

Music

I have gone into some explanation of how very important music and collecting records has been to me. So, as we get close to the trip portion of this book, I will say that in the different cities and bars I visited I could not help but comment on songs I heard. This was not only in gay bars (disco music) but also driving across country in my car, with country music being the most available. These were the songs that made an impression on me. They are therefore a musical slice of this time as well.

I have prepared a sort of playlist of this music, which can be found in the **Notes** section.

And I will say that I proclaimed the song "Remember Me / Ain't No Mountain High Enough" by Boys Town Gang as my song of the trip.

Ready for the Trip

Before I begin the actual journal, I will give a bit of a preface. Who Am I? I am, at age 75, a retired government worker, and for more than twenty years my passion has been gay history.

In April 1981 I was living in Norfolk, Virginia, where I had been working for a chemical company as an engineer. The company was having bad times and laid off about a third of the employees, including me. I had sold my townhouse, put my furniture in storage, and was renting a room from some friends. I had two things you seldom have in life: time and money.

So, when my dad (in Ohio) suggested I take a cross-country trip, it seemed like a great idea. He also suggested I keep a journal—smart man. Looking back on it, this was actually a pretty remarkable idea to come from him, as I can never remember him ever reading a book. He was a blue-collar worker, and his job consisted of assembling pumps. He was also a local union president for about twelve years, so I may have gotten some of my progressive ideas from him.

He met my mother during World War II, in Belgium. My family was always, always solidly behind the Democratic Party. When I was in college, I can remember him telling me that, as an engineer, I would probably end up being a Republican, because I would be making good money. Ha! He didn't figure on the much more powerful influence of being gay.

The following journal entries are my observations as I traveled through the south and west in a route that included stopping in about twenty-four states, visiting many gay bars (about 180) and businesses and newspaper offices. My work at *Our Own Community Press* had given me contacts and entrée to gay newspapers all over, and I took advantage of that to get a quick feel of a city.

Remember, this was 1981, and I had come out in 1978. So, I had already been able to experience three years of candy store, and I was familiar with picking up guys. But if you are expecting explicit sex scenes, this is not that book. It was never my style, and is not now, to go into detail about sexual experiences. You will not find any who-did-what-to-whom.

After writing such a lengthy introduction in these initial chapters, is this a memoir, or is it a travelogue? I think it is both. I was doing the trip solo, and making it work on my own.

My route was in a way like the outline of a butterfly. Norfolk to Raleigh, Atlanta, New Orleans, Baton Rouge, Houston, Dallas,

Albuquerque, Tucson, Phoenix, San Diego, Los Angeles, San Francisco, Salt Lake City, and Denver. From Denver I headed back south to Kansas City, and Houston again (you'll see why). From there I decided I wanted to do some visiting with folks I knew in the north, that included Ohio (family visit), Rochester, NY, Philadelphia, and finally back to Norfolk in mid-August, a four-and-a-half-month trip. Norfolk was my main reference point in my gay life up to that point.

I did have a few goals for the trip and some benchmarks. I planned to cover the events for the newspaper and send articles back. For example, in 1979 I had attended the 4th Southeastern Conference of Lesbians and Gay Men, in Chapel Hill, NC. During the time of my trip was the 6th Conference, in Baton Rouge, and I had registered to attend that.

In May, in Dallas was the second conference of the then-forming Gay Press Association. This was an early organizational event, and I definitely wanted to network with publishers and editors from all over the country, a rare opportunity for a gay publications nerd like myself. For Pride Month, well, of course that was devoted to San Francisco. How could I not make that my pilgrimage? The rest I made up as I went along, and let my networking uncover other opportunities. And, of course, there were changes in my originally planned route, but I allowed for flexibility.

I kept this journal because I wanted to capture my experiences during the trip, as I knew they would be of a nature I had not previously experienced. I did not write it with any expectation of it ever being read by really anyone, and had not re-read it myself in decades. This brought up areas I had not remembered in years, and even developments in my personality. So the thoughts are very personal and reflective, with dashes of self-therapy at times regarding things I was working through.

I am pretty sure I had by that time read *States of Desire* by Edmund White, a wonderful book, and a natural comparison to this journal, though written several years earlier. But of course, I was not trying to emulate any book, just keeping my own

Ready to see gay America... This guidebook helped me with my trip.

thoughts and observations.

Yes, this was all about forty years ago, and it now takes on a different light. I am very conscious of the place in history of what I wrote. I am commenting on a time of our culture just before AIDS hit us. This is a slice of that time.

Of course the grammar and punctuation have been cleaned up. Regarding content, I have not gone back and censored really anything, other than omitting the last names of those young men I met and got to know intimately. Some are still alive, some I know have passed, and many I would have no way of knowing their fate.

This is the trip I took.

Some images in this chapter courtesy Sargeant Memorial Collection, Norfolk Public Library.

Endnotes

1   In those days, political correctness did not dictate the alphabet letters GLBT to cover all bases…the word *gay* was sufficient.

2   *Our Own* issue with coverage of the March, Nov 1979: https://houstonlgbthistory.org/jd-book-links.html

3   My photos of the March at my history site, http://www.queermusicheritage.com/march79.html

4	*Our Own*, December 1979: https://houstonlgbthistory.org/jd-book-links.html

5	"Local Industry Survey on Discrimination Announced," *Our Own*, December 1979: https://houstonlgbthistory.org/jd-book-links.html

6	*Our Own*, March 1980: https://houstonlgbthistory.org/jd-book-links.html

7	See the cartoons in that issue, March 1980: https://houstonlgbthistory.org/jd-book-links.html

8	See **Notes** section for the resignation letter I wrote.

9	*The Other Side of Aspen* was a very popular gay porn film from 1978 from Falcon Studios, starring Casey Donovan, Al Parker, and Dick Fisk.

10	Some of the books coming on the market in those years are listed in the **Notes** section.

11	http://www.texasobituaryproject.org/122115whitlow.html

12	Read my article and see the doctored ad from *Our Own*, September 1979: https://houstonlgbthistory.org/jd-book-links.html

13	 Link to Sammy Williams article: https://houstonlgbthistory.org/jd-book-links.html

14	Diana R(h)oss interview (with great photo on the cover), *Our Own*, April 1981: https://houstonlgbthistory.org/jd-book-links.html

15	See a photo feature of the city's gay & lesbian bars in the February 1979 issue of *Our Own*: https://houstonlgbthistory.org/jd-book-links.html

16	https://www.queermusicheritage.com/apr2001tww.html

TWO

Beginning the Trip

Wednesday—April 1, 1981

Hello Journal,

    I am not really sure who this is addressed to, so "Journal" will have to do for now. Well, I have started the first leg of my trip—a short leg—three and a half hours to Raleigh. The weather was gorgeous, and the traveling was smooth. I got to the home of Jim Baxter and partner John at about 3 PM, as it was Jim's day off. He is ad production manager for *The Spectator*, a free, local straight newspaper that has an entertainment slant to it. He is also founder and editor of *The Front Page*, a gay newspaper. We talked shop (which we can do for hours) until his lover John (a lawyer) got home from work. I had met Jim at the 1979 March on Washington and we connected through our gay newspaper interests. During that March weekend the Washington Blade offered a tour of their offices and we both jumped at that chance, and we had kept in touch.

    We had dinner at The Rathskeller, on Franklin in Chapel Hill, a collegiate-type restaurant with some ambience. I understand the crowd is mostly locals, some gay but that was not the drawing card. The food was only fair, although I thought it interesting that the restroom had a blackboard in it. No chalk though; I suppose you had to bring your own or maybe check it out at the counter

like a library book.

After dinner, Jim showed me the office where *The Front Page* is put together. It is very nice, all sorts of interesting reading such as out-of-town gay papers and releases. He gave me a complete set of *TFP* for my archives, and also copies of Jim's interviews with Armistead Maupin and a report that Maupin has been to bed with Rock Hudson (who is, reportedly, hung) and also likes chicken (young guys). I also got to read Maupin's serial *Jackie Old*— which ran in five parts in New West last October through January. I kind of liked it, but it was not laugh-out-loud humor like *Tales of the City*. Jim says Maupin is listed in the San Francisco phone book and loves to give interviews. Damn, no tape recorder.

That night, John and I went to The Mousetrap (in Raleigh). Tuesdays are their only good night, and it *was* crowded. It is sort of a cross between The Cue (disco) and The Nickelodeon (of Norfolk, cruise bar). It had a front room with a bar and a mirror, a back-room disco, plus a small back patio. The crowd was kind of preppy, and for looks I would rate it about a five. I started a conversation with one guy who was nice-looking, but he had trouble sustaining the talk, so I got bored and rejoined John.

Today, Jim and I visited his former office, and I met his ex-boss Arthur Sperry, owner of the Capitol Corral and a new bar, Stage 4, to open this weekend. Art is kind of cute, but slightly full of himself (although not offensively so). If I stayed another day, I could go to a pre-opening party, but Jim does not want to go—he hates shows and is not on wonderful terms with Arthur. Oh well.

The Capitol Corral in 1993

Arthur is doing well though, as his Capitol Corral has been very popular since it opened in 1976. It's part Western bar, but it includes a disco with its own name and logo, Glitter Gulch. Per the description in Cruise Magazine, it's "decorated in a Western style with corral fences, saddles, and Marlboro men." That would work for me.

While Jim's clothes were drying at the Cameron Village Laundromat, we went to the camp card shop where I got heavily cruised by a cute clerk who practically followed me around the store. I admit I was not exactly trying to lose him. It was just playing, of course. Besides, his gray-haired lady boss did not look like she would allow any horseplay. I am sure there will be plenty of time for that later in the trip.

Tomorrow, on to Atlanta.

Thursday—April 2, 1981
Somewhere between High Point and Charlotte, North Carolina

I had lunch at a Waffle House, where there was very redneck, country music on the jukebox, like "Heaven's Just a Sin Away," (The Kendalls). There were two signs behind the counter, one of which said, "Our batter is made fresh every day in the back room," which sounds ominous or kinky, depending on your point of view. I mean, was that a baseball player? The other stated, "Shirt and shoes must be worn to be served," which may mean you also have to wear the waffles to get them served. I did not follow up on that story.

THREE

Atlanta

Friday—April 3, 1981

GOT TO Atlanta about 5 PM and went directly to the Gay Community Center. They gave me the scoop on the bars (which ones were popular, and on what days) and also called around to find me a cheap hotel. They also told me about a play in town at one of the bars, The Sweet Gum Head.

The play was *P.S., Your Cat Is Dead!* by James Kirkwood, and I saw it on the first stop of its national tour. The play was very good, but the turnout was really poor, only 15 people. The bar is normally a show bar, as in drag shows. It certainly deserved a better reception. After all, the play had been on Broadway, and Kirkwood had received a Tony Award for *A Chorus Line*. I guess great credentials do not necessarily translate into local hits.

After the play, I went to The Armory—a very hot cruise bar that shares the parking lot with Backstreet. I cannot ever remember seeing a hotter crowd—usually, in a crowded bar, there are about five people I would be interested in; in that bar I think I was interested in about a fifth of them. I got there about 10:30 PM and went to the bar for a beer. Less than two minutes later, the bartender, named Bobby Joe, sent me another beer. He was busy, but we talked for a little. Don't you just love it? Locals always know when there's new meat in town.

Other than a guy from the community center, I did not really talk to anyone else until about midnight. Allen G was the first person I cruised. He was with a friend but finally came over. He is really cute and really nice. We went to Backstreet for about an hour before going back to his place. My suitcase spent the night alone at my hotel. And, we have a date tonight. It will probably be a movie and whatever.

Back to Backstreet—it is a very hot disco and deserves its reputation as one of the best in the South. In layout, it reminded me a little of The Pier in DC. The crowd was really similar to that

Atlanta

at The Armory. At about 12, the crowd shifts from Armory to Backstreet, and probably The Bulldog, nearby. Allen lives about three blocks from Backstreet.

After catching almost three hours of sleep at my hotel, I took a walk on Peachtree Street. This was not worth it. I guess there are no trendy shop neighborhoods in Atlanta, so I went to scattered shops here and there. Lennox Mall is probably the nicest in the city, and the cruisiest. I recognized two or three people from the bar. The bookstore (a Waldenbooks) even sells *Blueboy* and *Mandate*! I am writing this in Piedmont Park, which is at times distracting.

Before I forget… The night before I left, I called my parents. During the conversation, my mom said, "Now, don't pick up any hitchhikers, no matter how good he looks." Now, knowing my mother, she used the term *good* to mean *safe* instead of *appealing*, but I thought it was amusing.

Saturday—April 4, 1981
Atlanta

Well, we did not go to the bars last night; after we ate, Allen and I went to bed early (8:30 PM *is* early) and stayed there until 11 AM. We went to the bargain matinee at the Tara movie theatre at 2:30 PM to see *La Cage Aux Folles II*. It was very good, but not as good as part one.

After that, we stopped for a drink at Crazy Ray'z, a nice cruise bar with a patio, and stopped again for a drink at The Armory. There that same bartender remembered what I ordered Thursday night and brought me a Miller Lite before I had a chance to order. He was so pleased with himself that I did not have the heart to tell him that I wanted a Coke.

That place has a patio too, where they were grilling free hotdogs. For a Saturday afternoon it was a nice crowd. I dropped Allen off and we said our goodbyes, and then I had a very expensive dinner at Gallus, which had been recommended to me. Then, to pass some time, I went back to Lennox Mall, again to Waldenbooks, which also had a good selection of gay books on its fiction racks (*The Lure*, *Tory's*, etc.), and has a whole stand for "alternative lifestyles" with the typical psych books, "Joy of Gay Sex" books, plus poetry and cartoon books—so *this* is the big city.

Monday—April 6, 1981
Atlanta

On Saturday night, I went first to Bulldog, a Levi-leather bar a block from Backstreet. It has kind of a trucker motif with gas pumps, wheel rims made into light fixtures, etc. I'll compare it to bars in Norfolk. It is closer to The Nickelodeon in atmosphere, thank goodness, than to Norfolk's The Paddock. Unlike The Paddock, this bar is nice, and has a good crowd. It is next door to Jocks, which I went in and out of in two minutes—a morgue. Then, back to Backstreet, which seems to be one of the city's focal points. This was the Saturday night crowd. Very packed, but, in my opinion, not especially friendly.

The DJ is very good, one of the best I have heard, and he didn't get too esoteric, either. The music was mostly familiar stuff. Two ones I liked that were new to me were "The Sound of the City" by David London (from *Can't Stop the Music*) and a great disco version of "Touch Me in the Morning" by Marlena Shaw that I didn't know existed. I must buy that record! All the cruise bars here seem to play taped disco music rather than use jukeboxes. I stayed at Backstreet until about 2:30 AM (the bars close at 3 here) and went back to my hotel.

Across the street from my hotel is Numbers, the afterhours club. Although really tired, I went. After all it's Saturday night and I may never be in Atlanta on a Saturday night again. Numbers is large. I'll compare it to the Late Show, in Norfolk. Numbers is about the same size but its dance floor is about five times larger and takes up most of its space.

It also has two or three side rooms with pool tables, lounge chairs, bars, etc. The place was very crowded, as it is the only after-hours bar. At about 4 AM I met Preston. He is a blond…I never get blonds! He was friendly—he walked up to talk to me and kissed me hello, a nice conversation starter. We left at about 5 AM.

On Sunday, after a too-short nap at my hotel I went to Crazy Ray'z at about 3 PM for brunch, which was very good. They again had a nice, and hot crowd. My bartender friend from The Armory was there. Like in Norfolk and probably most cities, if you go out a lot you start to see some of the same people over and over. I played Pac-Man (my favorite electronic game) with a guy from Baltimore for a while. He invited me up to his cottage this summer at Rehoboth, Delaware. Not a chance, I've already thrown away his address.

When I was at Crazy Ray'z the day before, I saw a very hot man. We cruised each other but it went no further since I was with someone. Well on Sunday, he was there again, and it went further. His name is Don D. We spent the rest of the evening and the night together. From the Small World Department: Allen and Preston work for the same bank, and Preston and Don live in the

same apartment complex, in neighboring buildings.

From Crazy Ray'z we stopped first at Texas Drilling Co., which seemed like a decent Levi's bar, although there were hardly any people there at this time of day on a Sunday. Then, to Bulldog for a drink. It was crowded. I didn't mention before that at various spots along the ceiling of the main bar are hooks with underwear (mostly jockey shorts) hung from them. Don told me that the bar had a quaint custom of every so often tearing the underwear off someone if they caught them wearing any. I would like to see that. He says they burn the collected trophies about monthly. There were probably 20 or 30 pairs hanging up when I was there.

Then we went to Backstreet, which, since I was with someone, I liked much better. When we got there, the place had a very large crowd—at 7:30 PM on a Sunday! At about 9 PM, Vickie Sue Robinson came out and sang four songs (you know, "Turn the Beat Around"). She looked awful; I've seen better looking drag queens, even in Norfolk, but she sang fine. I think there is a "name" entertainer here every week.

Generalities time: Except for the Levi's bars, the Atlanta bar crowd has a definite preppy tone—lots of alligators with those button-fly jeans. Joking about one bar in particular, one guy I talked to said if it didn't have air conditioning, the customers would suffer from Halston-dioxide poisoning. The bars are not very mixed here. There were very few black men except at Numbers and women only at Numbers and Backstreet (of the bars I went to).

Atlanta seems to be a very gay city. Gays are *very* visible here. Everywhere you go it seems you can't help playing spot-the-queer. This is at the malls, while driving, everywhere. I guess if you're gay in the South, you move to Atlanta. It would definitely *not* be a hardship. On the con side, it's not near any other major city, so you would be stuck on an island.

I went to visit the *Gazette* office this afternoon. It is owned by about three people. I talked (for about four hours) with Mike Jameson, the editor, who seems really nice. Their office is in an upscale apartment complex. The paper pays for room and board for the three who live there. It's a three-level apartment with a lower level set up like a den. That's the paper office. They have a small Varityper for headlines and lease a typewriter-like typesetting machine for $260/month.

They have no trouble getting ads and, though only six months old, have been very successful. It's a weekly with over 5,000 copies per issue (but their printing bill is only around $300+ for 16 pages). Mike says we (*Our Own Community Press*) have permission to use anything we want from the *Gazette*, including ad graphics.

Comparing this to the budget challenges of *Our Own*, well, I cannot imagine it having the funds to produce a paper and also rent an office large enough to house three people.

Atlanta also has two bar rags (*Cruise Weekly* and *Sunset People*) which are all vying for advertising—all seem to get it too. Here, there are also your standard personality and political problems. I guess you can't get away from that. We swapped stories about problems with the bars, and other issues.

Mike and one other person will be at the Dallas convention I plan to attend. Their ad rates are very similar to ours—I got one of their rate cards. Mike also gave me a copy of a new South Carolina paper called *Gay Charleston*, which started in February. The *Gazette* also pays several ad reps (by commission, I think) and pays the writers for its columns; all that pretty much solves the problem of getting volunteers, which made my work at *Our Own* so difficult.

After the paper, I had dinner at Crazy Ray'z. Yes, I like that place—it kind of has an atmosphere a bit lower key. As it was more of a restaurant it was more calm, and they did not play disco. I met the owner, who recognized me from yesterday and came over and spoke to me. Also, two of the waiters are from Norfolk. One is Lane, a friendly, hot blond who used to live near Bob Scott (a psychologist friend), part of Norfolk's A-gay crowd. He remembered seeing me at Bob's. The other former Norfolk resident was Kevin, who used to be Kenny H's lover. I remembered him from Norfolk, too—very hot and with attitude to match. In Norfolk they had both been out of my league. Kevin has been here two years and Lane has been here one year. Lane, when asked what he *doesn't* like about Atlanta, said that sometimes it's almost *too* gay. Such a problem.

Atlanta

Tuesday—April 7, 1981
Atlanta

From Crazy Ray'z I went to the Armory. Monday is one of their busy nights. Earlier in the day I checked out of my hotel. Since I haven't spent any nights there yet, I figured I would take my chances tonight, something I've never done so consciously. Well, jackpot. I met just an incredibly handsome man, Bill A, who is definitely in the "unattainable" league. Fortunately, he has no idea how good looking he is. It was *really* nice.

Bill A

So today, Tuesday, after leaving Bill's around noon, I shopped most of the afternoon. I went to a nice trendy boutique (Sparkles), the gay bookstore (Christopher's Kind) and spent $40 on books. Then I went to Blane's Art Gallery, and ate lunch at a nice gay restaurant called Gabriel's, on 10th and Peachtree. I decided to check back into my hotel since my body is telling me that at least a nap is essential. I plan to leave tomorrow morning for New Orleans.

More from the Small World Department: While driving around this afternoon, I was waiting at a red light when the driver of the car in the next lane spoke to me. He said he noticed my Norfolk city sticker and that he used to live in Norfolk. In the space of time before the light changed, we established that I liked Atlanta and had been doing the bars and that he used to work at the Oar House and the Cue, though I didn't remember him.

Later, after my nap, I went to Pharr's Library—a disco whose best night is supposed to be Tuesday, which is tonight. It was not as preppy as I heard it was, although the crowd is a tad younger. It is a nice place, decorated like a library with shelves of books on most walls. The dance floor was small, but the music was really good. That *Bits & Pieces III* record ("Let's Do It," a medley) is popular here and at Backstreet). No one really interested me in particular, although two people asked me to dance.

Oh yeah, before the disco I ate dinner (yes, again) at Crazy Ray'z, as they have a very good prime rib special. Again, the place had a very hot crowd. I just can't get over all the hot men in this city, much more than I saw in NYC or Miami (last year). Disneyland is not in California—it's here.

Tomorrow: New Orleans.

FOUR

New Orleans

Thursday—April 9, 1981
New Orleans

Well, it took 8½ hours to drive from Atlanta to New Orleans—the traffic from Mississippi onwards was seldom less than 65 miles per hour. I checked into Lafitte's Guest House (as advertised in *The Advocate*). It is *very* nice, but also very expensive, but it seems all accommodations here are. It is at the corner of Bourbon St. and St. Phillip, which puts it within two blocks of the two most popular bars, and almost in the heart of the French Quarter. I ate at the Fatted Calf on St. Peter and then walked around for a while. Bob O (who was a good friend in Norfolk before he moved to Miami last January) is in town on business for a few days. We got together about 9 PM and started out to see the town.

Bob and I went to the three most popular bars, and frankly, we were very disappointed. New Orleans so far has not captured a piece of our hearts. First however, we walked around the Quarter for a while. Bourbon Street is blocked to traffic at night, so it's people everywhere. It's hard to compare New Orleans to anywhere else—it has elements of Times Square, Key West, SoHo, and a state fair. There is constant noise as you walk down the streets, and it is just a barrage on the senses. You might hear

Lafitte Guest House

jazz, rock, country, zydeco, or disco from any doorway. It is mostly bars, restaurants, galleries, antique shops, and tourist shops, all slightly tacky. The city is very rundown and dirty. I'm not at all impressed. Two days will be plenty. I'm glad Bob is here to "enjoy" it with me.

Anyway, we went first to Jewel's Tavern on Decatur, a dark cruise bar, then to the legendary Café Lafitte in Exile, a dark cruise bar which upstairs has The Corral—another bar, a pool room, and a balcony. Lafitte's is supposedly one of the oldest gay bars in the country (since 1933). It is one block from the hotel. I guess for a Wednesday night it had a good quantity of people. But alas, quantity does not mean quality.[1]

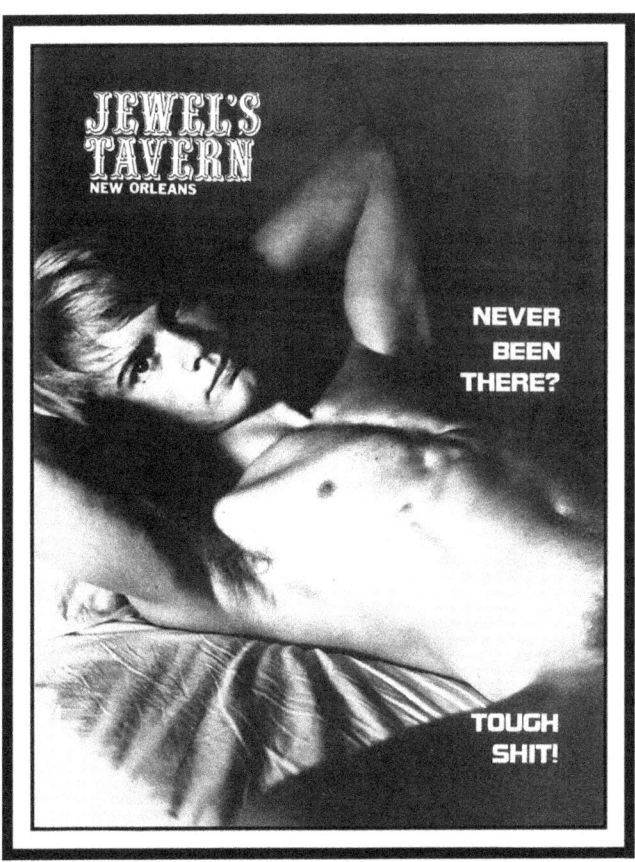

Then we went to the Bourbon Pub, a dark cruise bar, which upstairs has The Parade, the only disco in town, and also a balcony. Neither floor was at all crowded. The disco was kind of electric—all neon and mirrors—a little much. Scratch that, a lot much.

Bob and I figured that at all three bars there were one or two decent looking men and a couple that were marginal. Unlike Atlanta, there were almost no clones[2] (my preferred type, I just love clones). At about 12:30 AM we gave up.

This morning, while Bob was working, I walked around with my camera for about an hour and a half. Jackson Square is kind of nice. It has a very photogenic church and park, which faces the Mississippi River (which is *not* photogenic). Then, after lunch I took a very thorough walk around the streets and window-shopped. The French Quarter *does* have some interesting architecture. I finished up a roll of film easily. So far, I've asked three different people which bars are the most popular and they all name the same two or three bars, quite depressing.

As I was walking, I noticed a guy standing on his balcony, wearing a robe. He grabbed his crotch, I guess as a come-on signal. And I laughed out loud, which probably did not boost his ego.

I picked up a copy of *Impact*, the monthly gay newspaper of New Orleans. It's about 34 pages, in its fourth year, is typeset, and has lots of ads. It is quite good and would probably slightly edge out *Our Own* in quality.

Later: Well, Bob was supposed to meet me at Lafitte's at 7:30 PM. While I was waiting, I met Wesley C, a really nice-looking man who worked for two years as a go-go dancer in a gay bar when he first came to New Orleans. He was *really* persistent. He knew I was waiting for a friend and didn't have a lot of time. He wanted me to go into the john with him, but I would have none of that. It was about 7 PM when I decided that it wouldn't hurt Bob if I was a *little* late, so we went to my hotel for an hour and then back to Lafitte's (which you may remember is only a block away).

At about 8:30 PM, I am *still* waiting for Bob. So, I started up a conversation with a very cute and hunky man named Allen D, who has lived in New Orleans about three years (and is *not* a big fan of the city). He is an accountant and also does carpentry work for the owner of Lafitte's and The Refuge. At 9:30 PM we decided to walk back to my hotel to see if Bob left a message (which he just had a few minutes earlier; he had to work until about 9 PM). I discreetly let Bob know I was busy. Actually, since Allen was standing right beside the phone, I kind of hemmed and hawed until Bob guessed what was going on. No problem. Bob said he would have dinner and then hit the bars. Allen and I also had dinner at a nice gay restaurant called The Coffee Pot.

We stopped briefly at Lafitte's and The Refuge (a cowboy bar), and got back to my hotel around 11 PM. And yes, if you are keeping track, that is two tricks in the same day.

Addendum: I talked to Bob this morning. He says he hit the bars until about midnight and then gave up. He is really over it. He arranged for a friend from Miami, Miguel, to fly up and join him for the weekend.

Another side note: When I met Allen, I walked up to him and asked him where he was from. I told him that I was curious since I was trying to determine how far the style/fad of leaving the bottom button of button-fly Levi's open had gotten. I know it's been the style on the East and West Coasts. My friend Michael Collins in New York City had told me about it last year. I wasn't specifically cruising Allen, just making conversation. The fact that he was cute had nothing to do with it…well, maybe a little to do with it. Anyway, Allen's interpretation on what that style means is the same as mine. It means you're available, and he commented that he definitely was.

Endnotes

1	As of 2021, Café Lafitte in Exile is still open, making it *definitely* one of the oldest gay bars in the country. See the discussion here: http://peterga.com/kbar-gay.htm

2	"Castro Clones" was a slang term in the late 1970s and 1980s for the fashion of many gay men (nationwide), including short hair, moustache, form-fitting t-shirts and tight Levi's 501 jeans, usually commando.

FIVE

Baton Rouge

Saturday—April 11, 1981
Baton Rouge

HELLO, Journal. Well, it's 10 AM Saturday morning. It only took about 1½ hours to drive to Baton Rouge. I registered at the conference (Southeastern Conference of Lesbians and Gay Men, at LSU) at about 11 AM. This was the 6th annual conference. I had attended the 4th annual event in Chapel Hill in 1979 and fondly remembered it. Highlights for me were the concert performances by Charlie Murphy and Therese Edell. I came out of that conference with rave reviews, and detailed those in an article I wrote for *Our Own* (May 1979 issue).[1]

Friday, as you might expect, is a slow day because not everyone is here yet, so I just mingled a little at the cafeteria. I got hooked up with some Atlanta people and ran around most of the day with them. Gene, who I met in Atlanta and runs Christopher's Kind Bookstore, was selling books here, as were the Houston Wilde 'n Stein people. Ray Kluka, a nice, sharp man who directs the Atlanta Gay Center, was with Gene.

Ray and I went to the Gay Crisis Lines workshop Friday afternoon. It was okay; it was the only one I was even remotely interested in during that time slot. The workshops, in general, seem very dry and serious, hitting heavily on the political, religious, and medical angles. There are no "skin hunger," or "fun" workshops, and also none in particular for someone just coming out—such as Coming Out to Parents, etc.

I've noticed so far that I tend to be very critical of this conference; however, I suppose they did a fine job considering the college environment. I guess I'm used to the professionalism of the conferences my Norfolk friends would give at Old Dominion University.

Unfortunately, the conference seems slightly closeted. When I walked into the student union, there were no signs directing anyone to where to register or, really, any clue that a gay conference was being held. The nametags and the t-shirts do not have the word "gay" or even a lambda on them![2] I'm sure the student body knows there's a conference going on. It's been quite controversial. But I would prefer a more "out" appearance.

The conference staff people are working really hard, but it's evident that some of their attitudes are still coming along—I heard the SFGA president comment about one of the Louisiana sissies, "Just too many earrings! And he's a *man!*" I guess they need more exposure to the movement before they could be expected to be completely politically correct.

The keynote speech by Larry Bagneris that night was good—he's a Houston gay politico and was their first gay delegate to the Democratic National Convention. [And, as I would learn later, was chair of the Pride Committee and in 1982 would be elected President of the Gay Political Caucus.]

Later, there was a play, which was just incredible....incredibly bad. It was *Dearest Mommie*, put on by a New Orleans performing troupe. That's about all I can say kind about it. It turned out to be a four-person drag show with an excuse for a plot strung between such songs as "Fame," "Angel of the Morning," "Steam Heat," "This Is My Life," "Money," "Maybe," "Saved," and "Heaven Is Just a Sin Away." It was in extremely poor taste and concluded with a scene involving Joan Crawford's daughter delivering a baby fathered by a Polynesian island chief, where they had been stranded after the *Titanic* sank. (I *told* you the plot was thin). They used the song, "You're Having My Baby," therefore offending anyone with any sympathy for the women's movement.

I talked with a couple members of the conference staff later, and they were quite embarrassed. They did not know what kind of play it would be, and had not seen it. Their fault, of course. Isn't that just amazing? A pure drag show would have been better. It is ironic that in the conference program[3], they made such a big deal about this being a non-ERA state and recommending only going to their list of pro-ERA restaurants.

After the play, Ray, Chris, and I went to George's Place, allegedly one of the best (out of four or five) gay bars. It was small but was fixed up nicely. A local man I talked to said the crowd that night was about double normal, obviously due to the conference. If that's the case, I am so glad I don't live here. Oh, Ray and I did find time to play for a while.

Sunday—April 12, 1981
Baton Rouge

It was a long day, and I did not get to any of the 9 AM workshops. At 11:30 AM was the general assembly with Ann Toups as keynoter. She's a New Orleans psychotherapist and was in the 1979 ABC special *Close-up: Homosexuality*. She was an excellent speaker. A Creole-Cajun lunch was served in the student union cafeteria—okay, but *much* too spicy for me. (Remember, I'm a Yankee). Went to the Sexism and Racism workshop in the afternoon. It was useful that these issues were introduced, but they are hard subjects to cover in this setting.

Baton Rouge

For dinner several of us went to a gay bar/restaurant—The Cock & Bull Story—which happened to be next to my hotel. I was told that men and women usually hang out in separate parts of the bar...the *cock* part for the guys and the *bull* part of course for the dykes. Cute, huh? They served a free drink to all conference people, and the barbecued ribs were delicious.

For the evening assembly Michael Denneny was the main speaker, and his keynote address was on Gay Identity.[4] He is an author, and editor of *Christopher Street*. I talked to Denneny a little afterwards about the book and newspaper business, and he told me that gay books almost never make money, including popular ones like *The Lure* (Picano). He says *The Native* (NYC) is doing okay, with a circulation of about 6,000. The concert afterwards featured Robin Flower and Nancy Vogl, who played a kind of bluegrass/jazz. Vogl would make a good keynoter—having heard her talk on various occasions, I think she's really sharp.

After the concert I went to the disco The Emporium, which reminded me of a VFW hall (no, that's not a compliment). I guess the crowd was large enough, but in quality I would rate it about a 3 overall. Every bar I have been to in Louisiana has been *much* too dark, as was this one. The music was average or less. You're right, I'm not at all impressed with this state's bars.

Sunday, the conference consisted of a general feedback assembly and some goodbyes. It was approved that next year's conference would be at Tampa, and Atlanta perhaps the year after. Also, a man from Tampa who is going to the LA conference asked for input. He, I suppose, is representing the new network formed at the conference for Southeast states. Finally, the assembly agreed to ask the national group to put more emphasis on strengthening local groups and to resist state and national marches.

This conference ended with 200 people from 16 states, and about twenty-five percent were women. Financially it ended $1,600 in the red. The poor attendance was chalked up to the location and lack of publicity. Nevertheless, I was grateful that the Louisiana Sissies were here. They brought a feeling of brother- and sisterhood that was needed at an otherwise businesslike conference. They are from the group Louisiana Sissies in Struggle (LASIS), a collective formed in New Orleans in 1977.

For lunch, the Atlanta group I had hooked up with and I went to the gumbo place again—this time, I ordered a hamburger—Cajun/Creole food is just *too* spicy for me!

Endnotes

1   At the link is a May 1979 article I wrote for Norfolk's *Our Own* covering the conference.
https://houstonlgbthistory.org/jd-book-links.html

2   In the early 1970s lambda became a symbol of gay and lesbian unity and pride. Though its use has fallen out of widespread use it is still today common to see it as a symbol or part of an organizational name; for example, Lambda Legal.

3   Program for Southeastern Conference of Lesbians & Gay Men, 1981
https://houstonlgbthistory.org/Houston80s/SECLGM-81.pdf

4   The keynote address Michael Denneny gave can be found in the 2023 book *On Christopher Street: Life, Sex, and Death After Stonewall*, pp 114-127. Sadly, he died a month after his book was published, at age 80.

SIX

Houston

Monday—April 13, 1981
Houston

THE DRIVE to Houston took five hours, and I checked into the Plaza Hotel on Montrose upon arriving. It was expensive, so I arranged to spend the rest of the week at the Houston Guest House on Avondale. I had dinner at Baja Sam's, a nice gay bar/restaurant, classy but not overdone.

Tuesday—April 14, 1981
Houston

Drove around Montrose yesterday morning, mostly stopping at record stores. Montrose has a gay ghetto atmosphere you can sense. It has some similarities to Ghent (Norfolk) but is bigger and much more commercial. There are at least 15 bars within walking distance of the Guest House and many others not much farther.

Of course, not all of these are bars you would want to go to. For example, the Midnight Sun is a hustler bar—hustling is very common in this neighborhood. Even I figured out immediately what those young guys were doing loitering on those street corners.

Wilde 'n Stein, the legit gay bookstore, is about three blocks away, and it appears that there are also a few interesting shops nearby. As I write this, I am sitting on a lounge chair on a deck by the pool, and what appears to be some sort of gecko…about 4 inches long…just crawled by. Okay, these are new to me.

One myth about (at least this part of) Texas has been destroyed. Houston is very green. Except for an occasional yucca, it could pass for Ohio. I guess I was brainwashed by all those Western films into expecting sagebrush and tumbleweeds and lots of brown. This is probably a common belief held by many northerners.

Yesterday afternoon I sat for several hours on the porch talking to people and writing the article for *Our Own* regarding the conference in Baton Rouge. A fellow guest—Small World Department again—was born and raised in Youngstown and has relatives in my hometown of Salem, Ohio, and was even there a couple of weeks ago. He works as a travel agent in NYC now is a nice guy, really well-read. He knows Frank Kameny, and was at Stonewall (wasn't everyone?).

I had dinner a few blocks away at The Godfather—the food was excellent, although I was tempted to tip the piano player to stop playing. He was ruining so many songs that I like. After that, I walked down to "Disco Kroger" for some food for today's breakfast. They usually play disco music, and of course, there were lots of queers there.[1]

Later I walked to the Montrose Mining Company, a Levi's-Western bar with a sprinkling of Lacostes. It is also the first Levi's bar I've seen that also had a DJ. It had a decent crowd, for a Monday night. I would not have wanted it any more crowded. I would rate that crowd about a 4 or 5, but there was one very hot man that I liked named Norman C who works as an orthopedic technician at the Medical Center. What a wild night—just about the best sex I've ever had—and he said about the same thing. It was one for the record books. We have a date for tonight.

So far, I like the Houston Guest House—it's convenient and the atmosphere is pleasant. If you stay at least a week, you get a rate reduction—from $30 to $25 per night. I'm in the red room, which is aptly named as everything—walls, rug, woodwork—is the red color palette.

For lunch today I stopped at a nearby Italian place, Marini's Empanadas. I guess an empanada is a doughy-like covering with almost any type of filling (meat, fruit, asparagus, etc). I didn't order one of those, but I had a drink called a *licuado*—kind of like a milkshake, but thicker and with real fruit blended in. They sold banana, blackberry, black raspberry, and bing cherry, but I got brave and ordered guava. I won't go as far as to say I would order it again, but it *was* interesting.

Well, it looks like I will be here at the Guest House for two weeks. Stewart McCloud, the manager, offered me a rate of $20

Houston Guest House

per night if I stay that long. It seems that he is going out of town for a few days, so it is worth it to him to know that someone reliable will be there and that the room is booked. I guess he feels the place will fall apart when he's gone, so he wants to tie down as many loose ends as possible. While he's gone, a friend of his, Charles Gillis, will be minding the store. Charles, who I met at the Baton Rouge conference, owns the Wilde 'n Stein bookstore.

Houston

Wednesday—April 15, 1981
Houston

Last night Norman and I had dinner at a very gay restaurant called Baba Yega, and then went bar hopping. First to the Wildwood Saloon, Home of the Sundance Saddle Club—obviously a Western bar. It had a nice back patio. Almost all the bars here have patios. I love this. It's a chance to get away from the smoke and noise, and the atmosphere on a patio is more laid-back.[2]

Next, on to the Galleon, which was nice. It is not quite a Western bar, although there seems to be at least a Western element everywhere. Finally, to the Brazos River Bottom—definitely a country Western bar. There is C&W music on the jukebox, such as "You Ain't Woman Enough to Take My Man" (Loretta Lynn) and sometimes a live band. I got to see guys fast dancing to C&W music, which I can't quite describe—you have to see it. On the patio is a mud bath for the mud wrestling bouts on Saturday afternoons. Most of the customers dress kind of Western—cowboy hats, boots, with t-shirts and Levi's. Lacoste shirts would be pushing it a little, though. Cowboy hats on guys in Houston are common enough that after a while you do not even notice them.

As I was sitting here on the pool deck of the guest house writing this, I just met two visitors—one from here, who almost immediately gave me his card in case I want someone to "run around with." I think he has more in mind. The other guy is from LA and told me where I should stay when I get out there (*his* number I asked for). He offered to show me around a little in LA.

I drove out to the Galleria this afternoon. It's a huge shopping mall about four miles west on Westheimer Street. Very impressive. It has three levels. On the ground level is an ice-skating rink in the median area between the shops. Later this afternoon I took a long walk from the guest house out Westheimer Street, which is the main commercial street in Montrose. I walked for a number of blocks. There are several interesting trendy-type shops (gift shops, galleries, card shops, clothing shops, etc.) and many,

many restaurants, which if they aren't gay-owned might as well be by dint of their location.

While I was walking, a kid in a pickup truck stopped and asked me where the bar Montrose Mining Company is. I guess I looked like I would know (I did). Farther down the street, I walked by an older man using a pay phone. As I passed him, he blew me a kiss. Of course he was a troll. Such is life.

During my walk I stopped at two more bars. They are everywhere in this neighborhood. First was Mary's, which, I gather, is somewhat of an institution in the area. But, as I had heard, it was a dive—there was a German Shepard (named Sam) walking around inside, playing with a plastic trash can lid. The patio was ok, but the bar was dirty and seedy. It is a block from the intersection of Westheimer Road and Montrose Boulevard. Next bar I went to was Dirty Sally's, which is a block from the Guest House on Avondale, a residential street with many big fine homes.

Now, imagine one of the houses converted into a bar and you have Dirty Sally's or several other area bars. It and the others have a high wood fence all around the property starting with the inside edge of the sidewalk. The front and back yards are therefore enclosed patio areas. It is quite nice. The whole first floor of the house is the bar with smaller rooms used for lounges, a DJ, or pinball machines. Houston is the first place I've seen with bars with a live DJ but no dance floor. Dirty Sally's had a fair-sized crowd considering it was 7 PM on a Wednesday night.

Thursday—April 16, 1981
Houston

Well, I didn't go out last night...you have to rest sometimes. I was going to go to Babylon, one of the two most popular discos—it's two blocks away. It and Parade are only open Wednesday through Sundays. Babylon used to be called Numbers.[3]

This afternoon I visited the *TWT* (*This Week in Texas*) offices...or, should I say, suite of offices. Very modern and impressive. They employ about 20 people, but that may also include the other part of their business. They are owned by Montrose Ventures, which also sells poppers and lube. They have all the modern newspaper equipment, and from what I saw, a very cute staff. I talked to Chuck Patrick, the editor, but only for about 15 minutes. Even though this was supposedly a slow day, people were very busy. *TWT* (or as everyone calls it, *Twit*) has a weekly bar-mag type format but is much better than similar ones such as *David* (Miami), and it's state-wide. It has a decent balance (~60% ads) and mostly Texas news (by design) with some national news. Overall, it's a very good publication, with sections for sports, reviews, comments, humor, and serious articles.

After I left the *TWT* office (which is about three blocks from The Guest House), I went afternoon bar hopping— to Mary's, Montrose Mining Company, the Barn, and Dirty Sally's. The only one I hadn't been to before was the Barn, a Western bar, which, as I had heard, had an older crowd.

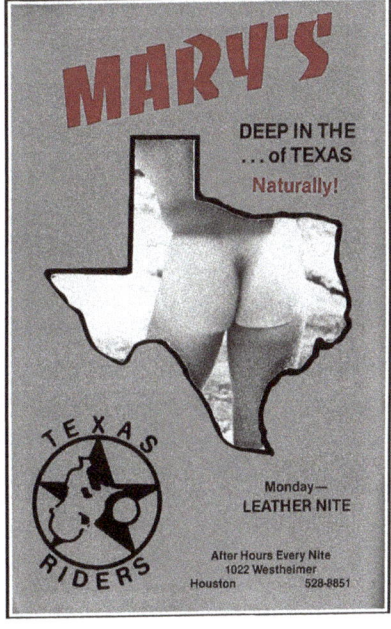

I just met a guy from the Montrose Sports Association—the softball committee had a meeting at the Guest House. He said the MSA has over 600 paid members. He mentioned that there are eight softball teams and 70 bowling teams, and also volleyball teams and probably other sports, too. That is very impressive.

Friday—April 17, 1981
Houston

I went to Babylon last night (the disco by that name, that is), and it was amazing. It has a huge dance floor with a very large raised stage off to one corner. The decor is sort of hi-tech with lots of mirrors, electric lights, and CO_2 jets. There are two or three bars around it, and there is a second level mezzanine lounge with a bar that overlooks the dance floor and stage. That lounge is glassed in, which kind of gives you the feeling of being removed from it all. The music was good, especially the new Disconet records. Disconet is a custom service for DJs only, often featuring remixes of recent hits. But one that especially grabbed me was a disco version of "Ain't No Mountain High Enough," which was *really* good. I don't know the artist's name, but the DJ told me it would be released in three or four months. Remember, you heard that here first![4]

The crowd was a little light, as it was a Thursday night. I guess that the same number of people placed in a medium-sized bar would make it very crowded. This place is big. There were only two guys that I thought were especially good-looking—one was Steve, a very cute bartender, and the other guy (whom I took home) was John, my first tourist of this trip. He and his roommate are driving cross-country from LA to NYC to move to the city. He was very knowledgeable about disco and told me of his favorite record store in LA. He is also a terrific cuddler.

Oh yeah, performing at Babylon last night was disco singer Celi Bee. I had never heard of her either. She had a couple of dance chart recordings. She was okay, but the four dancers with her were very good, almost distracting attention from her. The performance lasted about 45-minutes, and the only song I had heard of was "Superman," but not by her. The Herbie Mann version was the one played in Virginia.

Saturday—April 18, 1981
Houston

Yesterday afternoon I sat by the pool for about 2-3 hours. I got a little sunburned, just enough to feel it. I had dinner at Barbecue Ranch again—really good food, big portions, cheap, and gay-owned. There I met Bobby, with whom I went to Wildwood Saloon and Mary's. Although Mary's is very sleazy and dirty, I kind of like the patio. From there I walked back to the Guest House to take a nap, somehow managing to not stop at Dirty Sally's along the way.

I woke up at 1 AM—just in time to get ready to go out. This *was* Friday night, and I went to Parade, which is I guess the most

popular disco. It is part of the same firm that owns Parade Disco in New Orleans. This one was much, much better. I liked the layout, very large and with the dance floor in the center. It is very hi-tech—lots of lights and mirrors. The lighting was very good. The music was just average, and the DJ, I thought, adequate.

Some of the popular songs (as in the other cities) were "It Feels Like I'm In Love" by Kelly Marie, "It's Not What You've Got, It's How You Use it" by Carrie Lucas, and "On and On" and "Lay Your Love on Me" by ABBA. One interesting song was actually from last year, though I guess it was regional and did not get to Norfolk. It was the Goombay Dance Band, from Germany, with "Rain." This one just packed the dance floor. Musically it reminded me a lot of the Skatt Brothers ("Life at the Outpost," 1979).

The crowd at Parade was large and there were a lot of pretty people there, but, like at Backstreet (Atlanta), was not particularly friendly or cruisy. Everyone seemed to be paired up or partying with their friends or high on something. I have found for many dance bars, if you are there to cruise, that's a tough objective. This is because most of the crowd is there to party with their friends, often with the help of drugs. They are not there to cruise.

At 2 AM they announced last call, and that they would start to serve liquor again at 7 AM. At about 3:30 AM they passed out free popsicles and fudgesicles, which was interesting. I think I talked to a total of three people while I was there, including the waiter from Babylon (whom I would like to kidnap…*so* cute). At 5 AM, when I got back to the Guest House, the assistant manager Billy was still awake and talked me into going swimming. Why not?

Later that same day… Well, I have just now returned from Brazos River Bottom and what will probably be one of the most memorable spectacles of my stay in Houston. Every Saturday afternoon at about 4 PM, they have mud-wrestling bouts. I would have given $10 to have had my camera with me, because I'm sure what I saw was a classic. It lasted about two hours and there were about

Houston

seven or eight bouts, mostly customers volunteering. The bar provides gym trunks and towels. It's held in an about 6 x 8 wading pool on the back patio. One of the bartenders (Abe) emceed and was also in several matches.

The highlight had to have been an unplanned match. During the afternoon they had been teasing Charlotte, a rather large lesbian, to get in a match. She is owner of another bar, The Saddle

Club. Well, she refused until Abe came over and put mud in her face. She pushed him into the pool. Then, while standing, they started doing something resembling arm wrestling—him in the pool and her out.

This was until someone else snuck up behind her, grabbed her, and they both wrestled her into the pool (she was dressed, of course). She rightfully got pissed and proceeded to dunk the one who snuck up on her. She was basically a good sport about it though. I wish I had it on film. But I did find an ad for the bar showing the wrestling.

A little later during a bout with two guys the emcee got pulled into the mud too. As if this wasn't enough, out of the crowd came this old man, about 60 years old and buck naked (a rather quaint expression, don't you think?), to join them. So, there were four of them wrestling. Of course, during the show there were the usual catcalls and jokes from the sidelines, and a couple of the wrestlers were very good looking. It was very enjoyable.

Time out for a culture comment: Much more so than Atlanta or New Orleans, if you're gay, you wear button fly jeans with the bottom button left open, and usually commando. I kind of like it. Also, I don't think I've ever been cruised so much—in the bars, on the streets (especially) and in shops and restaurants. People speak to you on the streets. Everywhere in Montrose it is pretty much assumed you are gay, which is fine with me. I do realize that in most gay communities they recognize when someone is from out of town and is fresh meat.

Sunday—April 19, 1981
Houston

Last night seemed to have been Dallas Night here. First, I met these five guys from Dallas that were staying at the Guest House—they drove down for the weekend. They invited me to go over to The Mine (Montrose Mining Company) with them. Well, they were a trip. They spent the whole time dishing each other and carrying on. They didn't look like queens, but they sure could camp: You know, "her" this and "girl" that. By the time we came back (after only about 45 minutes), I had my fill. But it *was* interesting.

Then I went to Venture'N, a cruise bar closer to downtown. It was not what I expected at all. It was downtown on Main Street (kind of like the Nickleodeon in Norfolk was) and I expected a slightly sleazy, dark and dirty bar. Wrong! It was very hi-tech—I liked it. There was a mezzanine on the sides you could stand on to look down onto the first level. Also, it had a pool table and pinball machines on the mezzanine and disco lights and glitter balls hanging from the ceiling.

Another interesting…er…feature of the Venture'N is found in one of their restrooms. Instead of a row of urinals there is

about a five-foot long trough, for those needing to pee. There is room for three guys to stand in front of it. Above the trough is a chrome panel, about two feet high, and polished like a mirror, so those who want to see the details of who else is peeing, from the neck down, can. And they can do so without their faces giving away where they are looking. It's sort of an exhibitionistic, voyeuristic thing.

On the bar's second level, I started a conversation with a guy named Kelly N from Dallas who told me later that he had noticed me when I came in and had (discreetly) followed me upstairs so he could meet me. Isn't it amazing how these things work out? Well, he is a *very* nice guy and very interesting. He is a gay Mormon (my first) and is also good friends with Leonard Matlovich. He told me that Matlovich used his settlement money to buy a pizza parlor about 60 miles north of San Francisco.[5]

Kelly just broke up with a lover (of 2½ years) about two weeks ago. It was a completely closed relationship, so I'm the first person he's been with since. He's cute and very sweet and almost too nice. I think he might be the type to become easily attached to someone they like. That makes me a little wary, but I did promise I would visit him in Dallas.

This afternoon I had Easter lunch at Steak and Eggs on Montrose Boulevard. Based on the customers, they can have my business anytime. Then, walking back, I happened upon the Annual Easter Sleaze Bonnet Contest. This is where guys in drag, heels, and outrageous bonnets dress up. Judging is held at five or six bars during the afternoon, and the whole motley group travels from bar to bar—by foot if it's close enough or by pickup truck if it isn't. They stopped at most of the cruise bars I've mentioned thus far.

This time I had my camera—but almost only coincidentally. I knew the contest was going on but figured it would be too hard to catch it at a particular bar. I went out just to take pictures of Westheimer Avenue and stumbled upon the procession—around 20 contestants and their entourage—walking from the Montrose

Mining Company to Midnite Sun.[6]

Well—these queens love to pose[7], and I think I got some priceless (if not tasteless) shots. I followed the troupe to Dirty Sally's, The Hole, and Venture'N. I got the best shots at Dirty Sally's since the judging was on their patio. I asked one of the judges if he would get them to pose for a group shot. He must have thought I was some official photographer or something, because he called out, "All right, line up for the photographer." They of course loved it and hammed it right up. I think I shot about 40 or so slides of this "event," including an occasional one here or there of the men in the crowd who caught my attention.

Later this evening I went to Dirty Sally's again—I cannot decide whether or not I like that bar. It has a strange mix of contrasts and features. It is probably the only bar that can be rightfully called a neighborhood bar. The others all have some tone to them: Western, disco, sleaze, uptown, hi-tech, etc. Does this mean that Dirty Sally's has *no* personality? That's almost it. The layout is fine, a nice, converted house and patio around the front and back. The DJ is accessible for questions (and not up in somewhere or

Easter Bonnet March at Dirty Sally's

encased in glass and too special to be approached) and both DJs I have heard there are certainly acceptable.

The crowd has perhaps the widest age span of any bar, and the youngest crowd. However, the 18 to 20-year-olds are not the navy or preppy types that we're used to in Norfolk. They are of the long-haired hippy or young queen variety, *not* appealing, at least to me. In fact, in general I've not seen a very attractive crowd here. The bar's location is very good—near Babylon, Montrose Mining Company, etc. This place *should* be a good bar—but it just is quite not.

Oh yeah—I heard another disco record I want and probably will never get, a really good disco version of The Beach Boys' "I Can Hear Music" by California. The DJ at Dirty Sally's told me it only came out on promo around two and a half years ago and he tried to get an extra copy at the time but could not.

I ran into what might be called "bar games" tonight, two examples. In the first, I started a conversation with a nice-looking man at Dirty Sally's named John. He wasn't that easy to talk with; the conversation was ragged. I decided that there was no rapport at all and no future in this one. He went to the restroom and when he returned, I told him that I was going to get a sandwich or something and (to see where his head was) asked him if he'd like to join me. Complete turnabout—he wanted to know if we could go back to my hotel. This was too drastic a change for me. I still hadn't gotten a grasp on whether I liked him yet. He had been very stone-faced, almost tense.

He said he'd already eaten and thought if he would stay and have a couple beers while I was gone, he could relax a little. But he asked several times that I come back and meet him there. He seemed genuinely interested by now. We also kissed and groped a little, so I agreed. Well, I was gone an hour cause restaurant service was very slow, and (you guessed it) he wasn't there when I got back. This was probably just as well. I just couldn't get a fix on his personality; at least at first impression he didn't seem very warm.

Bar Games II—this time it was at MMC (which stands for Montrose Mining Company, or The Mine). It is definitely one of the better cruise bars, and just 8½ blocks from the Guest House. There were only one or two interesting looking men (to me) in the crowd tonight. One I semi-cruised a little—that's looking in his direction and looking him over, but not going for the hard eye contact. No progress, so I moved on. About an hour later I was walking through the bar in the direction towards the door when he puts his arm around me as I walked by—I didn't even see him. He was immediately very touchy-feely, which although a little abrupt (okay…a lot abrupt). I guess that was okay, and I certainly didn't discourage him. His name was Larry (probably still is).

He wasn't too subtle about wanting to get together, but at the same time just vague enough to avoid asking the question. This took about five or 10 minutes; and then he just seemed to lose interest. His friends decided they were going to Parade Disco. He had already asked me to come along, and I had told him I just didn't feel like going to a disco. He then decided to go with his friends but again extended an invitation.

Strange—he was interested enough to make a very bold gesture to meet me (grabbing me as I walked by would be considered bold—don't you think?) but then could not decide what to do from there. He was very cute, but lost points for being wishy-washy.

Monday—April 20, 1981
Houston

This afternoon I visited the radio station that airs the gay programs here in Houston—Station KPFT, 90.1 FM. The gay show is normally broadcast on Thursday nights, but they were having a special all-day program as a fundraiser; and they had an open house at the studio, which is just three or four blocks from the Guest House. Ray Hill is station manager and is also known as the father of Houston's gay movement. I did not really talk to him, as he was very busy, but I watched him in the studio give part of a news broadcast. He is very articulate—to hear him talk on the air, you would swear he had the copy written in front of him, and yet he did not, it was all him.

He is very involved with the court hearings in a case in which a gay activist (Fred Paez) was shot at point blank range by a cop. The activist had been doing a lot of research into police discrimination against gays. The shooting was just before Gay Pride Week last year.

Ray's lover is Kent Naasz, whom Michael Collins (someone I had visited last year in NYC) suggested I look up in Houston. Kent happened to be the first person I talked to at the station, so it was kind of coincidental that we met that way. The station of course is all volunteer (except for Ray) and as expected, they program gay news, interviews, group discussions, records, and about anything else they can think of. It seemed like they had their shit together. Of course, the station does not do all gay programming, usually one show per week.

Addenda: Later, I did get to talk to Ray Hill for about an hour when he saw me at a nearby restaurant and sat down at my table. He is very interesting—I told him he should write a book on his experiences. Talking with him is a little like interviewing him, except that he is doing all the talking.

Houston

Endnotes

1   In 2021, the building housing that Kroger was demolished, a part of Montrose history.

2   Smoking was banned in bars in Houston in 2006.

3   Babylon was open for about a year and then once again became Numbers, but as Numbers #2. It's still open though it has not been continually open during these decades.

4   Current note: This was by Boys Town Gang, and I adored that record.

5   Matlovich is the Air Force Sergeant and Viet Nam war vet who came out, was drummed out of the service, and fought the ban. He was a gay hero and was on the cover of *Time* magazine, and a movie was made about him.

6   I had avoided the Midnite Sun so far because it is pretty much a hustler bar.

7   Easter Sleaze Bonnet Contest 1981 photos: https://houstonlgbthistory.org/houston-easter.html.

SEVEN

Houston…and there's a love story

Wednesday—April 22, 1981
Houston

LATER, on Monday, I stopped by Stadium Bowl near Rice University. The Montrose Sports Association (MSA) was having their weekly Monday night bowling—55 teams. Last week I met one of their members who invited me to stop by. Why not? Where else can you see over 250 men under decent lighting?

The alleys also had automatic scoring (bowling scores, thank you)—first time I'd seen that. I didn't go there to cruise, instead just to see another part of the gay community other than the bars… But, you guessed it, I did get picked up by one of the MSA members. His name was Clark W—a former policeman & currently an insurance adjuster. He is a very nice guy, and *great* in bed.

Tuesday, he took the afternoon off, and we went to Galveston Beach, about 50 miles away. It has a gay section like 21st Street of VA Beach, and it wasn't bad for a Tuesday. Naturally, we both got sunburned. We stopped for a drink in Galveston at Mary's II. I suppose that bar is connected to Mary's in Houston, but it is not as sleazy. We played a couple of games of pool and generally acted trashy. I remember the bartender giving us free drinks, so he could watch us lean over the pool tables in our skimpy shorts.

So, there was some heavy play there, and all the way back to Houston, which ended in about two hours of afternoon delight (damn, he's good). We had dinner at the Barbecue Ranch and went to Baja Sam's and The Bunkhouse for drinks. The Bunkhouse is sort of a neighborhood bar, which I liked, although there were only about three other customers there. The bartender bought our second round of drinks (probably, like the bartender at Mary's II, because he enjoyed watching us clown around as we played pool).

Wednesday, after sleeping till noon, I went on errands. I ate at Steak and Eggs, went to the bank, went to a record store with an excellent oldies 45 selection (Third Planet) and went to a gay clothing store called The Manhole (on W Gray Street). They serve their customers complimentary cocktails. I bought two t-shirts that I had been looking for: One saying TALK ME INTO IT for me, and THIS IS NO ORDINARY HOUSEWIFE YOU'RE DEALING WITH for my close friend Fred, back in Norfolk.

Houston...and there's a love story

Thursday—April 23, 1981
Houston

Last night, Clark and I had dinner at the Brasserie, a gay restaurant on West Alabama Street. It was very nice, and reasonably priced, too. Then to Baja Sam's for drinks with some of Clark's friends, most of whom also went to The Copa later. This Copa is not to be confused with the one in Ft. Lauderdale, by any means. In layout it was okay, with a small piano bar lounge as you enter, and a large disco beyond with a dance floor. The dance floor is surrounded by several platforms and four bars. The lighting effects were adequate but nothing special. It was 20-cent drink night there, which is a good deal. What was wrong for me was the crowd. It was very young. If you like long-haired chicken, this is the place. Although the size of the crowd was okay, I did not see *any* men I thought particularly attractive.

I thought the music was average or below average. To be fair, this was a Wednesday night crowd. I gather that the Copa is very popular, with frequent high profile drag shows. Last Sunday they had Texas drag royalty Tiffany Jones, Donna Day and Ernestine. Other frequent headlining icons include Naomi Sims, Tasha Kohl and Hot Chocolate (Larry Edwards). Anyway, last night I guess we left The Copa before midnight, and stopped at the Galleon, which I had seen very briefly about a week ago. It is a nice, neighborhood-type bar.

Friday—April 24, 1981
Houston

We had dinner last night at still another gay restaurant—The House of Pies—which was good, with great desserts. Then, on to Babylon, the disco, where Grace Jones was doing a show that night. The 10 PM show started at 11:30 PM, but the music before the show was excellent—the DJ played "Remember Me/Ain't No Mountain" (Boys Town Gang) again.

Grace Jones came out in sort of a black bulky double-breasted suit, with sunglasses, and her head almost shaved on the sides and about 1½" long elsewhere—almost mohawk style. She did a song I didn't recognize which featured her banging on cymbals violently to the beat and finally knocking them over. Her expression during this and most of the numbers was very deadpan, with a cold, blank, mean stare—what an effect! Her movements during the songs are very slow, deliberate and unorthodox. During "Love Is the Drug," she came out wearing a long, reddish-orange hooded robe with big round padded shoulders—very haunting.

She went up to several people in the audience and kissed them or pretended to grope or fondle them; she called a couple guys up to dance or bump with her. The stage at Babylon has four or five wide steps arching down from it and she was all over the steps. Clark and I were sitting on the floor near the center-right against the steps. During one number, she stood in front of us, motioning for one of us to come up. I pushed Clark up (I

was not *about* to do it), and she had him sit on his knees with his back to her (he faced the audience).

She then straddled his head with her legs as she faced the audience while singing. He didn't know what she wanted him to do (and was embarrassed too) but not too embarrassed to bite her on the ass. She jumped up, hit him on the back of the head, and said, "You're going to lose those teeth!" The crowd (and I), of course, loved it. Other songs were: "The Hunter Gets Captured," "La Vie en Rose," "I Need a Man," "Breakdown," and the encore, "Bullshit." She was on for 45 minutes and it was just a *great* show—I wish I had it on film. No, she didn't sing my favorite of hers, "Do or Die."

We danced for about an hour after the show...with shirts off. This *is* the big city. Later two guys tried to pick us up—it was kind of interesting. We walked by them at the bar and I thought I heard one of them say something like, "Look at those two." As we were standing by the bar they came up and one started a conversation with, "How did you like the show?" or some such remark. They introduced themselves (Jerry and Mark) and then asked, "Are you two lovers?" We said no but Clark put his arm around me—body language at work. Even before they asked that, it was obvious they wanted a foursome or something. Jerry said he and Mark were lovers.

Clark and I were not interested and quickly said, "Well, see you later," or something. That's the first time I had ever been approached like that—by a couple while I was with someone. They were cute, sort of—but no big deal. If I were alone, I might have been interested in one of them. But that night, no thank you. As I told Clark, I am much more interested in quality than quantity.

Oh, I did want to make one negative comment about Grace Jones. She was over an hour late starting the concert and made not one word of apology. She just started the show, like keeping a club full of people waiting was something to which she was entitled. I thought that was rude.

Today (Friday), we slept till 11 AM and then ate (at House of

Houston...and there's a love story

Pies) and ran errands. Clark had some insurance field work to do, so he didn't go into the office this morning. I went with him to check the scene of an accident at some intersection in NE Houston. I watched him measure it out and take pictures.

One thing I meant to comment on earlier was the general attitude of a lot of people that everyone just automatically wants to (or is planning to) move to Houston. I've had at least a half a dozen conversations where it had already been said that I was on vacation, when they would ask, "Are you moving here?" I suppose part of that comes from the statistic that 6,000 people move here every month.

General observation time: Houston has a lot going for (and against) it. It has an established gay ghetto that is very comfortable. Parts of it are very nice and other parts (just as many or more) are very run down or perhaps not yet renovated. Houston is not an attractive city (as is DC or SF) and does not have the appeal of being near the water, as does Coconut Grove/Miami. The city—at least Montrose and a wide, wide area around it—has a lot of gay presence... *lots* of trendy, obviously gay shops and restaurants; *lots* of clones (yeah!). There appear to be lots of jobs available and rents do not seem as high as other large cities. I am not in love with the bars here. They don't appear to be as nice as in Atlanta; many are downright sleazy—apparently by design—most notably Mary's, naturally. Actually, Mary's, Naturally is its official name.

The gay community here is justifiably one of its big attractions—it has its shit together. *TWT* is an established and strong entity in the city (and state). There is a long list of gay groups of every description (at least 40), including The Montrose Sports Association and The Gay Political Caucus, which began in 1975. Currently there are several committees involved in planning the 11-day Gay Pride Week (with its parade, guide, etc.). One of the few gay radio programs in the country is here.

I haven't mentioned yet the other gay publication here, *The Montrose Voice*. I haven't visited their offices yet, something I can't quite get the incentive to do because I just don't like the paper. It is not very gay. It has community news that is non-gay (which is fine), but it also has lots of straight syndicated features like movie reviews, horoscopes, photography columns, cartoons, theatre and art listings, etc.—all that you could just as easily read in the Houston city papers like the *Post* or *Chronicle*.

I find no excuse for this laziness, since there is no shortage of gay copy. Plus, the layout reeks! No imagination— it is obviously just slapped down to just get it done. On one page of news articles, they had the headline at the bottom of one column and the copy starting at the top of the next column. Just absurd.

One more observation—around Montrose you get the impression that the phrase "gay waiter" is redundant.

Saturday—April 25, 1981
Houston

Last night, Clark and I had dinner at Jasmine, a gay restaurant—it was a nice place, although I didn't care for what I ordered, a spicy marinated steak. Then to the Briar Patch for a drink. It is a nice bar that has an older crowd. I have heard it called The Wrinkle Room. We next went to Mary's to go in their store, which is only open after 9:30 PM, to look at their t-shirts. They have one of the better selections, although they were out of the only shirt I wanted. It said in small, typewriter-like type A GOOD FAIRY.

We went to The Different Drum to see if their store had it… nope. The Different Drum is the leather bar. For the image it is trying to invoke, it does a really good job. I wouldn't be comfortable there, but it thoroughly succeeds in its image. We also went to Venture'N, which had a really nice-looking crowd. It is one of my favorite bars here. Then to a party put on by the MSA softball committee. It was held in a hotel lobby and bar of a former hotel. There was an open bar and a DJ for dancing.

There was this one hot number there that Clark liked. I thought he was the best looking one there too, a short Italian

clone named Benny. Clark got his phone number for future reference. Grass does not grow under Clark's feet. A little later, Benny came over to both of us and talked a little. Clark and I were obviously together. I was sitting on his lap, but that doesn't seem to bother people here. After getting introduced to me about the third sentence out of his mouth was "Are you two lovers? Are you into three-ways?" No to both questions, but it was interesting, and nice to be asked.

Today we went to the Westheimer Arts Festival, held twice a year along 11 blocks of the street. There were lots of crafts, etc., and an interesting but not particularly hot crowd. I took pictures of course of all the clones I could, and even two dykes, and a couple of the interesting crafts. I bought a very nice ink drawing of a man's torso. Activist Bob Kunst from Miami had a table selling his Oral Majority stickers and buttons. He had been very active in the Anita Bryant protests in 1977. It stated to rain around 4 PM, which closed the festival a little early. We were already back in the hotel room for some playing.

Later, I went bar hopping from about 6:30-8:30 PM, which turned out to be great for the ego. I turned down three very nice-looking guys. Even if they weren't quite my type, it is nice to be asked. I just went to Mary's and was out on the patio, as I never stay in the bar area of that bar. A guy named Ron came

right up and gave me the line that while he's not attracted to too many people, he sure thought I was good looking and would love to get together with me. I was friendly but noncommittal. Two of his friends came over shortly and he introduced them as Mike and Rick. I had met Mike last week at the bowling alley. They all left soon for the Mining Company.

About an hour later I was over at the Mine on their patio (I love patios) and a man named Reed came over to talk. I had noticed him earlier giving me a thorough cruise as I walked down Westheimer on the way to Mary's. He was about 6'2", broad shoulders and chest, mustache, and beard—very nice looking, but I'm just not attracted to that body type. I like men my height or shorter. We talked for about 15 minutes. He rubbed my leg a little, but I did not reciprocate (I am *not* a tease). When he finally asked, I told him I thought he was really good looking but just not my type. He finally gave up and left.

Mike, Rick, and Ron had been standing about eight feet away during all this and (although they couldn't hear us and weren't deliberately watching) knew what was going on. Rick came over and said, "Now *what* was wrong with him?" I said Reed just wasn't my type. Rick asked if he himself was. Rick has a very attractive face, but a very muscular chest, too much so for my tastes. I probably will kick myself later for passing up that one. Yes, I can be picky.

One thing about the men in Houston is that they sure are assertive. There seem to be fewer games in the bars. If they're interested, they'd come right up to you—which is good. And you kind of sense that these are the ground rules, so you feel comfortable doing the same thing.

On a separate note, last night I had a fight with a waiter! It was at the Italian restaurant, The Godfather, where I went for dinner on Saturday after the arts festival. Granted, the restaurant was busy due to the festival, but the service was just terrible. It's one of those places where they automatically include the tip in your bill (this is stated in the menu) so when I went to pay the bill I said I felt the tip should be left out. He had already written it in and said it was automatic. I proceeded to enumerate what was wrong with the service: I never got a menu, I had to ask for silverware, I had to ask—twice—for a glass of water, I had to ask for bread which I never got, I had to ask twice for the check. He was arguing too, but gave up halfway through my list, which I finished anyway. It also pissed me off that never did he apologize for the service.

So, I didn't get charged for the tip, and on the way out I stopped by the neighboring table to mine. The party of four there had also complained about the service, and I pointed out to them (which they didn't know) that the tip would be billed to them and that they might question that point. They thanked me, of course. I kind of felt good about the whole thing; I guess it was one of those little victories. I had never had an argument in a restaurant before. And, no, of course it wasn't the amount of the tip, it was the principle!

Monday—April 27, 1981
Houston

Monday morning, 6 AM. Clark just left for work. What a great weekend!

On Saturday night after going bar hopping from 6:30-8:30 PM, I went out again about 11:00 PM. Clark went to a movie and dinner with several friends, which had been planned before he met me; so, we had planned to meet the next day at the festival. I went to the Venture'N, the downtown cruise bar. And although it's only about 8 blocks away, because of the neighborhood you don't walk it. It and the Mining Company are probably the two bars where I would most likely be found.

Around midnight, Clark walked in the bar (I saw him from the bar's mezzanine). He had thought he would find me there, which I thought was *really* nice. And he came right over and asked me if I was ready to be picked up. I certainly was. I also thought it was nice that after spending the last five nights with me, he still wanted more. I later teased him that I was surprised to see him on his "night off". We stayed at the bar for a while to watch the people—it was certainly a pretty crowd, and I would rate it overall about a 6 or 7.

Sunday, we went to the festival again—to watch the people, of course—and the crowd was even larger that day, with about the same atmosphere, or better. There were two or three "gay" booths selling gay pride t-shirts and other merchandise. There were lots of clones, of course, and I took three rolls of film. I'm sure I got several classics, especially one of a drag queen who posed with her wig off. I think I saw everyone I've met in the last two weeks at the festival, which is a lot of people. It made me not feel like a tourist.

The two best places to loiter around (to see clones) at the festival are almost at opposite ends of it: at Mary's and near the booths outside of Babylon. We spent adequate time at both, where I took lots of pictures. It is interesting that people inside of a gay bar or on its patio don't seem to give a shit if you take their picture, and lots of people had cameras. I can't imagine doing that in Norfolk.

Although it might have been due to the festival, the bar crowd was friendly, and I did find it very easy to talk to strangers. However, the bars were extremely crowded. Remember, they are either *on* Westheimer or within two or three blocks of the heart of the festival. The Mining Company was also very packed. You had to almost grope your way through the patio—it was awful.

Sometime around 3 PM we met a friend of Clark's who joined us in our travels—a very good-looking man from Colombia named Jader A. He's 23 and comes from wealthy parents in the diamond business. He's been here about two years. His father sent him to live in America after he (Jader) accidentally caught the father in bed with the father's best friend—a man. Isn't that interesting?

I guess that nothing was ever said about it. The father just conveniently decided it was time to send the son to America.

Jader is about 5'8", slender, cute and a real sweetheart—you feel like hugging him every five minutes. And his sense of humor is such that he is very fun to kid. You crack a joke and (although his English is pretty good) there is just that slight hesitation before he catches it that is neat. It tickles you to be around him—just a delight.

Around 5 PM we were at Babylon and decided to walk back to Mary's, but first walked back to my room to put away my camera. Once there (I'm still not quite sure I believe I did this), I said to them, "How 'bout a threesome?" Jader was ready, and Clark was a little surprised but also ready. I guess the rapport between the three of us had been so good that it just seemed right. It was! I had figured—correctly—that Clark and Jader had already been to bed together. It was a very nice experience. It more than made up for my other threesome last summer in Norfolk, which I did not like.

We all went to Mary's afterwards, then The Mining Company, and finally to dinner at Brasserie. We dropped Jader off around 10:30 PM. What a perfect day, and weekend.

By now you're probably wondering what's going on between Clark and I. After all, eight days in a row (counting tonight—already planned) must be some record for me. Well, I'm not in love. I don't think with my current frame of mind—what with my life being so much up in the air right now—that I would let myself fall in love. But I feel kind of attached to him and thoroughly enjoy being with him (not just for sex, of course, although that part is *great*). On his part, he has said that he'll miss me, that he likes my gentleness, my sense of humor, and ability to clown around, the way I handle myself in the bars (the fool thinks I have my act together). And he thinks I'm hot. He actually *likes* my body—takes all kinds. All these things were communicated in a matter-of-fact manner and without things getting heavy, which is exactly the way it should be.

He is a very "together" guy. He has a very outgoing personality, and I gather he goes out a lot—he seemed to know most of the cute guys at the arts festival (and those he doesn't know he will soon). He's really interesting to watch at work. Last year in his bowling league he was voted "Mr. Sportsman"—I think he was a good "sport" with someone on every team.

I feel very comfortable with him, and I don't think I have any hang-ups or insecurities about it. That should be obvious if I was comfortable enough to have (even instigate) a threesome with him. I think that around him I start to feel that maybe I do have my act together. He has made Houston special.

Tuesday—April 28, 1981
Houston

Yesterday afternoon, I went out to the Galleria to get Clark a birthday present. He's 36 today. And I had to run other errands, too (post office, bank, buy film, etc.). At the t-shirt store I ran into the young man whom Clark and I talked to at the Grace Jones concert. He's the one (about 21, blond, and twink cute) who had a teddy bear in his back pocket and said he thought Clark and I made a gorgeous couple. I'm sure he would go to bed with either one of us in a heartbeat. His name is Billy.

Also, while I was walking through a department store men's department, I passed within about 20 feet of two young straight-looking male clerks behind a counter. As I passed by, one said something to the other. I couldn't quite catch the first thing he said—it was something like *"look at that one"* or *"look at that queer."* But the second thing he said was, *"Did you see his bottom button open?"* The other replied affirmatively, *"Uh huh."* They were probably playing spot the faggot. I give them credit for that one. The tone in his voice was not malicious though, just matter of fact.

When I got back to the guest house, I got a nice surprise. It was 3:30 PM and Clark was supposed to meet me at 5 PM. Well, he was already off work and waiting on the porch. I was really pleased; he said he wanted to spend as much time with me as possible while I'm here.

He said that when he got there he went up to the front door, which was locked (as it usually is) and one of the part time employees asked him if he wanted to be let in his room. Clark told him no, he would sit on the porch. I had already joked with Clark that they were going to charge me for double occupancy.

We had dinner downtown at the Spaghetti Warehouse, which was very good. It's about the best Italian food I've had here, and very reasonably priced. I went with Clark to watch him bowl (his Monday night league), which I enjoyed. I got to talk again with some of the people I met last week and met some new ones.

Of course, I probably got extra attention because I was a new face in the crowd. Four of them let me know they were interested. In Houston it doesn't seem to matter if you're with someone or not; people still feel free to at least sound you out. Some of them are even more blatant: When we were at the Jones concert, Clark and I were sitting on the stage steps (very obviously together) and a man walked by and reached over and handed Clark his phone number. He did so without saying a word and was just as quickly gone. Clark had never seen him before. We thought that was really tacky.

Wednesday—April 29, 1981
Houston

Tuesday afternoon we went downtown to take pictures. We went up in two or three of the tall buildings and got nicely thrown out of several offices who were very firm about people taking photos from their windows. One secretary and one maintenance man did let us into offices with windows though, so we didn't fail completely. Then we went to the revolving restaurant in the Hyatt Regency, called the Spindletop. Although not very tall, it seems to be the only observation deck available to the public. We also saw part of one of the tunnel systems, which was full of underground shops.

Tuesday evening Clark took me to a birthday party for him that some friends were giving. There were about a dozen guests. The hosts, Norman and Reggie, gave him a nice Kodak instant camera and he got a few other gifts, some naughty. Reggie, who is a great cook, prepared lasagna. Of course, there were cocktails, and the usual trashing of each other during the evening.

I enjoyed myself even though I really didn't know anyone. I had only met Frank, who is Clark's cousin, and also Norman and Terry very briefly. I got Clark a personalized Montrose t-shirt and some bay rum cologne for his birthday. I had the shirt personalized with the number 77, for being my 77th trick, but of course you don't know that without asking.

Today—Wednesday—I checked out of the Guest House and will stay with Clark until I leave for Dallas on Friday. Also, yesterday I met at the Guest House Scott Anderson who is associate editor of the *Advocate*—a non-clone, believe it or not. He's probably 35, blond, just slightly stocky and no mustache—kind of nice looking in a 30-ish preppy way. He's going to the GPA (Gay Press Association) convention, and is also in Texas to try and hire a freelance writer to represent Texas for them. It seems that Texas is a big gay market, but it is currently untapped.

According to the Guest House manager Stewart McCloud (who interviewed for the job), there's only one newsstand that sells the *Advocate*, and it sells only 18 copies a month. *TWT* has a very strong hold on Texas readers—probably justifiably so. Stewart said he isn't likely to get the job because he is too opinionated. I think he won't get it because he's too flaky. When I was introduced to Scott, I told him I work on a gay paper in Virginia. He right away said, "*Our Own?*" I felt proud that he seemed to know about us.

Regarding *Our Own Community Press*, it *did* get a lot of attention. Way back in 1980, when I had just finished my stint as editor, the paper found itself embroiled in a white-hot controversy. We were distributed in all the bars, many restaurants and logical places, and in the Virginia Beach Library. The bible bigots found this to be unacceptable. It turned into an ACLU lawsuit, and we could not have bought all the publicity we got. Across the country people knew Norfolk had a gay newspaper. Ultimately, the compromise was to have non-distribution copies available for reading, but you had to ask at the library's information desk for them.

Thursday—April 30, 1981
Houston

Yesterday afternoon we took pictures in Warwick Park of the Mecom Fountain and other objects. Okay, we clowned around a little. I probably should not have climbed on that statue. We caught the 5:15 PM showing of *La Cage Aux Folles II*. Yeah, I know, I saw it in Atlanta, but Clark hadn't seen it. Then we had dinner near Clark's house at a home-style restaurant. When I checked out of the Guest House, Stewart exclaimed, "Oh no, my firstborn is leaving the nest!" I *did*, after two weeks, kind of feel like I lived there. At 10 PM. Clark dragged me to bed—I really fought.

Friday—May 1, 1981
Houston

On Thursday, my last full day in Houston, Clark took off work early again; we went window shopping at a mall, played pool for a couple of hours, and he took me to my first 25-cent movie at a newsstand. (Translation: dirty bookstore). This is a movie shown in a private booth, and you feed the machine with tokens you buy at the front desk. I assure you that whatever mystique those movies have is completely shattered when you see one. They last about a minute on this little screen and the doors didn't even have

locks on them. What a rip-off!

That evening we went out for pizza with Clark's cousin Frank. He hasn't been "out" very long, and he is fun to tease. I told him I was going to take a compromising photo of him to his mom in Missouri on my way back east. Since Clark and I planned to get up early on Friday, we went to bed around 10:30 PM.

On Friday, after running a couple of errands, we finally left on schedule around 10:30 AM. The drive to Dallas took just under 4½ hours. Clark was also going to Dallas that weekend to visit friends (I know, how convenient), so we caravanned up there and then had a late lunch and some making out (maybe more) in my hotel room before he left.

Less than five days ago I wrote how nice I thought it was that things between us had not gotten heavy. I must have been kidding myself—I think we've both fallen a little in love with each other. I know that I feel that way. We talked about it in a way—sort of talking around it, knowing that there is something between us, but, because of the circumstances, not wanting to really acknowledge it.

Neither of us has said it, but reactions, phrasings, and things not said have said a lot. We both realize that there may be some element of "shipboard romance" or fling to it and that I have a long way to go, in not just miles, on my trip before I find (if I do indeed find) what I'm looking for.

We've been holding back our emotions trying not to let things get carried away. But I know he thinks an awful lot of me. And as for him, he makes it very hard to say goodbye to, and to not say, "Okay, hang it all up, I'll move to Houston."

I don't think I've ever had a relationship quite like this. He is just what I would want someone to be—he is very affectionate, considerate, he makes me feel good just being around him. We spent almost every hour of 12 full days together, during which I've never wished I was with someone else or alone. I haven't even gotten a little tired of him!

And with all that going for him, he is also good looking, intelligent, and a complete sexual turn-on. This is why I'm so confused: He seems like Mr. Right, and yet I don't know if I'm ready to put such things in perspective. My life is hardly in a normal state. He has made it clear that he would very much like me to stop in Houston on my return trip. I can't deny that it isn't tempting, but we both know that I shouldn't promise that now, what with so much ahead of me yet.

He left the hotel at 6:30 PM and we said goodbye in the room and again in his car before he drove away. I didn't think I would cry, but at the last minute I started to, and quickly got out of his car and walked away. I couldn't even wave goodbye. As for what comes after this, time will tell.

EIGHT

Dallas

May 1, 1981
Dallas

Later, the Round Up Saloon had a reception/barbecue for convention attendees this evening. There were about 20 of us here early enough to attend, while the rest are probably arriving late tonight. I've talked a little with Joe Di Sabato of Rivendell Agency, Scott Anderson of the *Advocate*, John Fauling (*Fifth Freedom*, Buffalo), Henry Mach (*First Hand*, NYC), and Harry Losleben (*TWN*, Miami). Harry and I met when I was in Miami in January and he brought me up to date on the publication's problems: a production manager being forced to quit, and another, Rico, being close to that. And there are lots of power plays and fights over editorial policy. Sounds like home!

After the barbecue I stayed at the bar to watch the country dancing—The Round Up is a real Western bar with country DJ and line-dancing. It was entertaining to watch, and the dance floor was always full. While it looked like fun, I'm not ready to try it yet.

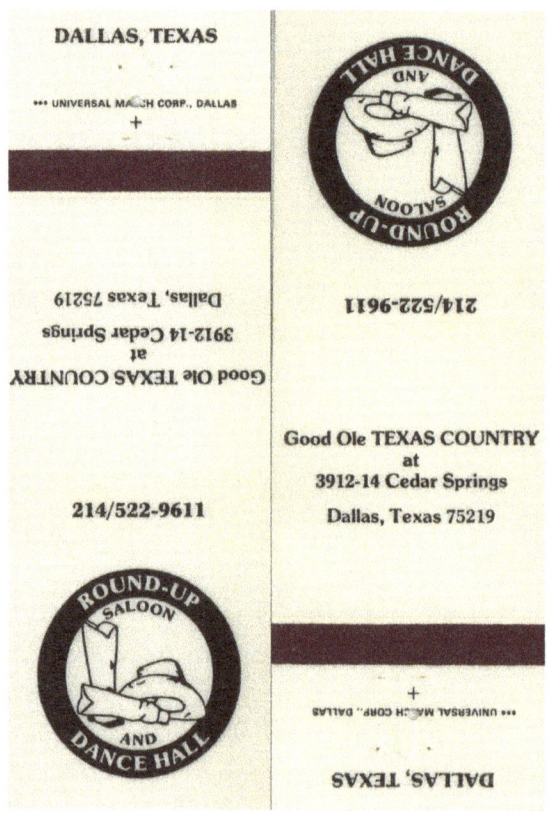

Sunday—May 3, 1981
Dallas

Well, the Gay Press Association convention is over, and it certainly was an interesting and enjoyable experience—about 50 people attended, representing about 25 publications.

While the business aspects were important and neat to be a part of, I was much more enthusiastic about the opportunity to meet the editors and staff people involved in various publications from across the country. I almost wish it could've lasted longer so I could have gotten to know some of these people better. And there were some I didn't get a chance to talk to at all.

I'll try and comment on some of the people I met; or at least list them:

Joe Di Sabato—organizer of GPA and was elected first president. He was a nice guy, and he seems sharp. He handled the meetings well, I thought, especially considering some of the issues, like organizational and regional representation, and membership rates that could vary on the size of the publication.

Mark Segal (*Philly Gay News*, Publisher)—Elected vice president; didn't really talk to him. He seems to be on the ball although perhaps a little pushy, or let's say, very self-assured.

Sally Tyre (*Philly Gay News*, Associate Publisher). She was the only woman to stay for the whole convention, and another I did not meet was there for Saturday morning. Sally was elected as a board director at large. She seems competent and I don't have any issue with her election, except that it gives that paper two of the 11 board seats.

Phil Nash (*Out Front*, Denver)—Elected secretary. I talked only briefly with him. He took notes for all the sessions and did a good job.

Morgan Pinney—A freelance writer living in NYC. I talked quite a bit with him at the cocktail reception sponsored by the DGPC (Dallas Gay Political Caucus) and had dinner with him and Rance Pearson, another freelancer from SF. Morgan was elected treasurer, in part because he's an accountant by degree. I liked him—he was very interested in the perspective of the small papers, and I think our talk helped him understand some of our problems. I was glad a freelancer was elected as one of the main officers so a different view (as opposed to just the big papers) could be presented.[1]

As for the meetings themselves, they were kind of dry. Saturday was comprised mostly of getting the group's bylaws ironed out. Remember, this was the organizing meeting of the new organization. A committee had roughed them out, but they were only tentative. Major points included voting rights and dues along with membership requirements. I thought these discussions went smoothly, despite the competing interests. Naturally, there were occasional debates over phrasing. What else would you expect with a room full of editors?

I lost interest in the presentation regarding usage of the computer for a proposed gay wire service because it was just too pie-in-the-sky for any small paper like Norfolk's. The election of officers went smoothly. I pretty much agree with all the choices made.

Mark Segal, Phil Nash, Joe Di Sabato, Morgan Pinney

(Photo courtesy of GCN.ORG.00283, Gay Community News Photograph Collection, The History Project, Boston)

Sunday's reports were on insurance and benefits, credit (collecting ad money), ad standards, affiliations, communications, the writer's task force, and the seven-page standards and ethics proposal. The ethics proposal is very much stricter than those of us from Norfolk are used to, especially concerning the usage of other paper's articles, photos, and graphics without permission. Many of us in publications have, in the past, violated these rules a lot. We do a fair job of crediting articles, but we haven't always asked for permission to even use the article. Our worst abuse is probably the stealing of graphics.

On Saturday evening the Dallas Gay Political Caucus hosted the GPA at a cocktail party, which I enjoyed, as it gave me the opportunity to talk to fellow attendees (such as Morgan Pinney, and the *GAZE* staff). I socialized a little with the DGPC's president Don Baker[2] (defendant in the Texas 21.06 sodomy lawsuit challenge) and one of the group's lesbians, Doris Taylor. She and I talked for at least a half hour comparing impressions of our respective gay communities, and she gave me a copy of the local Texas women's newspaper.

At Sunday's afternoon session I joined GPA, as an individual. I didn't think I could commit *Our Own* to a $100 membership fee (even paid on installments) without asking. Conversely, the individual rates are $50 for a founding member, and $25 for a general member.

The convention was thankfully not all business. On Saturday night after the cocktail party and a late dinner (with Rance Pearson and Morgan Pinney), I hit the bars. First to JR's, which I had heard is the most popular bar at this time. I thought it was an attractive place. It was fixed up nicely, kind of rustic with, unsurprisingly, a touch of Western without being sleazy. It's a cruise bar (as opposed to a disco, or cowboy bar). It is even fairly well lit. It has a DJ playing disco, no dance floor though.

Next, I went to the Throckmorton Mining Company (TMC), which is next door. Many of the bars seem very close together in Dallas. It is almost identical to the Mining Company in Houston—same layout (except no patio or DJ) and same decor and atmosphere. Even the owner is the same, Frank Caven. Then back to the Round Up Saloon—I really enjoy watching the Western dancing. I ran into Clark again there (as I did on Friday night) with the friend he was visiting, Steve. I watched them dance to several songs, and then we all walked back to TMC for a beer before last call (2 AM in Dallas).

Something that I meant to comment on is in the Houston

section was the rivalry between it and Dallas. It's real. According to Houston, Dallas is "uptown," unfriendly, with plenty of attitude. Vice versa, Houston is "low class" and seedy. When I was in Houston about one week, I tried to find a Dallas newspaper at a newsstand because I knew I was going to Dallas next. Well, forget it. I stopped at every newsstand I happened by for the next two weeks and never saw a Dallas paper…the *Detroit News*, the *Birmingham* whatever, the NY *Times*, but never any Dallas. It was like this city didn't exist. I wonder if, just for comparison purposes, I would find a Houston paper here.

Another thing I meant to mention was a Texas expression I just love: "I'm a-fixin' to…", as in, "I'm a-fixin' to call him" or "I'm a-fixin' to get groceries," or whatever. It's very common.

Monday—May 4, 1981
Dallas

Last night I had dinner at a Western-style restaurant—Tolbert's—across from the Melrose Hotel in Cedar Springs. I had Texas-style

Melrose Hotel

chili, which was really hot! Later I called up Mike Rutherford (*Out*, DC) to see if he was going to the bars—there were probably only about five of us from the convention staying Sunday night. I had met him but hadn't really talked to him, so I enjoyed a chance to exchange views with him on the convention and the people. He is a really nice guy. We talked shop about three hours, the last two of which we were at TMC; and I thoroughly enjoyed it. He is one of the board members, so it was also good to exchange views from that respect.

You may also recall that I said earlier that Mike was by far the cutest person at the convention. You guessed it—after the bar closed (2 AM) we continued our "discussion" in his room till about 3:30 AM, and I got back to my room about 7 AM

I had planned to meet Clark in my room at 8 AM—no rest for the wicked! He was visiting friends this weekend, but we wanted to see each other again (alone) before he left. We cuddled for a couple of hours, and talked a little, and in general just tried to soak up each other's company. It will be at least July before we see each other again, as the tentative idea is for him to meet me on my way back East. We had lunch and then sat in his car in the hotel parking lot for about 20 minutes trying to say goodbye. It was almost as heavy as Friday's goodbye. This time I noticed that Clark got a little misty too. Needless to say, I will miss him a lot.

And, yes, you read that correctly. The tentative idea is for him to meet me on my way back East. It surprises me that I've reached this level of commitment.

Tuesday—May 5, 1981
Dallas

On Monday afternoon I walked around Oak Lawn and Cedar Springs for a couple of hours taking pictures, and I also went up on the roof of the Melrose Hotel to take some. All this wasn't as easy as it sounds—as I gather from the locked doors, they don't want people up there. I found one stairway which also had a window on the roof level that was about eight feet from the floor with a 4" ledge about five feet up. I climbed up and out the window onto the roof. I walked all around the roof taking photos of Oak Lawn and the downtown skyline, expecting to be caught and arrested for trespassing at any moment. But no one saw me apparently. Fortunately, the doors could be opened from the roof level, so I didn't have to climb back through the window. I was glad, since climbing up from a 4" ledge is surely easier than climbing down onto one.

At 4 PM I went to visit Richard Rogers at the *TWT* Dallas office, which is in his apartment. As I already mentioned, I was impressed with him at the convention—he is very sharp, a nice guy, and has a very outgoing personality. We talked for a couple

Dallas

Two views of Cedar Springs

Richard Rogers and friend

of hours—more b.s. than business. He showed me a pair of gym shorts he just bought that, besides being of thin material, had a design based on the Texas state flag. Naturally, I asked him if he was going to model them. He didn't need encouragement and continued to model three or four other pairs of shorts, some not very discreet. This of course was thoroughly enjoyable—Richard is good looking, has a nice body, and is a solid 6'4" tall. The whole show was kind of like a mini seduction, which I really got off on. Next, as seemed appropriate, we went to bed.

Richard is the first person I've been to bed with that was so much taller than me, which was kind of different. As I said, he's 6'4"; I've probably only been to bed with about two or three others taller than me, but they were not more than an inch taller.

Around 8 PM he had some errands to run, and I went along. He visited a friend to borrow some leather chaps, boots, and a vest. This weekend he is going to be a judge in the Mr. Leather International contest in Chicago. Next, we went to visit some of his friends just down the street, who are also his landlords. They live in a $350,000 house, which is just awesome—one is a realtor and the other is VP in an interior design company.

On a side note, the realtor just turned 40 and bought himself as a present an evening with porno star Al Parker (who cost $500 plus expenses from California). Richard also met Parker that weekend and went to bed with him at no charge. This means that I've been to bed with someone whose been to bed with Al Parker which is close enough for me.

Richard's friends invited us to stay for supper, which was very nice—there were about seven of us there. When we finally left around midnight, we then went to Sassy's, a women's disco, at which Richard had to collect some ad money for *TWT*. He is Regional Sales Director. Then to the Club Baths for a quick tour. Richard was their manager for four years before he worked for *TWT*. The Baths are fixed up very nice—maybe even nicer than the ones in Miami. There were hardly any customers there, though, since it was about 1 AM on a Monday night.

Oh yeah, while talking to Richard at various times, I also learned some more background on two more of the GPA's new board members. One is Chuck Renslow (*Gay Life,* Chicago) who owns the Gold Coast (one of the best known and oldest leather bars in the world) and Man's Country. The other is Henry Mach (*First Hand*), who wrote a lubricants humor article that got read over the radio in Cincinnati and started a big controversy there.

I stayed at Richard's that night, and we slept till noon, sleep I sorely needed since I got only about a total of eight hours sleep the last two nights. Also staying with Richard that weekend was Allan Lozito—a drag comedian from NYC that gave a routine for entertainment during lunch Sunday at the convention. He comes on stage with face painted white and wearing flowing kaftans and strange hats and wigs and insists he is not a drag queen, but a "drag-goon" (that *is* more appropriate).

Allan is a trip—really off the wall. His comedy is at times very funny but starts to wear thin after about 20 minutes. He also had kind of a nasal voice and is very thin, and usually very spaced out on one drug or another. Off stage he is a little easier to take but still comes across as a bitchy queen. He is kind of like Fig Newtons—you like the first two or three you have, then realize you don't want any more for a long time! I guess he is very popular in the big gay bars. He plays all over the country—NYC, Miami, LA, etc.

Later tonight I went to six bars in two hours, which isn't hard in Dallas since the bars seem to be in clusters. These were all on Fitzhugh Street. I know it was a Tuesday night, but still, none of these bars impressed me at all. First was Studio 69, a small disco which was having a drag show when I walked in. I stayed for three numbers and then walked next door to Crews Inn— you guessed it—a cruise bar which I suppose would be good on

Dallas

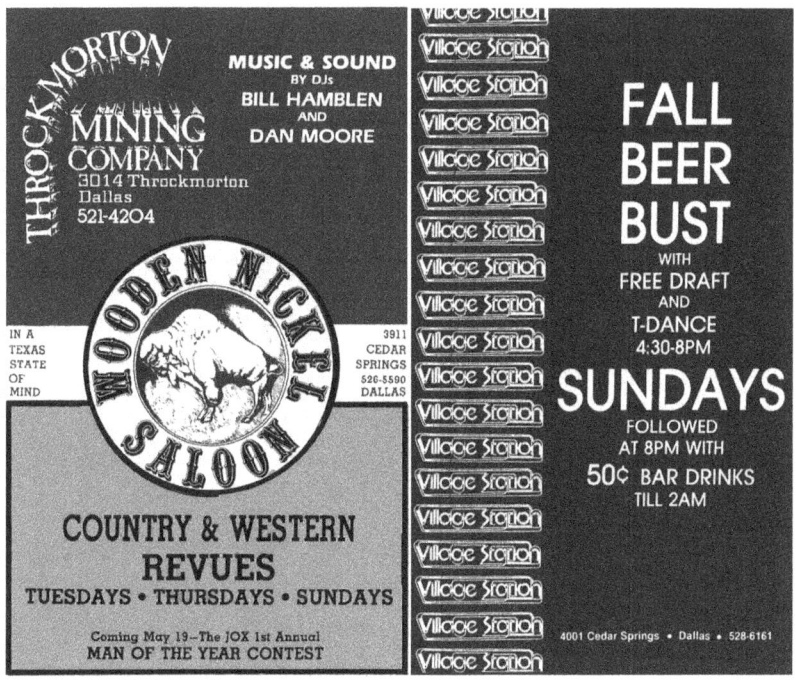

weekends. It had a fair crowd for a weeknight. Across the street was Fraternity House, a disco with kind of homey decor—fireplace and bookshelves. Farther up the street were three more bars in a row—Eight Day, No Name, and Wild Crowd Saloon. All three were really dead. They are a small disco, a small cruise bar and a Western bar, respectively. Four of the six bars seemed to have young crowds. The cruise bars had a wider range of ages. I suppose Crews Inn was the best bar of these. Of course, this was not a good day of the week to make fair comparisons about these bars.

Wednesday—May 6, 1981
Dallas

Well, this afternoon I sat by the hotel pool for about 3½ hours writing my report on the GPA convention[3], to send back to *Our Own*.

The Village Station

Then I called Kelly on the phone. He is the guy from Dallas whom I met on April 18th in Houston. He had made me promise to visit him here, definitely not a hardship. He invited me out to dinner with some friends of his named Joe and Guy. It was a nice evening. They are lovers and extremely friendly people. We went to an Italian restaurant called Sergio's that had an outdoor piazza for eating—good food and good atmosphere. I tried escargot for the first (and last!) time. I didn't order it, thankfully. I had the fettuccine alfredo, which was great. Kelly dropped me off at the hotel at about 9:30 PM.

I wanted to go to the disco tonight, so I changed into my red TALK ME INTO IT shirt and off I went—first to The Round Up, then Dallas Crude, then JR's. Dallas Crude and The Round Up weren't very crowded, as it *was* a Wednesday. Dallas Crude is kind of a Western cruise bar. JR's had a decent sized crowd—it always seems to, and usually a good-looking crowd. It's also the first bar I've seen with three TVs, and *Star Trek: The Motion Picture* was on (just the picture, no sound, thank goodness). The DJ was playing disco per usual. I hit these three bars from about 9:30 to 10:30—

Dallas

Dallas Crude

Under Arrest / Bronx

Union Jack / The Round Up

they are all on the same block.

Then to the disco, Village Station. It has one of the best layouts that I've seen for a disco and a versatile atmosphere that can combine both allowing one to party or cruise—not all discos can do that. For instance, Backstreet in Atlanta and Parade in Houston are good, maybe great, discos. But they are *not* cruisy. Village Station has a large center dance floor and platforms (about 2' high) on two sides. On the other two sides there is a mezzanine level over the main level so you can look down over the whole place. It has three bars and a good lighting system and a kind of rustic decor—corral-type fences around some of the dance floor, and the platforms. The corral decor and the disco lights somehow fit fine together—you wouldn't think they would. On one wall was one of those Times Square-type message boards where words travel across electronically to announce the bars coming events—I never saw one in a bar before. There was a big crowd—it was 10-cent drink night; and the atmosphere was one of the best I've seen. Oh, yeah, me? Not much of a drinker, I nurse a beer all evening. I always order beer as opposed to a well-drink, as it's easier to carry, and easier to hide that I'm not really drinking.

I can hardly believe the guy I picked up there. Technically he picked up me, I guess, since he spoke first, but I placed myself in a location to make it easy for him. I had already decided about a half-hour before we met that he (Tim) was by far the hottest man in the place—about 6'1" (another tall one), dark hair and mustache (clone personified) and nice body. He was really the only one in the bar who interested me. We left the bar about 12:30 PM and he took me to see another disco, Alcatraz. It was dead on that night. Everyone was at Village Station, but I am glad I got a chance to see it. We played a few games of Pac Man—my favorite electronic pinball game. Then we drove by the local gay cruise park, Reverchon, near Turtle Creek Road and Maple.

Tim said there is heavy cruising and some sex in the park night or day. Then we went to my hotel for a quickie. That's the way it had to be since Tim has a lover and he was expected home shortly after the bars close. He said they have been together for three months and that I was the first one who tempted him enough to cheat on his lover. This was really flattering, especially since this guy was *very* good looking.

Regarding the process of being picked up in a bar; I think going to another bar rather than straight to their place is done in order to give the person more time to make up their mind about you. I've had that happen before. Then again, they may have just not quite been ready to stop partying.

Furthermore, have you ever noticed that some guys are cute but not handsome, some are handsome but not cute, and some are hot and not quite either cute or handsome? Some are also cute or handsome, but not hot. Some have two out of the three. This guy had all three. He also seemed like a nice guy, and he liked to cuddle, although we didn't have much time for that. He thought it interesting that I was the same age as his lover. Tim is 25 (I am 34).

Thursday—May 7, 1981
Dallas

This afternoon, after running some errands (Kwik-Copy, post office, etc.), I stopped by Reverchon Park again. It is really pretty, with a creek running through it and stone arch bridges, and a big hill with many, many paths running up and down. The paths have stone steps and walls and benches, all nestled in the trees and bushes. You could not sit down and design a cruisier park. I took a few pictures and *did* see a little cruising; it was interesting. I just watched, thank you.

I was supposed to meet Kelly at his place at 4:30 PM. I still had some time to kill, so I went to JR's. That bar, as I have mentioned, is a very nice and a very popular cruise bar—probably one of the best anywhere. By now I would rate it, The Round Up Saloon, and Village Station as my favorite bars in Dallas, and they all are of different categories, so they really don't compete with each other much.

JR's is on the corner of Cedar Springs and Throckmorton. The side on Throckmorton is probably about 80' long and has big, slightly smoked, glass windows the whole length, so you can see in, and especially, out very easily, which is usually interesting viewing since TMC is next door and Village Station is across the street. I had a beer at JR's and played two or three games of Pac Man—which is about all my nerves and arm could take. You've heard of tennis elbow? Well, there's now also Pac Man arms. And since I played a few games last night at Alcatraz with Tim, my arm can feel it.

The last couple of days I've been listening a little to C&W music on the radio—trying to soak up some local color. I just love C&W song titles…some of them tell the whole story in the title. These include the previously mentioned "You Ain't Woman Enough to Take My Man," and also "My Shoes Keep Walking Back to You," and "Old Flames (Can't Hold a Candle to You)." This could be the next craze in party games.

Friday—May 8, 1981
Dallas

Well, I'm staying at Kelly's now. As you may recall (see entry for April 18th), I met him at the Venture'N in Houston. He's 25, a gay Mormon, works nights at a data processing outfit, and spent two years as a missionary in Mexico. He's from Idaho originally. He lives in a beautiful mobile home in Lewisville, about 20 miles north of Dallas. He is also a good friend of Leonard Matlovich, who is also Mormon. Kelly says that Leonard has invested most of the settlement money he got from the government in his lawsuit. He had been kicked out of the Air Force for being gay and filed a lawsuit. He bought a pizza parlor in Russian River (Guerneville, 65 miles north of SF). I guess he's always wanted a pizza parlor.

JR's

Dallas, as seen from the roof of the Melrose Hotel, May 1981. The art deco Esquire Theatre was torn down in 1985.

Kelly also was in a touring dance group for a year or two. That group was giving a performance in a nearby town, so we went tonight. Since he was part of that group five years ago, there was no one still in the group he knew, but he still wanted to see it. Sure, why not? The performance was held in the cultural hall of a Mormon church. Can you imagine *me* in a Mormon church on a Friday night?! It was so-o-o wholesome! The show was okay, a mix of folk, jazz, and ballroom dancing with about 30 performers—18 gals, 12 guys, all around 18 or 20 years old. It was held in Plano, which is supposedly the fastest growing city in the country, It is seemingly a very wealthy place. It appeared to be a sprawling suburb of 100,000+ houses, most of them brick and all very nice. But since almost all the houses were new, and the trees were still small, the streets seemed very monotonous.

Saturday—May 9, 1981
Dallas

This afternoon we went to one of the new malls in North Dallas—I think it was called Prestonwood Town Center. We also ate at my first real Mexican restaurant, and I had beef tacos, rice, and refried beans for the main course. The tacos had soft shells and real steak for the meat, rather than the Taco Bell-type with hard shell, hamburger, salad, and cheese. It was good, but I didn't like the beans or the side helping of salad, as they must have soaked the tomatoes in hot sauce. They look innocent enough, but lookout! For dessert I had an empanada, which is a warm pastry shell filled, in this case, with bananas, pecans, and raisins. Delicious!

After dinner, Kelly took me to a party. The host must have been fairly wealthy, as it was a catered affair for about 150 people. While the crowd seemed to be on the older side, it was nevertheless a good mix of ages. I met some nice people.

When we got home, Kelly called Leonard Matlovich on the phone so I could "meet" him. He seems really nice. His pizza parlor should open in a couple of weeks. I think it is called Stump Hollow Annie's, in Guerneville.

Sunday—May 10, 1981
Dallas

Today Kelly and I went to Six Flags Over Texas for about six hours with two of his friends—Olin and Louis—whom I met at the party last night. They both are quite friendly! Olin is a real character and Louis is kind of clone-ish; both are nice-looking. They are on-and-off-again lovers, I guess.

Six Flags is very much like Busch Gardens (Virginia) in a lot of ways—similar rides and shows. We went to the dolphin show, a 3-D movie, and a very good dance hall show, which was like a Vegas performance with good dances, songs and costumes. It was all quite well done. They tried unsuccessfully to get me on the Six Flags version of the Loch Ness Monster called Shockwave. We did ride the water flume and a mild (but not mild enough for me) rollercoaster, and there was a tunnel ride called The Cave. I sat between Olin and Louis and, okay, our behavior bordered on *trashy*.

For dinner I took Kelly to the Spaghetti Warehouse downtown. It was just as delicious as the one in Houston.

Some final thoughts regarding the Dallas-Houston comparisons: Ultimately, I'm not sure I can confirm the stereotype of Dallas being more "uppity" since I only went out one night (Wednesday) on my own, and the rest of the time I seemed to always be with people I knew—either Kelly and his friends or ones from the convention. Still, it didn't quite seem as friendly as Houston, but Oak Lawn was cleaner and fixed up nicer than Montrose. It was also smaller and a less gay atmosphere. I met friendly people both places of course. I guess Dallas is okay, but it didn't really win a place in my heart. I was impressed with three of its bars in Oak Lawn (JR's, Round Up, and Village Station), but that is not enough to really make it a good gay ghetto.

Endnotes

1 See **Notes** section on the other representatives to the Gay Press Association meeting. This goes into too much detail for the flow of the book, but I believe it contains too much history on an important time in our culture to not preserve it.

2 The "Don Baker case" tried to challenge the sodomy law in Texas and went rather far in that journey but ultimately failed. Several more efforts would fail before the Lawrence v Texas case in 2003 would settle the issue, and for the entire country.

3 Article in *Our Own*, June 1981, on the GPA convention. https://houstonlgbthistory.org/jd-book-links.html

NINE

Albuquerque

Monday—May 11, 1981
Albuquerque

Well, I got off to an early start today. I left Dallas (actually, Kelly's house in Lewisville) around 8 AM. It took 12 hours to get to Albuquerque, and surprisingly, I'm not really that tired. I didn't get drowsy driving at all. I stopped a lot though, usually very quick stops to buy a Coke or to take a picture. The landscape from Dallas through Amarillo to the Texas border is very flat. Let me repeat, very flat. About 15 miles before the border, it abruptly becomes hilly with those beautiful flat-top hills. The scenery from the Texas border to Albuquerque is very interesting and has a bit of variety. It has a few of those tall, rock covered hills that the Lone Ranger always used to hide behind and some rolling hills with very stubby and sparse bushes.

Finally, about 25 miles from the city, you start to see the mountains—very impressive, although they are not the snow-capped ones of the Rockies. I bypassed Santa Fe, as it was a little out of the way, and neither *Bob Damron's Address Book* nor the gay guidebook *Places of Interest* listed any gay bars for it. Before I left on my trip, I joked with my friends that I'd probably fall in love and get married in Santa Fe. I'm in enough trouble as it is.

There were two other things of interest and irritation today that haven't happened to me in over four years. One—I got a speeding ticket about 35 miles inside of the Texas border for going 70 in a 65. Can you believe it? All the traffic goes 70 or over! Never mind. I had to follow the cop, who was very polite, a couple miles into a town called Vega to see the judge—a sweet old lady who surprisingly only fined me $10. I counted my blessings and was back on the road. The whole episode only took 10 minutes. I could hardly have paid it by mail that quickly. However, the ticket *does* go on my driving record.

Second, I got a flat tire about 25 miles from Albuquerque, but thankfully it only took about 20 minutes to change it. My car (a 1977 Buick Skylark) has one of those inflatable spares; I had never used before, but it was not hard to do. That's my first flat tire in this car—not bad for four years. Except now I must buy new tires tomorrow since the spare is only for temporary use. I expected that I would have to replace the front tires during this trip. Naturally, this was one of the back tires that I bought last August…oh well. While I'm mentioning my car, I will comment it is a Yankee car (bought in Rochester), so no air conditioning.

I called Clark tonight and we talked for 15 or 20 minutes…gosh, I miss him. I don't know whether talking to him made me feel better or worse.

Later: Well, now I've seen gay Albuquerque…and it's the pits. There is for all practical purposes one bar in town that people go to. It's *Foxes Booze and Cruise*. Cute name, eh? It's a medium-sized bar, and divided in halves, so, part bar and pool tables, part disco. I talked to a guy who used to live in LA and about the only positive thing he had to say about Foxes was that it had a varied mix of people and in LA the bars were very specialized. Well, I agree it was mixed…cowboy, Mexican, Lacoste, and a touch of leather and a few Black people and a few women, including a short dyke with stringy blond hair in denim and chains, across her chest.

When I left at 11:30 PM there were around 47 people, (okay, I counted) which I guess isn't that bad for a Monday night. But I would rate the crowd in looks about a 2 or 3. Good thing I

Albuquerque / Tucson / Phoenix / Las Vegas

Foxes

don't live here. This place makes Baton Rouge look like a Mecca. That guy from LA said there were also two other bars—one is a private club for mostly the older set (he's heard), and the other is a chicken disco. No, thank you.

Tuesday—May 12, 1981
Tucson

Well, although I wasn't pleased that I had to buy new tires, at least I was able to buy them, get them put on and amazingly be on my way by 9 AM. While they were being installed, I ate breakfast and also went to a GM dealer to get a new tire air cylinder. By luck these three stops were all in the same block.

Driving through New Mexico was very interesting. It has great scenery, and I stopped here and there to take pictures. When I checked out of the Motel 6 in Albuquerque, I had them reserve me a room at their motel in Tucson, so that was out of the way; with a $12.95 rate nationwide, you can't beat the price. Some of the scenery included Elephant Butte reservoir, and several rest areas in NM with rolling or rocky hills, where I saw actual tumbleweed and mini-dust storms. Yucca trees are very common in NM, and finally, just outside of Tucson, I saw a real cactus in the wild.

About 50 miles before Tucson, I figured I still had enough daylight left to take a side trip—25 miles south off Highway 10 to Tombstone, Arizona. All the way there I was afraid that Tombstone—"the town too tough to die"—would be dead, but, luckily, good old American commercialization came to the rescue.

In all seriousness, it was rather pleasant and not really too overdone from the tourist standpoint. True, the OK Corral has been walled in so they can charge $1 to see the site (it was closed for the day, and I wouldn't have paid it anyway). But the streets were very scenic. Best of all was Boot Hill, which was open and was on a donation basis. It was rather interesting. I took pictures of the Clanton Brothers' graves and a few others.[1]

Later: Well, I've now seen all three of Tucson's bars. I started off at the Hair 'Tiz. I hate that name! It's an already feeble joke ran further into the ground by them answering the phone with a loud, campy *"Hair 'Tiz!"* It took me about a half hour to find this place, due to all the one-way streets in this town. It was a typical old downtown bar. The bartender, whose nickname is "Mother," is a sweetheart.

The local newspaper, *Arizona Gay News*, used to be located next door, so I asked the bartender if he knew where they moved to. He said that the editor was expected there around 10 PM (it was 8:45 PM) and he called him to make sure. So, I had one drink and went to another bar for a while.

The next bar, Dale's Graduate, wasn't too far away. It is also a downtown-type bar, nestled next to a car dealer. I guess it's okay. It was semi-crowded—not bad for a Tuesday night. A semi-troll sent me a drink, which I didn't touch (either one). Then, back to

---

1   The Clantons clashed famously (and cinematically) with Wyatt Earp and Doc Holliday.

Albuquerque / Tucson / Phoenix / Las Vegas

Hair 'Tiz, where I met the editor of *AGN* (Bob Ellis) and his lover (Gary Clark), one of the writers. I liked them both. Gary is about 25 and probably has fairy tendencies.

He knew activist Faygele Ben-Miriam when they both lived in Washington State, and knows Charlie Brydon (NGTF co-chair). Bob is about 55. Both are very nice. He immediately offered that I could stay with them tomorrow night (if I stay in town that long, which I doubt). They have a three-person staff and are a weekly. We talked shop, naturally, for a while, and I told them about the convention. I gather from Bob that most of the gay groups in town have petered out…apathy rules.

They then took me to see the other bar, a disco called the Back Pocket. Before I forget, bars close here at 1 AM and there are never any cover charges. The bar had, I thought, a good size crowd for a Tuesday night, any more would have been too crowded. The crowd tended to be young, but there were all ages and a good mix of types. It is by far *the* bar in town. I liked the layout and decor was very compelling, with a bar and dance floor inside the main room, and beyond that a large patio, and a side bar like a lounge where you couldn't hear the disco. I found the disco to be too dark, a pet peeve of mine, but the lounge was well enough lit. A lot of people came up to Bob to talk—some to talk and some obviously to meet the new face in the crowd…me. So, I got a couple of free drinks (which I didn't really want) and got to talk to a few people. I wasn't really engaging in any cruising, but also I didn't really see anyone there extraordinary looking.

Wednesday—May 13, 1981
Tucson

This morning I got to the Arizona Gay News office early, around 10 AM, and Bob showed me around and we talked shop some more. His publisher, George Rederus, stopped by around 11:30 AM. He is about 45 and very interesting. He is an electrician by trade and has started up many gay bars over the years, and of course, seems to know everybody. He spent about the whole afternoon showing me around. First, he bought me lunch at The Back Pocket. They have a good Wednesday buffet.

Then he drove us about 15 miles west of town to the Saguaro National Monument, which is just breathtaking. He says it's the most beautiful park in the state…I believe it. I never would have even known about it. It's about the only place in the world where the Saguaro Cactus is plentiful. That's the cactus that grows straight up, with branches on the side arching upwards. Some are 30 to 40 feet high and they bloom only in May. Looking out onto the rocky hills and valleys dotted with these plants was awe-inspiring, and I got I think some good photos of some of the vegetation.

George should be a tour guide—he's so interesting. He is completely psyched on the area (he's from Iowa) and tells lots of very interesting stories about the local sites. One is how the Indians take the fruit from the saguaro cactus, boil it, and make jelly. Another was how he and his lover fished a 150-pound javelina out of their pool. A javelina is a wild pig, that is almost blind and tame unless cornered, and roam in packs. The adult javelinas can weigh 300 or 400 pounds!

He told how their house once belonged to a woman architect who loaned it to Clark Gable while he was in Tucson making a movie. And on and on—he was just full of interesting stories. He lives in a very impressive house near the park, with some nice varieties of cactus all around it. He has two videotape machines and many tapes I would love to copy (*The Ritz*, Bette Midler's HBO special, *Norman, Is That You?*). Unfortunately, they are VHS and he doesn't have any way of making Beta tapes—damn!

While he was running some errands, he also showed me one of the adult bookstores, the legit bookstore (Books Brothers) and what he thinks will be the next gay bar. Then back to the Back Pocket for a drink. The disco part of the bar is called Joshua Tree and is closed during the day. He was hoping a bartender friend would be there, as he usually is around 4 PM, because he thought we would like to…er…meet, that we would like each other just fine. I guess the guy is really hot; but he didn't show up, so I'll never know.

I just can't get over how hospitable he and Bob were. Had I wanted to extend my visit another day I certainly could have stayed with either one of them. They really made me feel welcome and I probably saw more of gay Tucson in one day than most people could see in a week. I almost wish I had stayed another day, but I already had prepaid reservations in Phoenix, so I left Tucson around 5 PM.

Phoenix

It was an easy hour and 45-minute drive there, and the road was especially scenic. I checked in at the Motel 6, Central on 24th and Van Buren, which seems to be a good location with respect to the bars. Phoenix appears to be laid out very logically, with even blocks and nice wide streets, and very flat. For dinner I went to Sammy's Steakhouse and Saloon, one of the bars on the bar map Bob gave me from an issue of *AGN*. However, I only stayed about 5 minutes since, despite their name, they don't serve meals after 8 PM. It seemed like a nice bar though; fixed up quite well, with a separate room for a disco and bar, another room for a lounge, and a pool room.

After I ate (some chain restaurant) I went to a bar called Tommy and Clyde's, which was part cruise bar and part dance floor, with taped disco music. Wednesday night is their strip contest, so I figured that would draw a good crowd, which it did. Almost right away I got into a conversation with one of their bartenders, Steve, who was helping with the contest rather than serving drinks. Steve was very nice (also hot) and introduced me to the owner and the bartender and several other people, which made it easier to socialize during the evening. He even made sure I met one of the contestants that I thought was cute. Now, that's a good bartender.

The contest was interesting but certainly not exciting. Of the eight entered, only one (Mike) was cute (but he was *really* cute). He's 25 and was probably the only one to enter because he needed the money (first prize was $50). It was obvious that he was nervous and felt out of place in the contest, but he did well. He came in third (his prize was a bottle of booze) but he got three $5 tips. The contest was not a complete strip contest (that's illegal)—it was down to bikini briefs or a jock strap or whatever. And they danced to two different disco songs while they stripped on a long platform about a foot off the dance floor.

I thought the other seven contestants, and the bar's customers in general, were just average, no one at all I thought interesting. I danced with one of the other contestants after the contest, and while I guess it's nice to be asked if I wanted to fuck him. I certainly didn't. For the record, the cute one—Mike—went home alone (he had finals the next day…he's a sophomore in college), and so I also went home alone. Did I mention that bars are only open until 1 AM here?

Thursday—May 14, 1981
Phoenix

Today I ran errands (post office, took the film in) and went to the Desert Botanical Gardens in Phoenix. It was very pretty, and it gave me a chance to take more cactus photos (I think I have enough now). I even got a picture of two lizards fighting! I stopped briefly at Club Phoenix to see if they have t-shirts, but they don't—the guy at the desk was slightly embarrassed that I recognized him as one of the dancers from last night.

The temperature was 98 today! It got so hot in my car the other day that it melted one of my contact lens solution bottles. It didn't burst but now the bottom is rounded, and it barely stands on end. I went for a swim in the motel pool also. The water was like bath water, almost too warm.

At the pool I met a Belgian couple who live in Montreal.

The wife was born in the same village as my mother—Tienen, a very small village indeed. The woman's maiden name was Gerda Maes and most of her relatives live near Tienen in Hoegaarden. I only asked cause I'm sure my mother would shoot me if I didn't. Gerda and her husband are very nice; we talked for at least a half hour. Her accent reminds me a lot of my mother, so that was nice.

I went to two bars tonight: Taylor's and Connection, which are on 7th Street on the same block. Taylor's is sort of a neighborhood bar, only it looks like someone's den or a basement that has been fixed up nicely. The bartender said that the crowd was very slight for some reason and suggested I try Connection. I thought that was unusual, but I later found out that they were owned by the same person.

I guess Connection is a Western-leather bar, but it doesn't lean too heavily in either direction. It has a rustic decor and seems like a good cruise bar. It is supposedly one of the most popular bars at the moment, maybe *the* most popular. It had a good-sized crowd, although I didn't think it was a particularly attractive crowd. The age mix was right, but no men that I would consider to be really hot. The bar is medium sized, but I understand there is another large room (with a leather shop) that is only open on weekends, which would make it a rather large bar indeed.

I met a nice young man named David B (age 22) and, after we talked for about an hour, brought him home, well, to the hotel room. I haven't made a practice of detailing sex acts so far, but this was kind of interesting. I love to nibble on ears and his were so sensitive that he climaxed while I was doing so. Apparently, I did something right, because he said that had never happened to him before. Rather than be upset because it was over so quickly, I thought it was flattering that I could turn him on that much. He's a Phoenix native and, of course, cute, about my height, thin, and a semi-clone.

Saturday—May 16, 1981
Phoenix

The last two days have been more restful than eventful, especially since I didn't go out Friday night. It was one of those cases where at 9 PM you decide to "lay down for an hour," the alarm goes off and you ignore it and wake up at 1:30 AM, by which time everything was closed. In the afternoons I mostly just drove around the city. I went to a couple of malls and picked up my film. Naturally I had to buy a viewer so that I could immediately look at all 300+ slides, figuring out of which ones (mostly of Clark) that I wanted to have made into prints.

This afternoon I stumbled upon a good used record store called Antiques Forever on North 12th Street. They have about

Albuquerque / Tucson / Phoenix / Las Vegas

60,000 used 45s, all fairly well categorized by artist. I spent about an hour searching for a few records that I've been wanting, most of which are really obscure. I found a couple of those and bought only a total of five $1.50 records, which for me is probably amazing. There were also many, many boxes of miscellaneous or unsorted records that I didn't have the patience to look through.

Afterwards I went to South Mountain Park, which is about eight miles south of the city. It contains over 15,000 acres of peaks, canyons, strange rock formations and trees, shrubs and cacti particular to Arizona, and a drive to Dobbins Lookout (2,330 ft.) which affords an excellent view, so says the AAA book. All true. It was a very nice drive, and the park was free, if you don't count being forced to take another 10 or 15 pictures.

For my impressions of the city so far, I would say that it is clean and very new looking, and very flat. The streets are all wide and most of the buildings low. However, all this neatness leads to the city having very little personality. It all is kind of boring and all looks the same, like the commercial strip through almost any modern suburb.

There is no gay ghetto, and, while there are 15 or 20 bars, they are kind of spread out. For example, Connection, perhaps the ruling cruise bar is on 7th Street and the ruling disco, Hot Bods, is on about 34th Street, with one 2 or 3 miles farther north of the other two. If there are any trendy gay shops, I certainly haven't found them.

The city is reportedly very conservative, and from reading *AGN*, I do not see much evidence of there being an active gay community. What *is* very visible are the prostitutes (female and black) that are in abundance as you drive down Van Buren Street at night. It seems odd that, while they are so obvious, the cops seem to focus their attentions on enforcing the speeding laws in the city. I have seen an amazing number of patrol cars stopping speeders. I guess speeding tickets are less paperwork.

Later: Well, it's now 1 AM and I'm back at my motel. I hit

three bars tonight. First, to Connection. I wanted to see the rest of the bar, including the leather store that is only open on Friday and Saturday nights. The other room is even larger than the first and, in a way, better. It's kind of like a large garage or small barn (and decorated similarly) with a bar, a raised platform, and a loft. Lots of barn wood and bar posters. The leather shop is adequate for leather but they carried no unique t-shirts like some other bars do. There is some country on the juke box, such as "Tonight the Bottle Let Me Down (And Let Your Memory Come Around)" (Merle Haggard). And there was one I think I want to buy called "You're the Reason God Made Oklahoma" by Dave Frizzell and Shelley West.

At Connection some guy started talking to me. My TALK ME INTO IT shirt must have encouraged him, but he didn't have a prayer. As we talked about the bars, he commented that Connection probably drew the hottest crowd. As he was saying that I was thinking, *"If that's so, this city is in trouble."* Granted, it was a little early (10:30 PM), but there were enough people to give an indication that it was not going to be a good-looking crowd. I would rate the crowd about a 4. The same applies for its crowd last Thursday night. However, I liked the layout of the bar a lot. I guess that technically makes it a good bar.

Next, to Hot Bods, a disco on McDowell and 34th (five miles from Connection, I measured it). It has a layout like Babylon in Houston, with the high-ceiling dance floor room and DJ booth on a second level. In short, it's a big bar. The light effects were just marginal, however. And it is one of the darkest discos I've ever seen, much too dark. It had a side bar in a separate room however, called the "no smoke saloon" which I think is a great idea. It also had a $2 cover, which it certainly can't justify.

I was warned that the crowd was a little *GQ* (read: preppy). I wasn't warned how young the crowd was, which was very disappointing. I forced myself to stay 45 minutes and then left—the place was too dark and too young. I really didn't get enough impression to comment on the quality of the music. When I got to my car there was a note in the windshield: *JAD 24*(my license number)— *I'm from VA too. Tom Fiesta, WGM-192. I'm from Richmond. Hi.* I am not sure what I was supposed to do with that information, but it was amusing.

    I knew there was another disco not far, Farrah's, so I went there. It had no cover and was a much better bar. It is of medium size, and, though I would only give the crowd about a 5, it was the best crowd I've seen in Phoenix. This city is hurting! The DJ's taste was ok, but he couldn't mix for shit. I met a nice, good-looking guy named Patrick. We talked for a while and danced once, and it seemed fitting to go home together, but he had slightly different ideas. He introduced me to his lover, who, I suppose, was nice looking, and they asked if I wanted a threesome. I said no, but I would be glad to have him come to my hotel. I told him that I'm really cautious about threesomes and won't do it unless it feels exactly right. Stalemate. He tried again and I said no, so that was that. We parted amicably. I could tell that his lover was surprised I said no when Patrick told him. This was right at last call, so that ended the evening.

Planning Vegas

Sunday—May 17, 1981
Phoenix

Well, it looks like I'm going to Las Vegas tomorrow. I spent about an hour and a half yesterday trying to track down a Las Vegas newspaper so I could see what entertainers were in town. I went to the airport newsstand, and no luck. There are no regular newsstands listed in the phone book. Finally, I stopped at a library. Even they, in their main branch, didn't have the paper (which seems odd) but the librarian really went out of her way to help me. She telephoned hotels and finally found a travel agent with the information. Playing this week are Don Rickles, Kris Kristofferson, Wayne Newton, Anne Murray, several others, and…are you ready for this... *Diana Ross at Caesar's Palace!*

I called the 800-number for info and found that they only accept reservations one day in advance (strange), so this morning I called for Monday night. Obviously, I didn't intend on even passing through Vegas if I couldn't get reservations—it's not exactly on the way to San Diego. Fortunately, I was able to get reservations, or at least I think I did. All the clerk asked for was my last name, first initial, and which show I wanted to attend. That didn't seem like enough.

I was ready to give my credit card number and all that good stuff. I started to ask her if this was confirmed, since I was calling from Phoenix. She just said be there at 11:30 PM, she wasn't supposed to accept reservations for just one person. So, I didn't push it. I'll just go and see what happens. I asked for the 12:30 AM show. I figured it wouldn't include a meal and might be cheaper. As it is, tickets are about $35 each, and I think you're expected to buy drinks.

Afterwards, I went to the Motel 6 office to see if I could reserve a room at their Vegas branch, and I got it right away. This has been just too easy! I know that Vegas hotels are very expensive and would expect an inexpensive one to be booked for months in advance.

Monday—May 18, 1981
Phoenix

Yesterday afternoon I swam and sunbathed for a couple of hours—I now have not a tan-line, but a burn-line. It's a start. Then I went to the Nu Town Saloon for their Sunday afternoon barbecue which, for $1.50, was a very good deal. The bar had 30 or 40 people, a decent afternoon crowd. It's a Western bar by décor, but everyone was in t-shirts and jeans. I guess the bar was okay; it has a nice patio. Then on to Trax, reportedly a leather bar but there were more bartenders there than customers, so I couldn't verify its reputation. It seems Sunday afternoons are not

Albuquerque / Tucson / Phoenix / Las Vegas

their bag, but the layout was nice enough.

Then, for lack of any other inspiration, I headed to Connection for my third visit there. It's obviously the most popular bar in town—because it had a good-sized crowd at 5 PM and that was with no buffets, cheap drinks, or gimmicks to draw them there. Behind the patio in a fenced-off portion of the parking lot, several people were getting the grounds ready for an annual carnival next weekend sponsored by the bar. One of the guys working there was good looking (my basic clone) and I said about 10 words worth of small talk to him in passing but didn't really think much more about it and went back inside. About a half hour later he sends me a drink. He apparently was outside and told one of the bartenders my description (wearing a red Dallas Club Bath shirt probably helped) and had them give me the drink.

I'm sure it was no problem for him to do this since it turned out that he was the owner of the bar, and of Taylor's Bar, down the street. Naturally, I went out to the patio to thank him. His name was Dale Williams, and, after talking for a while, we went out for dinner. On him, as it turned out…which I don't feel guilty about after seeing his house, probably in the $200,000 range. He seems to be doing quite well. Turns out dinner included breakfast. He is a fascinating guy and quite dynamic. Unlike most bar owners he is supportive of the gay community and backs it up with money.

One of the things he would like to do is start his own newspaper in Phoenix. He would be the backer and would hire a full-time editor and supply all the equipment. He just needs the right editor. I got the impression I would be considered if I wanted it—talk about having a dream handed to you on a platter. It is too bad I don't really like Phoenix, or it would be tempting. He wants his own paper because he doesn't think *AGN* (which is based in Tucson anyway) is professional enough. I agree it *could* use a lot of work.

He says that after a year he would turn his paper over to the editor, keeping 25%. There are some things he's a little naive about though, since he doesn't have any newspaper experience. For example, he was surprised when I told him that very few gay papers do any better than just break even. And he had never heard of the major gay magazine *Christopher Street*. But I do not doubt that if he wants to pull it off, he will. I suggested he contact the *San Diego Update* people for advice. He certainly can't go to Tucson, and I suggested he advertise in the *Advocate* for a managing editor. Lastly, I told him about the Gay Press Association.

Later…much later: I am exhausted! What a day! I spent about 12 hours on the road going from Phoenix to Las Vegas via the Grand Canyon, which adds at least three hours to the trip. The side trip was worth it though. I had my doubts, but you can't deny that the Grand Canyon *is* impressive. I took about another 20 pictures; the canyon is *so* photogenic. I got a couple of sunset pictures about 20 miles south of Hoover Dam—they should be interesting if they come out. I reached Hoover Dam after sunset, so I couldn't take pictures, but it did look impressive, as did the lights of Vegas as you approach the city.

I called Clark from a Stuckey's near Williams, Arizona (just west of Flagstaff). It was good to hear his voice, but also hard, because it makes me miss him more, and he said about the same thing. Also, for the record, during that call it was the first time he directly said, "I love you." Geez, I miss him. He's thinking of meeting me in Kansas City when I'm on the way back to Houston, and he can also visit his folks up there.

Las Vegas

I finally got to my hotel at about 9 PM, which gave me no time to spare. I showered and changed (and wore for the first time in two months, something other than my 501s…my brown cords). Ate at a chain restaurant called Carrows, then drove to Caesars. It took 10 minutes to find the box office, that place is so big, and confusing. I got in line around 10:30 PM, about two hours before the show was set to start. They started seating at 11 PM.

Albuquerque / Tucson / Phoenix / Las Vegas

It is amazing what a big tip will do: $20 got me a seat just left of center (about 20 ft to the left) and six feet back from the stage. I got within about eight feet of Diana Ross! And what a show!

A comedian (George Wallace) was on first, and was pretty good, and then she came on (with "I'm Coming Out") about 1 AM It seems so trite to say it was fantastic, and it still doesn't seem real that I really saw her. She was all in white and was on for just under an hour. I'll try and list the songs: "I'm Coming Out," "Upside Down," "Theme from Mahogany," "Reach Out and Touch," "The Boss," "My Man," "Ain't No Mountain High Enough," "Touch Me in the Morning," "It's my House," "Remember Me," a medley during a film including bits of "Baby Love," "Stop In the Name of Love," "Love is Like an Itching in my Heart," etc. I'm sure there were more I've forgotten. I know here was a ballad called "Home" from "The Wiz," and one I think called "Lady Sings the Blues." She closed with "It's My Turn" and encored with "I'm Coming Out."

I just can't believe the whole evening. Getting a seat that close to the stage at Caesar's Palace to see Diana Ross is just hard to really believe, when two days ago I was in Phoenix, had no plans to come to Vegas at all, and had no idea who was playing here.

Tuesday—May 19, 1981
Las Vegas

I spent all afternoon at Circus Circus, and I thought all the carnival-type games on the mezzanine were really interesting. The first quarter I put into a machine was for Pac Man—probably the best buy in the place. I played the nickel slots all afternoon. I set a limit of not losing more than $25 (I know, big spender), but that can last a while if you use nickels. I won and lost for three hours and got back to within $3 of breaking even once; but, of course, everyone puts winnings right back in the machines. I stopped at one gay bar, The Red Barn, long enough to get the monthly Vegas gay newspaper (if you can call a four-page pamphlet a newspaper).

It's not impressive, but they use nice paper. The bar had only three customers. It was around noon though, and doesn't look like much, inside or out. I've heard that the two discos here are quite preppy and pretentious, in other words, piss elegant. Maybe I'll find out tonight.

Later: I took about a three-hour nap this evening (definitely needed), I could have used more, but forced myself to get up about 11:30 PM because this is the only chance I may ever have to go to the gay bars of Vegas. Yes, friends and neighbors, this is one of those times when even JD did not feel like going out. But, as I said, I forced myself; I was a trooper.

Before I went to the bars, I drove down to the strip to take some night pictures of the casino lights. Photographing marquee lights (especially flashing ones) at night is really tricky, so I hope the camera knew what it was doing (I didn't). Should be interesting. I stopped to photograph the Dunes, Caesar's Palace, Flamingo, Barbary Coast, Circus Circus, and Stardust. On the way back from Circus Circus, I walked back past Stardust in time to witness its big sign catch on fire. As I walked directly by it, I heard some popping (likely the neon bulbs exploding). I saw a security guard just starting to direct cars away from that entrance, so the fire must have started within five minutes of that.

It was a very small fire, involving only the lower part of the sign (the first two letters of "Lido"). About the time the firemen got there, they managed to turn off the whole sign's lights. After about 10 minutes they got the ladder up (a height of about three or four stories) and a man climbed up with a CO_2 extinguisher and quickly put it out. Although it was not a big fire, for once I was where something interesting happened *with* the camera. I hope those pictures come out.

Following this ordeal I headed to Gipsy, a disco with lots of mirrors. It has a sunken dance floor and a quiet back bar. I guess it was really kind of nice. There were only about 50 people there (four I thought attractive), but then, it was 1 PM on a Tuesday. The music and the DJ were good, meaning I liked what she played while I was there.

Down the street was the other disco I had heard about, The Garage. It was less classy and more crowded, and had three good-looking men, three of the four from the other bar—people bar hop here, as elsewhere. I imagine they may have been saying to each other, *"These bars suck…oh, there's that guy again."*

The bar was okay; it was smaller than the other one and the crowd included about 10 new-wavettes or, if you prefer, punk rockers. A little of that goes a long way. This crowd was slightly younger and about 50-50 men-women. They were having a female strip show later at 2:30 AM, for which I didn't stay. This bar also had three slot machines (the other two bars I was in didn't have them), so I played a quarter in one just for the sake of it. The crowd at neither bar was what I would call preppy or pretentious, as I had heard they were. Maybe weekends are different.

TEN

San Diego

Wednesday—May 20, 1981
San Diego

AFTER a five-hour, somewhat boring drive from Vegas, I've finally arrived in San Diego. I couldn't get in Motel 6, so I'm staying, for one night only ($26), at an International 8 Motel near the intersection of US 8 & 5. Tomorrow I'll find somewhere cheaper. I called the gay hotline, who recommended a hotel between downtown and the so-called ghetto (Hillcrest), near Balboa Park. I called the hotel, the Park 5th Avenue, and they said they could likely find me a room for around $20 if I stay through the weekend. If I like the place, I may take it—remember, this is Memorial Day weekend and rooms are hard to find. The Motel 6 is booked through September! When the clerk asked me how I heard about them, I told him I called the gay info line. He said he was sure they could get me a room. Something tells me he's gay.

So, this evening, I…
a) talked to my roommate Fred (in Norfolk) for an hour,
b) took a two-hour nap,
c) ate at the nearby steakhouse, and
d) hit the bars.

I went to two bars in the neighborhood since I figured I might as well while I was in this part of town. First, the Iron Spur. It's a rather small Western bar, and it was only by accident that I found that they also have a piano bar in the back and up a few steps. It's a restaurant too. I kind of liked it. The guy playing and singing was very good, and we chatted a little. Then I went a few doors down the street to San Diego's alleged leather bar, The Hole. Looked like a regular cruise bar to me (except that it had a leather shop). I suppose as a cruise bar I liked it. The bar is set back from the street and then down steps down a hill to the building. You really had to know it was there. There was a small sign at the street, but it wasn't lit up. Both bars are across the street from the Navy training center and Marine depot, although I didn't notice any military types in the bars. Neither bar was at all crowded.

Souvenir wooden nickel from The Hole

I technically met the managing editor of *Update* (Paul Burke) there. I say "technically," because we didn't meet in Dallas at the gay press conference but we still recognized each other. Naturally, we talked shop for a while—over an hour. He seems nice, and very competent. I'll probably visit their offices this week.

Thursday—May 21, 1981
San Diego

Today I went to Point Loma, which has nice views of the bay and downtown, and drove around a lot going to various shops. I went to International Male's store, which wasn't as impressive as the catalogue, but I still bought a khaki shirt. I stopped at Club Baths and bought one of their shirts and bought a swimsuit at a store called That Man. I also stopped at a couple of record stores.

I next went to the gay community center but wasn't very impressed. The guy working the desk didn't seem at all informed, but I did learn of a play that night.

Later I went to the play *A Perfect Relationship* by Doric Wilson[1]. I was very lucky to get in because The Gay Academic Union (a group of gay professionals) had bought out the performance, but they had a cancellation and sold me a ticket. The theatre only seats 50 and is about 30 x 30 feet with three rows of seats along two walls. The play, a comedy about gay sex in the 1970s, was excellent—well written and acted.

Next, I went to a disco, WCPC (West Coast Production Company), a few blocks from the theatre. It really wasn't very crowded, but I suppose it was okay. The layout of the place is really good—quite large, with two side bars. The music and DJ were excellent. I stayed about an hour and then went to another disco, Mr. Dillon's. Now *this* is a hot disco. It was large, very crowded and there were many very nice-looking men there. The decor was hard to describe, sort of Spanish-Western. The music was good there also. I ran into still another guy from Norfolk—a very cute blond named John who used to be a waiter at The Cue. He moved here last fall. We chatted about a half hour, and he recommended a couple of bars.

One thing John (along with several other people that I've talked to) commented on is how conservative San Diego is. This is something I didn't expect, and I don't know if this is really the case or if these people just perceive it that way in comparison to LA and SF. There *are* lots of bars, but I haven't really noticed an appreciable gay ghetto or any gay shops. And boy, I've looked.

Friday—May 22, 1981
San Diego

I slept in today till 1 PM—I must have needed it. This afternoon I drove around a little more, stopped at a porno shop and the legit gay bookstore; both are just okay. Then I went to Balboa Park and walked around a little and took some pictures. I went to the section John said was cruisy and could see where there were sufficient bushes to allow for some horseplay. It is really a very pretty park. I also called Clark again and we talked for 20 minutes or so.

I haven't told you yet about this hotel. The Park 5th Avenue is very tacky! Repeat, tacky. The walls of my room have large mural wallpaper—it feels like I'm in a forest in autumn. I think they did that because the walls are so rough. Also, none of the furniture matches. I've *given away* better furniture. It looks like odds and ends from a church bazaar. Worse, there's no electrical outlet in the bathroom, and the mirror is over the toilet instead of the sink. This place really has zero class. I keep telling myself that I'm lucky to get it for Memorial Day weekend, but I'm not sure I'm very convinced.

Saturday—May 23, 1981
San Diego

Last night after doing laundry and having dinner I went to a piano bar called The Caliph on 5th Avenue. It was decorated kind of Arabian-style, which I thought was tacky, and the bar was also too dark. Furthermore, I didn't think the piano player had a good voice. I didn't even stay for a drink! I instead went to Park Place, which is a much nicer bar. I gather it is fairly new. The

atmosphere is kind of classy but not piss elegant. The walls are dark green, and the high ceilings have skylights, and there are lots and lots of plants. There was a good-sized crowd. Its other half is a restaurant, which was packed. I also understand it has a patio, though I did not see it.

At Park Place I met a nice, good-looking man named Brad Truax who has a beautiful house on Sunset Boulevard, and the place almost looks like it came from the movie. Next to the pool is a built-in jacuzzi (which we used about 1:00 in the morning) and it has a nice view into one of the valleys. He never did tell me what he did for a living. He kept saying he was a hustler, which I don't believe. He's plenty good looking, and I think he's in the medical profession since I noticed a San Diego medical center notebook and a pager.[2]

I guess at Park Place I was being more blatant than I realized. I was leaning against the bar by the windows and did not notice that a beam of sunlight was focused directly on my crotch. That was his first comment when he came up to me. Honest, I didn't stage that.

We talked about the Hollywood set and who's gay. He said the following names: Rock Hudson, Jack Lemmon, Robert Redford, Burt Reynolds, Steve Martin, David Ogden Stiers, Lily Tomlin, Clint Eastwood, Tab Hunter, Richard Chamberlain, Jerry Brown and Linda Ronstadt, Merv Griffin, and more. Aren't rumors wonderful? I probably believe about half of those. Oh yeah, I mentioned that I worked for a gay paper in Virginia, and he asked its name. When I told him he said, "You're the people who had trouble with the libraries." Right! Isn't it nice when just an average person, who's not in the newspaper business, has heard of us, all the way to San Diego!

This afternoon I went to Black's Beach, the gay nude beach that I'd heard so much about. Most of what I heard was true—it *is* very hard to find. It's in La Jolla and there's a certain road you have to turn down to get to the so-called entrance. Even *with* directions I drove past the road twice and missed it. You see, you have to go down North Toney Pines Road 'til you get to the sign that says, "Salk Institute," then go past that 'til you get to the hang-gliding port. That just gets you to the parking lot. From there you go down a *steep* cliff to the beach. There are two so-called "trails" down the cliff. I say "so-called" because nothing that steep could rightfully be called a trail. I took the alleged "easy" trail, which took 10 minutes to climb down.

There were lots of people there. The beach was fairly crowded for a distance of at least 10 blocks. I walked all the way up and back twice. I would say about half the people, or a little less, were nude. I found, as I expected, that a nude beach is much more exciting in theory than in practice. It's just taken very matter-of-factly and is no big deal. There were a lot of straight people and women there too, which also kind of killed the atmosphere for me…all those floppy tits. There were a few people with cameras; I left mine in the car because I didn't want to be bothered with it and I was afraid it might get damaged during the climb—a very real possibility and definitely not worth the risk.

I think I saw only about eight or 10 guys all afternoon that I would consider attractive. There certainly are a lot of ugly naked people around. Some people brought coolers with them since there's no food or drink available on the beach (but I can't imagine carrying a cooler on that climb). One thing, once you're down the hill, you're there for the afternoon—it's just too hard a climb to be going back and forth. If you have to take a piss, either go swimming, or tough luck.

And of course, the rule of all nude beaches prevailed: those that you wish were naked were not, and those you wish weren't, well…were.

I found the water to be extremely cold, but nevertheless there were plenty of people swimming. It's quite a picturesque site, really. From the hill above they hang glide, so the kites are always just overhead. The winds must be just right, since they are able to stay up a long time, going back and forth, before returning to the same spot. The day was just a little cloudy, about 85 degrees and, although quite windy on the hill, very calm on the beach. I stayed about two hours and, in case you're wondering, did wear a swim suit. The climb back up also took 10 minutes. This time I took the "fast" trail, which is also steeper. I was glad I tied my towel around my waist, so I could use both hands to help climb. I'm not exaggerating how hard that climb was. When you get to the top it takes about 10 minutes to catch your breath. I'm glad I didn't take that trail going down. I know the view would have made me nervous.

I had dinner around 5 PM, my first food for the day, not counting a cup of coffee at Brad's and a popsicle on the beach. Then, since I was in the neighborhood, I stopped at a bar called The Nickelodeon. That was for sentimental reasons, since it shared the name with my first and favorite bar back in Norfolk, until it was turned into a parking lot. This bar was also a neighborhood bar and very similar to the Norfolk version. Since it was only around 6 PM, there were only four customers, semi-trolls, who all insisted on talking to me.

Sunday—May 24, 1981
San Diego

Today, after sleeping in, I had brunch at Boardwalk (the other half of Park Place). Although the service was slow, I didn't mind since the atmosphere was so enjoyable. The place is very well done. Then to Balboa Park to lay out in the sun for a couple of hours among the queens, and there were a few hot ones. There was one for whom I made a special trip to the car to get the camera. I hope that one comes out.

Then back to Park Place for their "kegger," from 4 PM to 7 PM. They have one keg that they give out for as long as it lasts. That isn't much beer, but it does draw a nice crowd. John L was there (the guy from Norfolk that I talked to at Dillon's). We talked some more and played a few games of Pac Man. I also talked to a couple of people I met at the bars Friday and met a couple of John's friends. It was very enjoyable. I also saw still another guy I knew from Norfolk, an ex-navy guy named Tim, another item from the Small World Department. I guess I spent about three hours there.

I suppose to summarize San Diego, I would say that it is probably okay. Although there is no gay ghetto, there are numerous, varied bars to suit most anyone. The city is not as pretty as I had expected but it's not dirty like LA. Highlights were the bars Boardwalk and Park Place, the Doric Wilson play, and Brad.

Endnotes

1   Doric Wilson was a pioneering gay playwright who (along with Lanford Wilson and Robert Patrick), founded in 1974 the first gay theater in the United States, The Other Side of Silence (TOSOS).

2   I found out later Brad Truax is a doctor.

ELEVEN

Los Angeles

Monday—May 25, 1981
Los Angeles

I<small>T TOOK</small> about two hours to drive to LA. The sky was very hazy—smog, I guess. I had a couple hours until I was supposed to check into my hotel, so I drove around a little in Hollywood and took a few photos in Griffith Park. I took some of that hill that has the big H<small>OLLYWOOD</small> letters, but it was so hazy I doubt they'll come out well.

The hotel I'll be at for the next week is the Coral Sands on North Western Avenue in Hollywood. Yes, a "gay hotel," advertised in the Advocate. I got a weekly rate of about $23 per night, which seems good. The location is great, since most of the bars I've heard about are in Hollywood or West Hollywood. The neighborhood is a little tacky…okay, a lot tacky, but the hotel is really very nice. The rooms are fine and the hotel has two connecting wings (two stories) that face each other over a long courtyard with pool, Jacuzzi, deck chairs, and workout equipment. And it's very cruisy and totally self-contained.

You would think it was a Club Bath, people walk up and down the walkways cruising and doors are left open. I was beginning to think there were no gay hotels that really were cruisy. None of the ones I stayed at up until now had been. I met a

nice guy from Belgium who didn't speak English very well. He asked me into his room for a drink, which to be friendly, I took, although I really wasn't interested in him at all. He wanted to take some pictures of me (dressed, thank you), which I let him. I suppose he'll tell his friends in Europe we had sex. If that makes him happy, I guess it's alright. A little later I was in my room watching TV and some guy just opened my door. It was unlocked but the chain caught it. When I went to the door he said, "Never mind, the chain answered my question." It did, he wasn't that cute.

Thursday—May 28, 1981
Los Angeles

Okay, I've been in LA for three days now and this is my first chance to write… Disneyland is not in Anaheim, it's along Santa Monica Boulevard in West Hollywood—also known as "The Great Gay Way" or "Boystown." Let's back up a little to Tuesday afternoon. Along Santa Monica for about eight blocks around The Motherlode and Studio One are, besides several bars, at least a dozen very trendy shops. And I hit them all…clothing, gift, card, books, etc. I also hit my Visa card pretty hard. One of the stores was called The Pleasure Chest. Once it was known as mainly a leather shop, and now it has everything…clothing, t-shirts, cards, leather, head shop, etc. A guy I met, Michael, used to work there and says the store gets a lot of celebrities: Dick van Dyke bought a $300 sling, Tony Curtis bought a gross of poppers, and Cher bought a vibrator. I have no idea if any of that is truth or just folklore.

International Male (famous for their sexy mail catalogs) has a branch there and other clothing stores (there are many) are Sports Locker and the PX and my soon-to-be favorite, All American Boy. All American Boy has one of the best selections of t-shirts I've ever seen, with printed sayings such as:

THIS FACE SEATS FIVE
MOUSTACHE RIDES, 5 CENTS
IMMEDIATE SEATING AVAILABLE
NOT A WELL WOMAN
FUCK 'EM IF THEY CAN'T TAKE A JOKE
CHOKE 'EM IF THEY CAN'T TAKE A FUCK
ALL AMERICAN BOY
MADNESS TAKES ITS TOLL
SPIT, SIT, AND SPIN
FREE SAMPLES

Silicone Is the Only Virtue I Have Left
Last Night in Town
More Than a Woman
…But What I Really Want To Do Is Direct
See Me, Touch Me, Feel Me…
Some Times You Feel Like a Nut, Some Times You Don't
What's a Mother To Do?
What in the World Are We Going To Do Without
                                          Walter Cronkite?

Drama Queen
Cheap & Easy
Do Unto Others as You Would Have Them Do Unto You
Debutantes for Human Rights
So Many Men, So Many Times
Surrender Dorothy
It's Not Easy Being Easy
etc.

    Yes, obviously I took notes.
    At All American Boy, besides buying two shirts, I met Michael MacKay, a really cute clone, I'll repeat, <u>really</u> cute. We spent most of that day and the next day together. He didn't get off work until 7 PM, so in the meantime I went to several bars. One was called Motherlode, and it was similar to Park Place (San Diego) except without the plants. It was very nice, popular in the late afternoon for the business crowd and also later. It's the first bar I've seen with a live daytime DJ. Michael says it's a S&M bar: "Stand and model." It seemed okay to me. Then to the Four Star Saloon, a Western bar/restaurant for lunch, and then to the Blue Parrot, which has kind of a tropical motif.
    I met Michael around seven at the Nutowne Saloon. They were giving Western dance lessons, which was neat to watch. From there we went to three cruise bars: The Spike, The Eagle, and The Rusty Nail. All were good, but I liked The Nail the best. It seemed to have a friendlier crowd. Of course, it didn't hurt any

Los Angeles

that Michael seems to know *everybody*.

The DJ is a friend of his and Michael had him play "Remember Me/Ain't No Mountain" for me. I had a really good time. The next morning, we had brunch at a very nice restaurant, the French Market Place, which has a patio overlooking the parade of gay life on Santa Monica Boulevard—very enjoyable. It's a mandatory gay tourist stop. We went to a couple record stores and shops in the afternoon and to a park with a neat Frank Lloyd Wright building (Hollyhock House) and grounds. We took a number of photos there.

Later, we went to The Jungle, a bar in Silverlake, which has a very hot patio—palm trees, banana trees, etc. I wanted one of their t-shirts (very military), but they were out. The bartender gave me a poster, so I didn't come away empty-handed. We also stopped by the LA Gay Community Services Center, which seemed quite nice and well organized.

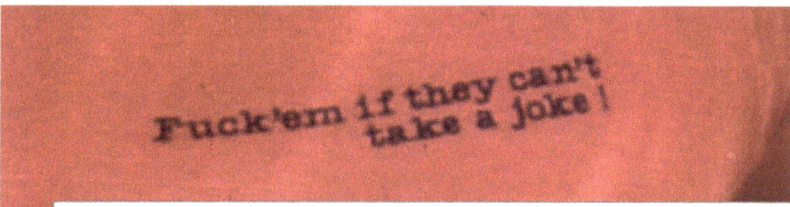

JD and Michael MacKay at Frank Lloyd Wright's Hollyhock House.

Los Angeles

(I found him so irresistible, I wanted to share another photo! — JD)

After dinner Michael and I and two friends, Billy and Dave, went to The Motherlode, Rusty Nail, and then to Greg's Blue Dot. Greg's on Wednesday nights has rock and roll revival (all early and mid-'60s 45s); very neat, and it drew a packed crowd, both inside and on the patio. The patio even had a campfire; and the place had about the hottest crowd I've seen in LA. They usually have a surprise guest every week, like the Shirelles or Martha Reeves, but not this Wednesday however (drat) because they had one over the holiday weekend.

After I dropped Michael and Billy off back at the Nail, Dave and I went back to my hotel. Dave is a hot blond with a beard. He has a hair salon in West Hollywood and has several industry clients: Warren Beatty, Scott Baio, Maureen McCormick, the girl that plays Erin on *The Waltons* (Mary Elizabeth McDonough), and several soap actresses with whom I wasn't familiar. Dave and I had brunch at the French Market Place with Suzy, who works for Dave. She's a very neat, good-looking dyke.

Later: This afternoon I sat by the pool for a couple of hours working on my burn line. Then I went to the National Gay Archives [1] to drop off the complete set of *Our Own Community Press,* which I had brought for this purpose. I talked for about a half hour to its founder, Jim Kepner, who was really fascinating. He told me about the evidence indicating that Abe Lincoln had

some gay experiences. So, I got to meet a gay icon.

This evening I went to the Vista Theatre to see two gay movies. The first was a 1964 French film, *This Special Friendship*, which was fair, though kind of corny. The second film was a Danish flick, *You Are Not Alone*, which I thought was awful. I left before it was over—something I rarely do. Both movies starred very young actors who must've been under 15…all Europeans must be chicken hawks. From the theatre I went to two Silverlake bars. The first was called Pure Trash—what a great name for a bar. I was hoping they had t-shirts, but they were out. The bar was almost empty but had a great patio, with platforms and a mezzanine. Then to the Detour, which was crowded, with a touch of leather, but for me the bar was much too dark.

Friday—May 29, 1981
Los Angeles

This afternoon I mostly shopped and ran errands. I had dinner with a nice guy named Glen. Remember, I'm still at the gay hotel. He's a fellow hotel guest from Oklahoma and is here for a cable TV convention. We ate at the French Market Place and then went bar hopping. But on the way we stopped at The Pleasure Chest because Glen wanted to buy a leather vest, which The Pleasure Chest sells very reasonably priced. Well, he got the last medium and talked me into trying on the last small they had. So help me, it looked and fit great—I had to buy it. I ask you, what is money for?

Then we went to a new bar, The Saddle Tramp, which was nice but almost empty. Next, we went to The Eagle, which was crowded. We stayed probably an hour. Glen met a nice guy named Michael and the three of us went down the street to The Spike until closing. It was even more crowded; a little too crowded for me, and too dark. Michael wants to take us to the Probe disco tomorrow night. It is a private club. I hope that happens.

Monday—June 1, 1981
Los Angeles

Busy, busy, busy… Let's back up to Saturday, if I can remember. Glen and Michael and I had brunch in a nice, although a little piss elegant, gay restaurant on La Cienega called The Garden District. It was very crowded but pleasant waiting and watching the people. There I saw the only pseudo-celebrity of this trip, Johnnie Ray, who hasn't been an actual celebrity for many years. Michael pointed him out to us. I surely would not have recognized him. He looks real worn and was half drunk (or more than half). If he were sober, I might have spoken to him, as I did like his music. Among his long string of hits were "Cry," "The Little White Cloud that Cried," and "Just Walking in the Rain," all from

the 1950s. From there we went to Aron's records on Melrose and, amazingly, I didn't buy anything!

Glen had promised some friends of his in Long Beach that he was going to visit them. He called and got us both invited to a charcoal-cooked steak dinner. I had a very good time. Glen's friends were really neat, especially Pat, who everyone calls Dorothea—a kind of earth mother Charlie Daniels.

After dinner we hit two of the Long Beach bars—Mike's Corral and The Mineshaft. Mike's, to be kind, is a nice Western/leather dive. The Mineshaft, certainly not to be confused with the one in NY, I liked a lot. It had sort of Western decor and was very crowded. It *was* Saturday night, and had enough hot men to merit several visits. It seemed friendlier than the LA bars, although that may be hard to gauge since we were with a bunch of people. The DJ was outstanding. The place didn't have a dance floor, but this guy was better than most disco DJs I've heard. One song I especially liked was "Cry to Me" by Precious Wilson of Eruption. We finally got back to Hollywood about 2:30 AM, a very enjoyable evening. Michael, who lives here, commented earlier (referring to Glen and myself) that, damn, every time he meets somebody nice, they're always here on vacation. I think he's exaggerating—I've met some nice natives.

On Sunday I got up around noon. I passed on an invitation to go to lunch with Glen and his friends, and sat by the pool till about 2:30 PM. I talked mostly with Dave S, also here for the cable convention. He is a New Jersey gay activist, involved with the speaker's bureau, etc. We talked for quite a bit about politics and the movement. It was refreshing to talk with someone so well read and informed. He is also very attractive, a very nice-looking blond. That's two in a row, now. We had, in his words, about a three-hour "tryst" in my room—very nice.

Then we went for dinner at Nutowne, where they were having a free, that's right, free barbecue. It was so good we had to have seconds. Glen and Michael were there, too. We all watched the Western dancing inside. They had a good-sized crowd, and it was around 7:30 PM on a Sunday. I just love watching the dancing. The crowd was very friendly, and really hot. I seem to think that the Western bars are friendlier in general. I will add again that maybe the bars seemed friendly because I was with other people.

Dave and I came back around 9:30 PM for a nap because we wanted to go boogie later. We got to Studio One around 11:30 PM. I had heard a lot about that place. It is one of those places you *have* to see. I thought it was really enjoyable. It's huge, and kind of reminds me of DC's famous bar, Lost & Found, maybe bigger. It is done in hi-tech, but they didn't get carried away. And has a large front bar, a side game room and bar, and large back restaurant and bar, everything done classy. In the middle is a very large dance floor. The music I thought was not particularly impressive, given the place's reputation. It was adequate. The place has a reputation also of being very young and *GQ* (preppy), which I suppose is true to a degree. Dave and I had a good time.

I think if someone went there alone, they might not find it too friendly.

This morning both Dave and Glen checked out. I went for lunch at a gay restaurant (where else?) called Yukon Mining Company. It's nice, kind of family style and in a small plaza right next to a Kroger, etc.—not somewhere you usually expect to find a gay restaurant. It was definitely gay though, even the female waitress had on 501 jeans. Then, some errands, mailing more records back home at the post office and picking up my Liza tickets.

Yes, you heard me, Liza tickets!

Then I went to yet another really good record store, the Record Connection on La Cienega and Santa Monica; I went crazy again and bought about 10 singles and two early Liza albums. I had been looking all over for the 45 of Liza's "All That Jazz" to no avail, and they had four copies (now they have two). I just wanted it on a 45; hey, I have a juke box at home. The prices were very reasonable—I was just making small talk with one of the clerks and she gave me a 30% off coupon (on the sly, so the boss couldn't see her…she saved me $8). As I write this, I'm sunbathing by the hotel pool. I figure I won't be able to do it in SF.

Monday—June 1, 1981
(continued)
Los Angeles

Yes! Liza in Concert!

Well, I've just returned from the Liza Minnelli/Joel Grey concert at the Greek Theatre. It's an outdoor theatre that holds about 5,000. My seat was not particularly good, especially not for $15. Fortunately, they rented 8-power binoculars, which made it worthwhile. It was a very good show. Joel Grey sang for 45 minutes; then there was an intermission. Then Minnelli came out for an hour and fifteen minutes. The highlights to me were "Yes," "New York, New York," "The Man That Got Away," "City Lights," "My Man," and "Bewitched." And then Grey joined her for "Welcome," "Money," and "Cabaret," the grand finale… just great!

So ends a week in LA. It's interesting—I really didn't think I would like LA, but I did. Of course, LA is basically defined for these purposes as West Hollywood and Santa Monica Boulevard, also known as "Boystown." It is very interesting and fun to visit…lots of very pretty men everywhere. I especially enjoyed the shops near the Motherlode and the bars, especially the Nutowne and Greg's Blue Dot. I met some very nice people. It is also interesting that of the four people I tricked with, I met none of them in the bars—quite unusual considering the quantity and quality of LA's bars. I also liked driving around LA. It was not at all hard to do so, as it had been rumored, for while the traffic is always heavy it is not overpowering.

It is also neat to be around all the studios and famous areas (even if you don't do the tourist route, which I didn't). I even noticed Goldstar Studios at the corner of Santa Monica and Vine—that's where Phil Spector produced all those classics that I love by The Ronettes, Crystals, and the Righteous Brothers, etc. The weather was not up to par, though. It rarely got past 80 and was overcast a lot—bad weather by LA standards, but nice enough to run around in. Tomorrow I start for San Francisco.

Tuesday—June 2, 1981

Cambria

Well, it took about 4½ hours to drive from LA to Cambria, just 6 miles from San Simeon. This is the site of Hearst Castle, which I'll see in the morning. Cambria sure is a quiet little town; the population is probably only a few hundred. I took some sunset pictures of the ocean nearby. I also called Clark again tonight, for the second time in two days—I can't help it, I miss him. He made his plane reservations today for his flight to Denver to meet me when I get there around July 3rd—he was flying out to join me on the trip back east.

Yes, this is a modification of my plans. We had been talking about his meeting me in Kansas City, but we both wanted to move that up, to sooner.

Wednesday—June 3, 1981

San Simeon

This morning I went on a tour of Hearst Castle in San Simeon. It was a very good tour. Took two hours and was very interesting, and worthwhile. It took about four hours to drive from there to San Francisco, stopping here and there for pictures. So, San Simeon was a very good half-way point in this part of the trek.

Endnotes

1   This wasn't the current location of the Archives. It was actually where Kepner lived, his apartment. His Archives did not merge with the One Institute until 1994. So, I had just looked him up in the telephone book.

```
HUDSON AV N                    90028
1625
  -4B HILL SHELLEY.............871-0309
  -102 CLARK E F CO ...........464-1968
  1654 Kepner Jas L............463-5450  <<
  1728¼ Macias Efren ..........467-3238
  1735 Jackson B ..............462-7085
  1740
    -1 SELBY HOTEL ............469-5320
    -3 Baird Deven ............469-9357
  1743 UNICORN PLAYERS ........464-8738
  1747 Johnson Lynn Walter ....465-2586
```

TWELVE

San Francisco

Wednesday—June 3, 1981
San Francisco

I CHECKED in the Atherton Hotel's guesthouse, a separate wing of the hotel. I got a very nice room (though with a shared bath) for $90/week, amazingly cheap for summer in San Francisco. It is on Ellis near Polk St.

This afternoon I walked about a dozen blocks up Polk Street, mostly just window shopping. I had dinner at a gay Italian restaurant, Anastasio's, which was only alright. There is only street parking around the hotel so I'm not sure yet what I'm going to do with my car. Just like New York, there are nothing but parking meters, if you're lucky enough to find one of them. I haven't spotted any garages yet, so I guess that's my project for tomorrow.

Thursday—June 4, 1981
San Francisco

Mission accomplished, but it was a little expensive. I found a 24-hour parking garage at Sutter and Powell (about 10 blocks away); it costs $115/month, or about $4/day. The daily lots charge from

$5 to $8 per day, so I can't complain too much. If I got my car towed away (easy to do here), it would cost that much or more.

I walked around downtown in the Polk area a little today, near Market Street. I noticed at a concert hall downtown that Minnelli and Grey will be here for a week in the middle of June, and it's already sold out.

This evening I met several of the guesthouse residents, although I am tempted to use the term "inmates." I ended up going to dinner with them downstairs at Suzy's Cafe, which is the greasy spoon it sounds like. The customers sure were colorful. I

think they all dropped out of a school for shopping bag ladies—couldn't make the grade. Two of the four guys I had dinner with I'm sure felt right at home there. One in particular—Tony (I don't care what his last name is) reminds me of Bowzer from Sha Na Na, only without the charm. He traded repartee with an Avery Schreiber character named Tim, who was almost just as insane. The first thing Tony said to me after hello was that I have a cute ass. All he'd ever be able to do, honey, is look! The other two sidekicks are Bret and Peter who, separated from this crowd, are probably decent enough. Dinner was a circus—I felt like I was in a sketch on *Saturday Night Live*. I was relieved when it was over and made a hasty retreat to my room.

Friday—June 5, 1981
San Francisco

This morning I played tourist…*avec* camera, of course. First, I walked towards downtown, then through Chinatown and finally on to Coit Tower. I wanted to get there early so I could take pictures facing the Golden Gate Bridge and avoid the sun's glare. It was about a 45-minute walk, and I got there a few minutes before the tower opened at 10 AM. The view from there is probably one of the prettiest views in the country.

From there I walked to Fisherman's Wharf. On the way is Pier 39, a very nice (and large) complex of shops. I spent about an hour and a half just walking around—none of this was here when I was in San Francisco in 1973. I got to see The Cannery and Ghirardelli Square, and I decided to walk up Hyde Street along the cable car route. And the word "up" doesn't say enough about that climb. I stopped at Lombard Street, "the crookedest street in the world," and then worked my way over to Polk and back to the hotel for a much-needed nap. Yes, my feet hurt—those hills are killers. I also did some gift shopping at Headlines, the best shop on Polk, and bought two more t-shirts and a Sisters of Perpetual Indulgence poster announcing their upcoming dog show.

Later: I had dinner at the P.S., a very nice, though a little expensive, restaurant-bar on Polk Street (hence its name). From there I went to the UUGC (Unitarian Universalist Gay Community) program. They have a special program every month as part of a "First Friday" series. The church building on Franklin and Geary (only five or six blocks from the hotel) is beautiful, very modern.

The program speaker was Peter Adair, who is known for his landmark film *Word Is Out: Stories of Some of Our Lives* (1977), which I had previously seen, and loved. This evening he showed the rough cut of his new film—42 minutes to be trimmed for a potential half-hour PBS show for the fall. It is about power and

violence and male bonding and showed three stories told by men. The working title is *Some of These Tales are True*. The first showed a black ex-con talking about violence and power in prison. The second a man spoke of his confrontation with an official at West Point while challenging the mandatory chapel rule. He very descriptively portrayed the official as a military egoist. Peter told the group after the film that the official is now Secretary of State. [This would be Alexander Haig].

I enjoyed the third section the most—it was a fictional segment with a man speaking of his experience on jury duty and how he confronted a fellow juror who tries to run the show and have his way. It was fascinating how, as he told the story, the speaker revealed himself as having the same aggressive, violent traits he criticized in the other jurist. The showing was the national premier of the film.[1]

After the program I spoke to Peter Adair briefly, and introduced myself to Joe Bryans, the UUGC group moderator. He knows my good friend Fred Osgood, in Norfolk. We went to a restaurant called Victoria Hausfraus afterwards for cokes and general b.s. Joe seems like a nice guy. I think we're going to go out for dinner or something this week.

Saturday—June 6, 1981
San Francisco

Today I walked to Castro Street. It was a longer walk than I expected, about 45 minutes. I guess I'll take the bus from now on. Along the way I stopped for lunch at Church Street Station, a nice gay bar/restaurant on Market Street. Its bar section is called Hideaway. The main Castro area is, I suppose, smaller than I expected—probably about six blocks long and two blocks wide. Yet, those are wonderful blocks, and the only thing that can compare to it is Christopher Street. And Castro wins.

I decided to try and get all my shopping done in one fell swoop, so the next time I hit the area I don't have to worry about

"Hibernia Beach"

carrying around things I might buy. Well, I hit every card/gift/ clothing store there, and those are about the nicest gay shops I've seen anywhere. Shops like Dear John, Does Your Mother Know (cards), Sports Locker, All American Boy, Leather World, Main Line, T's and Toys, The Store, Headlines, and The Obelisk. T's and Toys had an especially good t-shirt collection, and I almost missed them since they are an upstairs shop (552 Castro). I got their catalog for future reference. Of course, every shop had at least one really cute clerk, clone style.

While I was walking down 19th Street (this and 18th are the main cross streets of Castro Street), a gay wedding drove by! It was a parade of eight to ten decorated cars, honking their horns and waving, only the first car contained two brides in full wedding

regalia. Also, driving another car was a bearded guy with a bridal veil on. Even the locals stopped to stare at this.

I ate dinner at the Castro Café. It has good, cheap food and a great view of the pedestrian parade of clones on the sidewalk. I thought the weather today was cool—I wore a long-sleeved shirt and a jacket and wasn't overdressed—but I remarked to a clerk in one store, "Is this weather typical?" and he said, seriously, "It *is* a little warm." It was also very breezy. However, there still were many guys running around in just tank tops, and they looked damn good, too.

I have planned to go to the Sisters of Perpetual Indulgence Dog Show & Parade on Sunday, so staked out the location so I would be sure to find it. It is from 19th and Collingwood to the

Castro Station

Hibernia Beach. This isn't a beach at all. It's the sidewalk area in front of the Hibernia Bank. It's a localized cruise area where guys often take off their shirts, and just lean against the wall…hence the name Hibernia Beach. It's too bad there doesn't seem to be any cheap hotels in the Castro area; it really seems like the preferred place to be. I think I'll be riding the bus a lot.

Later: Now it's 3 AM and my trick just left. He's staying in the next room to mine at the guesthouse, which is, logically, where I met him earlier this evening. His name is Michael H. and he is an actor from LA here for a week to try out for a part in *Beach Blanket Babylon* (would I make that up?). He is kind of preppy cute, no mustache, and blond. That's three blonds in a row—chalk that up to California. He's a nice guy, although he doesn't seem tough enough for show business.

Michael and I went bar hopping tonight to the Castro area and hit what I have heard are its three best bars. First we went to Badlands. I love that name, so naturally I couldn't resist buying one of their shirts. The bar is very nice, kind of rustic and very crowded. Though it's too crowded to suit me, and a little too dark. But I still liked the place, I'll have to come back on a weeknight when it might not be so busy. Oh yeah: In the men's room, in addition to the urinal, was a bathtub one could piss into (and maybe be pissed upon) if so inclined. I was not, in either direction.

The next bar was the Midnight Sun, a smaller bar and even more crowded. The decor wasn't of any particular category. They had two TV monitors and one large 4x5 screen where they were alternating movies and rock acts, a few minutes of each. Tonight's movie was *Attack of the 50-Foot Woman* (1958), whose titular character ravaged a town before electrocuting herself by walking into a high-tension wire tower. (I know, bad planning). The rock acts I didn't recognize, although one looked a little like Tina Turner. Mind you, I would recognize Tina (I've seen her in concert), so I

Sylvester

Sister Missionary Position (who now goes by Sister Soami deLux) of the Sisters of Perpetual Indulgence

don't know who it was. Neither screen had the sound on. Instead, a DJ played disco. I saw a similar effect created at the Monster in Key West, where last January in two nights I saw the movie *Dumbo* accompanied by Viola Wills, et al.

The final bar was Castro Station. All three of these are within two blocks of each other. It had about the right size crowd to suit me, and one or two guys that I probably would have seriously cruised if I had been alone. The bar also had a rustic decor, and there seemed to be quite a few leatherettes there, but not an oppressive amount. I guess I liked it, too. I liked all three bars. We left just before closing at 2 AM and split a cab with two other guys who also missed the last direct bus back to near the hotel (so four of us split $4.20—not bad). Michael, by the way, is not particularly good in bed. Yes, that's subjective. Let's be more fair: I didn't think we were good together in bed.

San Francisco

Sunday—June 7, 1981
San Francisco

Today I got up early and walked to get my car and then drove to Castro (I took the car so I wouldn't have to lug the camera around all day). I took several general street scene photos before the Sisters of Perpetual Indulgence Dog Show and Parade began at 2 PM. It was, as expected, a hoot. They gave prizes to best body, legs, buns, smile, overall, and best match to owner. I met Sister Missionary Position and took photos of her. I also got pictures of three of the judges: Cleve Jones, Harry Britt, and Sylvester.

Naturally I also got a few random crowd shots. (Translation: photos of hot guys.) I went to three more of the area's bars: The Phoenix, Village, and Moby Dick. Phoenix was really nice, with very classy mirrors and very good, framed drawings (male nudes) on the walls. All the bars were crowded, and the streets had some very nice sights, indeed. 18th and Castro has got to be one of the gayest corners anywhere.

I had dinner at Duo, a gay restaurant on 19th Street. It was nice, although the decor was a little piss elegant…okay, a *lot* piss elegant. The lamps, vases, pictures, and flowers were all very tasteful (albeit ornate); it's just that they had enough decorations for three or four restaurants.

Some graffiti I saw (not there) that I wanted to record for posterity:

Q: What is in the air in San Francisco that keeps women from getting pregnant?

A: Men's legs.

Cute, huh?

An observation I wanted to make is that I've never seen a city where the neighborhoods can change so swiftly. You can be walking—down Grant, for example—and it changes from big city downtown to Chinatown to Nob Hill to Warehouses to the docks, all in about a mile. Also crossing that street is Broadway with its strip joints. The main gay drags—sorry, *streets*—appear and fade just as suddenly: Castro, Polk, Folsom.

Monday—June 8, 1981
San Francisco

This afternoon I went to the post office. The nearest branch is very well hidden, you have to go down to the basement in the City Hall building. There are no signs anywhere until you actually get to the bottom floor. It's not even on the building directory, which I was reading when a security guard asked if he could help. Anyway, I mailed two shirts to Fred, a card to Clark and a birthday card to my close friend Scott Wyatt. I think I bought that card for him about two months ago in Houston.

Since I was already heading southeast, I continued walking toward Folsom Street. I didn't see all of it but what I did see didn't look too appealing—it's a pretty seedy street. I joined it at 9th and walked northeast for four or five blocks. The only place I went in was A Taste of Leather—yes, a leather shop, and a very good one. It also sells cards (although even too tacky for me), and toys, and clothes. I bought a very nice tan, long-sleeved shirt with epaulets. They also had a very good collection of authentic uniform patches. I was amazed to see a Sebring, Ohio Police Department patch. That town is about 15 miles from my hometown and probably only has a couple thousand people in it. If it wasn't so expensive ($2.25) I would have bought it just for kicks. [A dollar in 1981 is worth about $3 in 2023.]

From there I walked to the Club Baths for t-shirts: one for me, one for Fred. They have very nice shirts. Their location, however, is the pits. It is nestled among several warehouses on a street about two blocks long (Ritch Street), maybe 12 blocks from the main Folsom area; certainly no place you would stumble onto if you didn't know it was there. And I certainly wouldn't walk there at night. I'm not sure I want to walk to Folsom *at all* at night.

San Francisco

Tuesday—June 9, 1981
San Francisco

Today I played tourist again with a guy from the hotel—Jean, from Vancouver, BC. We went to Golden Gate Park and the Japanese Tea Garden, to the hill above Cliff House and Seal Rocks, to Lincoln Park (which has a great view of the Golden Gate Bridge), and then to Twin Peaks (which has a great view of everything). Following that we went to the legendary (thanks to that CBS documentary) Buena Vista Park. We walked around Buena Vista, and I agree that it is ideal for cruising. There are bushes just *every*where. I just may have to go back there by myself.

This evening we went to a movie on Market Street a few blocks from the hotel. They were screening *A Very Natural Thing*, a 1974 gay film that was quite remarkable and advanced for its time. It had a little bit of politics but mostly it was just about the relationship between two guys, treated in a very natural way. And the guys weren't exactly hard to look at, either. Also, unlike some of those foreign gay films, they were adults. It was quite well done. This is a classic gay film.

Wednesday—June 10, 1981
San Francisco

I spent several hours this afternoon on Castro Street, mostly just walking and watching. I did go in another bar new to me, Bear Hollow, which I suppose is okay, nothing special. I spent a while playing Pac Man at Moby Dick's, where they have the only machine in Castro—and ta-da! I finally got past four rounds! In one game I got 26,370 points and seven, count 'em, seven rounds (That's two cherries, two oranges, two apples and a lime). With that I quit for the day.

I also got a haircut today—much shorter than I wanted. Thankfully I don't know anyone here. It's so short I can't part it.

Oh well. I also took the subway for the first time. What a great system—very fast and clean—and no graffiti! Just imagine.

Last night, at 12:30 AM, Bill F from Norfolk called. He found out my number from Fred. He'll be out here around the 25th and will be staying at the same guesthouse. He stayed here in May when he came out to interview, and he is planning to move into a house in August with Tim, Tony and Bret who all are staying on this floor. They were really surprised to find out that I know Bill, and vice versa…more from the Small World Department, I guess.

San Francisco

Thursday—June 11, 1981
San Francisco

So ends another busy day. This afternoon I drove to the Haight-Asbury District. You remember that, from the sixties. Well, it still has a Bohemian flavor to it, and lots of strange little shops. I stopped in two more gay bars on Haight Street, Le Disque and Deluxe. They were about empty, of course, since it was only two in the afternoon…but I was there, so I went in, just

to see them. Deluxe seemed like it would be a nice bar. It had lots of old car photos on the walls, almost a retro feel to it, very well done.

From there I went to Land's End, the gay nude beach of San Francisco. It is not exactly easy to get there either. You drive down a street (El Camino Del Mar) that dead ends in a tourist vista; then you go down a paved trail to the right for three or four blocks. Then you find a dirt path and start finding your way down a steep hill—for quite a distance—through some very winding paths. Lots of dense brush (and several nude sun bathers later) you get to the rocky beach area. Since it was a Thursday and a little cool, the beach was not too crowded, but it was still interesting. I met a photographer named Ken and we talked a while.

On the way back from the park I took a few cable car photos on Hyde Street and then went back to the hotel to change for dinner. Dinner was at Joe Bryans' apartment. Remember, he is a friend of Fred's that I met at the Unitarian Church last Friday. He lives with a straight couple (Leslie and Heinrich), very nice. To start the meal was artichokes—my first time, not bad, but a lot of trouble for a little food. Then a beef stew cooked in wine sauce over noodles. It was all quite good.

Joe and I had reservations to see the West Coast premiere of a gay play, *News Boy*, at the Rhinoceros Theater. While waiting in the lobby for it to start, I met Dan Curzon, the writer, and talked to him for about five minutes. The play itself I thought was just fair. I had seen a production of it in DC last year and I couldn't help but compare it. In the DC production, the casting and acting were just so far superior that it kind of made this performance less enjoyable. Joe also thought that the acting was a little uneven.

Since Joe lives in the Folsom area, after the play we went bar hopping there—something I had wanted to do. First, to The Stud, which had barn-like decor, and about the widest mix of people I've ever seen in a bar: Men, women, all races, leather, Lacoste, hippy, new wave, etc. If a Martian would have walked in, he (or she) wouldn't have raised an eyebrow. Then, very briefly, in and out of two leather bars—Febe's and The Brig. The Brig was *very* leather. We were definitely not dressed for it (a *cow* would have been underdressed). Then to the Arena and another milestone. Yep, sports fans, the Arena was the 100th gay bar that I've been to on my trip. It is also one of the ones I have liked best in San Francisco! It is very definitely a cruise bar. The decor was good and so was the crowd, but there was no unwritten dress code (Folsom is a very "leather" area in general). I bought one of their bar posters—they have about the hottest bar poster in the country—and, of course, a t-shirt.

Friday—June 12, 1981
San Francisco

Well, today was a long day. I took Ken (the photographer I met yesterday) up on his offer to see some of the beach areas south of the city. He knows them all. We drove about 60 miles down the coast on Highway 1, stopping at various places such as the nude beaches at Devil's Slide and San Gregorio, and then headed inland to the quaint towns of Cupertino, Los Gatos, and Santa Clara and Santa Cruz. We finally got back to the city just before dark and went to Treasure Island to take daytime, and later, nighttime skyline pictures at sunset and after.

    I used Ken's tripod, so the chances of good pictures much increased. I got some night pictures of the Bay Bridge, and Golden Gate Bridge as well. Ken and I lastly took a couple night photos of and from Coit Tower before I dropped him off at the bus station so he could return to Santa Clara. That sums up about 12 hours of photography.

Saturday—June 13, 1981
San Francisco

Saturday night on Polk Street started off with a delicious dinner at La Trattoria and then bar hopping, mostly on the west side of the street. There are five more bars on the east side of the street, all within nine blocks of each other. You can spend the whole night without crossing the street. But before you get too excited, I would say that they sure did not seem like anything special. Even on a Saturday night. The one I liked best was the Cinch Saloon, a Western neighborhood-type bar. While there I saw a guy play Pac Man and score 197,000 points in 20 rounds! I had never seen anyone get past nine rounds before—this guy was incredible. For the record, in order, the rounds are cherry, strawberry, two oranges, two apples, two limes, two spaceships, two ice cream sundaes, and then, apparently from the 13th round on—a series of keys.

Next, I went to Kimo's, a small corner bar with big windows and a mild African (or tropical?) motif; also, a very mixed crowd. They have an upstairs restaurant, though I did not check it out. Then, on to the New Bell saloon, which had a live Western band and an older crowd. The band was good. Next was Giraffe, which (like Kimo's) played taped disco music. Giraffe was much larger though and nicer. Logically, there were pictures of large giraffes all over. I guess it's a good bar, although I wasn't really in a disco mood. At least the place was well-lit. All the bars I went to tonight were. I went in the Polk Gulch Saloon, on the east side of the street, for just a few minutes. It has Western decor, a live DJ (disco) and is a small corner bar. It is probably better in the afternoons, but I thought it was still okay. Finally, to a bar on the corner of Ellis and Polk which I've passed numerous times—The Stallion. From now on I'll keep passing it; that place is a true dive.

Tuesday—June 16, 1981
San Francisco

On Sunday afternoon I had brunch at a Western bar, The Rainbow Cattle Company, on Valencia and Duboce, and from there I drove to Castro to buy t-shirts for my Norfolk friends Fred, Scott and (of course) myself. The last few days the weather has been beautiful, untypically warm, which for here means it got into the lower 80s. The natives are all dying of heat frustration, but I love it. Castro Street was very pretty—lots of clones walking around with their shirts off. Either Californians have better bodies or there are more of them to show them off. It *is* very distracting.

Still, my impression is that Castro Street itself is not especially cruisy. I could be wrong, but it seems that the guys are more interested in being seen than anything else. Also, I'm not that crazy about the Castro bars. I mean, they are okay, but nothing special. Badlands and Midnight Sun are always too crowded, and Badlands also is too dark. I guess my favorite Castro bar is Moby Dick on 18th Street. Although in fairness I haven't yet been to the bars on Market Street, like Patsy's and The Balcony. Oh, at Moby Dick they were playing "Step by Step," by Peter Griffin, a Euro record from last year but now re-released in a longer version on the Moby Dick label.

Sunday night I talked to Clark for about a half hour—these calls are getting more and more expensive. Then I watched a movie on TV in a neighbor's room. (*Audrey Rose*, 1977. I'm not sure why, I hate horror movies.) Finally, before I fell asleep, I read some more of the new Gordon Merrick book, *Now Let's Talk About Music*. I'm about halfway through it and it really sucks. The author seems to have forgotten that to like a book you have to like the hero, which so far isn't possible.

On Monday my plan was to walk to Hyde Street and catch the Powell-Hyde cable car down to Fisherman's Wharf. But I got there and instead of waiting, I started walking down Hyde. I got all the way there before a car passed me. I still haven't ridden one since the one back required at least an hour wait—the line is very long. So, I opted for the bus back to Polk Street.

While at Fisherman's Wharf, I went to Ghirardelli Square, which I missed before. It's an old chocolate factory converted into a multi-level complex of expensive gift shops. Kind of interesting, but not worth a special trip.

Back on Polk Street I stopped at the Cinch Saloon where I met a good-looking clone, Dennis M, and a friend of his, Alex.

We went from there to Kimo's and then to a small bar, The Wild Goose Saloon, which was kind of neat. Alex left us at that point (finally), and I went home with Dennis. His apartment is beautiful. It's on the 14th floor of a building on the corner of Franklin and Clay and it's a corner apartment with large windows facing south and east. The view is tremendous of the city, especially at night, with the heat waves from the city making the lights in the distance seem to twinkle. His view is of downtown mostly but also includes Alcatraz Island and Twin Peaks. He says his rent would normally be around $1,000/month, but he has a rent-controlled apartment (at $735/month). Dennis shares the two-bedroom place with his roommate. I spent the afternoon.

Tonight, I called Clark again and then walked downtown for dinner; there's a restaurant called Zim's near the garage (at Powell and Sutter) that I like. From there, I walked back to Polk Street. I didn't plan on it, but I ended up going into three more new bars. They are all on the east side of the street and just hadn't appealed to me before. I think now that it was mostly the people mingling on the street outside the bars who didn't appeal to me. There are a lot of hustlers on Polk Street, especially that side of the street and especially outside those bars.

Anyway, I went in Buzzby's and 'N Touch, two small discos, nothing noteworthy about them at all. Then I went into QT, which surprisingly, I liked, at least on Tuesday nights. I'll tell you why in a moment. First, there were in particular a lot of young hustlers (which is almost redundant) outside of that bar. I almost didn't go in, but I guess it was just because that bar had more customers in it at that time. It was about 9:30 PM. Anyway, inside the crowd may have been a little younger than average, but not to extremes. Also, the decor was the nicest of the three bars.

Now, why did I like QT's, and why on a Tuesday? Well, they have live entertainment, a different act every night (but an act will always play on the same day of the week). Tonight, on stage was 40 Karats, consisting of two women singers, a woman drummer and a male piano player/singer. I thought they were very good and stayed to listen for about 45 minutes. They had a varied song list: "We are Family," "Chapel of Love," "Fame," "At the Ballet," "Mr. Sandman," "Ooh Baby Baby," "Silver Threads and Golden Needles," and "He's So Shy" (which they dedicated to the boys out on the street). They did a good job on everything.

Wednesday—June 17, 1981
San Francisco

This afternoon I drove across the Golden Gate Bridge over to Sausalito. This was the first time this trip. I took a few pictures on the way, especially from the park just northwest of the bridge, with a great view of the city. I stopped in Sausalito's only gay bar, The Sausalito Inn. They have cute t-shirts that read TAKE A FERRY TO THE SAUSILITO INN AND TAKE A FERRY HOME. (No, I didn't buy one). It has kind of the atmosphere of a hotel bar, but definitely gay. Even if I hadn't heard about it, I probably would have found it.

I picked up (or got picked up by, depending on your point of view) a very cute guy named Hellmuth G. He is from Germany, but he's lived here 12 years. He still has a strong accent though. He said he is a wine taster at the restaurant on top of the Bank of America Building. His house is just gorgeous—on a hill overlooking The Sausalito Harbor, a fantastic view. It is easily a $200,000 house, probably more, since this is California. Have no idea if he owns or rents. Yes, some afternoon delight. And he offered me some cocaine. I declined.

Later, after putting the car away, I walked back to Polk Street and went in the QT again. This time a very talented woman named Lynda was singing, mostly show music like "All That Jazz," "Maybe This Time," "Send in the Clowns," typical fag stuff.[2]

Thursday—June 18, 1981
San Francisco

This afternoon, I walked downtown to find a lens hood for my camera. There is a concentration of camera shops on Kearney Street where Geary meets Market. I found one and bought a filter system. Isn't plastic money wonderful? I also stopped at Sutter's Mill (on Kearney between Geary and Post). It is one of two gay bars in the financial district, with the other being Trinity Place. I understand at five o'clock the place is packed with hot businessmen. The decor is beautiful—very nice and tasteful. They also serve lunches at reasonable prices.

Later, after having tacos for dinner, I went shopping on Polk Street and bought that Vito Russo book I've been waiting for, *The Celluloid Closet*, and a carrying bag for my trip tomorrow to Russian River.

Endnotes

1 Google doesn't indicate that this film was ever released.

2 *Typical Fag Stuff* is the title of a series of about 20 cassette tapes I've made for myself back in Norfolk, containing…of course…Broadway, disco, pop, movie, novelty, etc.

THIRTEEN

San Francisco, Part 2

Friday—June 19, 1981
San Francisco

I LEFT the city by 11:30 AM and drove right to Muir Woods, where I spent a couple hours. It is a redwood forest—not quite Sequoias, but still impressive. I have been here before. It was interesting that, while there were lots of people on the trails, everyone was really quiet. I think the park is just so naturally awe-inspiring that people act like they're in church. I stopped at several other points along Highway 1 to take pictures on my way to Guerneville. I sure wouldn't want to make that drive every day. Though pretty, it's very nerve-racking with all those curves and hills. You have to concentrate on the road every single second!

Guerneville is a small (repeat: small) resort town on the Russian River about 60 miles north of San Francisco. You may recall from the Dallas section of this epic (April 19th) that the guy I stayed a few days with (Kelly N) has a friend who lives here in Guerneville and has just opened a pizza parlor. When I was at Kelly's, he called his friend (Leonard Matlovich), and during the call Leonard invited me up for a visit. Since I don't have to be asked twice to visit a gay resort area *and* a gay celebrity, I called Leonard last week to arrange a convenient day for him; and here I am. When we talked on the phone, he said his restaurant was at the corner by the stop sign. After we hung up, I wondered if it mattered which way I came into town—turns out it doesn't; there's only one stop sign. I *told* you it was a small town.

I didn't spot the restaurant right away (much like the town, the sign is really small), so I went into Rainbow Cattle Company and asked. Obviously, that's a gay bar. There's one by the same name in San Francisco. Less than five minutes later in walked Leonard, so introductions were easy. I recognized him right away from his pictures. He was just opening his restaurant (called Stumptown Annie's) and he suggested I go down to Fife's to cool off. It was 108 degrees that afternoon there (only 80 in San Francisco when I left). Fife's is a very nice resort with a bar, restaurant, cottages, and pool. I pretended I belonged there, changed clothes in the car, and went swimming. No one seemed to notice I wasn't a guest, or I looked good enough they did not care. The bar also has a deck overlooking the pool, and there are huge pine trees all around; very pretty.

San Francisco, Part 2

Finally, I came back and ate at Leonard's restaurant and then walked around town a little, which doesn't take long. I went into another gay bar, The Sundog Saloon, which was okay, but very empty. I think Leonard said it closes around 11 or so.

Saturday—June 20, 1981
Russian River

As Leonard was working last night, I went to The Woods. That's the big disco in Russian River. It is a really *hot* place. The disco is quite large and hexagonally shaped. It used to be called the Hexagonal House, with an upper deck overlooking it. There's a huge patio area behind it which was nice, and several other rooms off it, like a restaurant, bar, pool table and game room, etc. On the grounds is also a pool that features a sign "Nude Bathing Permitted." I understand that after hours things get interesting. The complex also has cottages, so it seems to be an ideal place to stay.

I left The Woods around 1:30 AM, near closing time, and went back to the restaurant to wait for Leonard. It closed around 3 AM, which I guess is typical for a weekend.

San Francisco, Part 2

Leonard Matlovich

Okay, here I am with the possibility of tricking with a celebrity. It was already arranged that I could stay at Leonard's place that evening. I was relaxing on the dining room floor, talking with another gay guy whom Leonard agreed to put up for the night. That guy and I were chatting, and I think he must have been jealous of me, because he said, "You know, you're not sleeping with Leonard." I just said, "I don't know," because I didn't. Then less than five minutes later Leonard stuck his head out of his bedroom door and said, "JD, come here," while crooking his finger to me. I gave the guy I had been talking with a side look, though not a snide look, and went into the bedroom. Spending the night with Leonard was very enjoyable, high marks.

Today I slept 'til 3:30 PM. It was just too hot to get up, another scorcher like yesterday, which is one of the reasons I decided to return to San Francisco today. With Leonard running his business I couldn't really count on any time with him. Besides that, I had already seen the best of the bars yesterday. I got back to the city around 6:30 PM, stopping at the Golden Gate National Recreation area and at the marina to take some pictures and try out my new lens filter. That spot has one of THE best views of the city.

I had dinner at my hotel's new restaurant, which just opened last night. I'm very impressed… I had the beef burgundy, which was excellent. I didn't go out tonight, and I'm glad I didn't because Clark called, which was *really* nice.

Sunday—June 21, 1981
San Francisco

Today was a very laid-back day. This morning around 11, Brian O called from Miami and we talked for about an hour, bringing each other up to date on what's happened since we saw each other in New Orleans. He's volunteered to edit my journal; I'm sure he'd love that.

I read a little this afternoon: Finished *The Celluloid Closet* (very good, an essential gay book) and *Let's Talk About Music* by Gordon Merrick (awful). Then I went to the Walt Whitman bookstore to hear a reading by Armistead Maupin. (Can a paragraph get any more gay than this?)

The reading was very enjoyable. He read the next few days' worth of the new *Tales of the City*, being serialized in the *San Francisco Chronicle*. He writes only about two weeks ahead of what appears in the paper. He said the next book will probably be out in about a year. Even though I didn't know what happened previous in the story to what he read, I still enjoyed it.

He has a pleasant personality and is very funny. He's a little chunkier than I pictured him, but he is still good looking. I talked to him for a few minutes afterwards. I told him that part of his self-interview was read before the Virginia Beach City Council as an example of the perversion appearing in *Our Own Community Press*. He loved it. He autographed a copy of *More Tales* for me, which I had been wanting, but just never got around to buying before now.

I had dinner at the hotel again and got involved in about an hour discussion about homosexuality with a straight woman from Ottawa. It was interesting. She said she has never had a chance to talk openly about it with anyone gay. She has a couple friends she thinks are gay but wouldn't think of asking them. It's been a long time since I talked at length to a straight person. I enjoyed our talk.

When I talked to Brian on the phone, I tried to explain my impression of the people here. I can't quite put my finger on it, but I guess they don't seem as friendly here as other places. I'm not sure if it's my attitude or what, but something just isn't quite there. Granted, I've met several nice people, but in general there seems to be an aloofness or preoccupation when you talk to people. Maybe things are just too easy here. I don't know, I haven't quite defined it yet.

As a gay Mecca, of course, San Francisco has it all…a beautiful city that is very gay, and about the most comfortable atmosphere anywhere. It has more trendy shops than you know what to do with, several fine gay newspapers (and generally good treatment by the city papers), more gay activities and events than you could ever attend, gay celebrities in residence, etc. I'm not sure why the city hasn't won me over. I think I've been here long enough to get the feel of the city. I've found that, as with several other cities I've been to recently, like Houston, LA, and Miami, if I spent more than one or two weeks, I start to get, at least what I think, is an impression of what it would be like to live there. I'm comfortable here—just not won over.

Monday—June 22, 1981
San Francisco

This afternoon, really for lack of anything else to do, I took a long walk…down Polk all the way to Union, east on Union to Grant, then back downtown. I stopped in a few shops here and there.

While in the financial district, I stopped at Trinity Place, which I've already mentioned. It's the other downtown businessmen's gay bar (besides Sutter's Mill). It is one of those bars that if you didn't know it was there, you would never find it. It is in an alley (one block long) between Bush and Sutter, just west of Montgomery Street. It's a nice place, very classy, although I thought Sutter's Mill was nicer. Historically, this is just a few blocks up Montgomery from the location, at 710, of the famous Black Cat Bar, famous hang-out of Empress Jose Sarria.

Also, this afternoon my friend Bill F (from Norfolk) arrived, about two days early. He and a friend (CP) drove without stopping from North Carolina to Denver, spent the night there, and then drove 24 hours continuous to get here. His friend is here for a few days, but Bill has moved here, no job, no furniture, nothing. I hope he's ready for San Francisco. (I had dated Bill briefly in Norfolk, but now we're just friends).

Later: After dinner, Bill, CP and I went Castro bar hopping, mostly for CP's benefit, since Bill was here for two weeks in May.

We went to Castro Station, Badlands, Midnight Sun, Phoenix, and Moby Dick. I thought Castro Station was the cruisiest. Badlands was crowded and dark, as usual. Phoenix was almost empty, and Midnight Sun was *very* crowded—a line to get in. On their video screen tonight were clips from last year's gay parade, along with Bette Midler, David Bowie, Diana Ross, and the movie *Superman*. Moby Dick had a sparse crowd, but okay. A guy at Midnight Sun told us about a bar above a restaurant, both called Cafe San Marcos, that I didn't know was there—you can only get in either through the back of the restaurant or an unmarked door on the street. It has a sort of European flavor, I thought. I kind of liked it.

Across the street was another new bar for me, Patsy's, a Western bar named for Patsy Cline. There were only a few people there. I guess only the Castro Street bars do well on a Monday night—these two are on Market a block east of Castro. I don't think I saw anyone the whole night I thought was outstanding looking, but we had a good time. CP is very forward when he drinks, and is a cross between funny and embarrassing, depending on how flaming he is in that particular moment. He is, and looks like, a stereotypical flaming hairdresser.

Tuesday—June 23, 1981
San Francisco

This afternoon Bill, CP, and I went to the beach, to Land's End near Seal Rocks. I had been there the previous week and wanted to see it again, and it is definitely something CP should see while he's here. I acted as guide since I know what road to take and which trails to take down the complicated route to the beach. I had my camera and took some more nude shots. It was a very nice day. We stayed about three hours, long enough for CP to get sunburned and long enough for me to take a "walk" through the bushes.

Okay, you may not believe this, but today was the very first

The Castro Theatre

San Francisco, Part 2

time I had anonymous sex in the bushes. It's true, it's true. No, I didn't ask his name—somehow that would have spoiled it or been against *the rules*. It was, I suppose, okay, though more interesting than satisfying for me, since I had never done anything like that before—not in restrooms or at the baths, nowhere. I wouldn't want to make a steady diet of it, but it *was* interesting. Oh yeah, he was about my height, a little heavier, brown hair, blue eyes, mustache (of course), and kind of cute. Does this mean I'm ready for the big time? Just what *is* the big time for a somewhat nomadic introverted small-town boy from Ohio? Tune into some of these same stations for the next exciting adventures of…

But seriously, folks… Later the Virginia two (Bill and I) had dinner at a gay Mexican restaurant, Casa de Crystal. I'm sure it was good Mexican food, but I couldn't appreciate it, too spicy for my gringo tastes. I guess I'll just stick to my Taco Bell.

Tonight, I took the subway to Castro to go to one of the gay film festival showings—Vito Russo's presentation of *The Celluloid Closet*, a talk and showing of film clips of how the movie industry has poorly represented gays in the movies since the beginning. It was just an excellent showing (as was the book). And I am delighted to have had the opportunity to see him give this presentation in person. He was touring the country giving these talks and they are legendary.

The Castro Theatre is very interesting—I'm not sure I can describe its decor. Regressive piss elegance? Anyway, there is lots of gold leaf and two huge murals showing some Roman scene in 1920s style.

And I got a photo of the bookstore Paperback Traffic, 535 Castro, mainly to capture the men lounging/cruising on the steps, typical of everywhere.

I caught the bus back to Polk. I think everyone on board was gay. Standing in front of me was a very drunk lesbian and three of her friends, all of whom looked like extras from the cast of *Cabaret*. They were on their way to The Stud, which seemed logical.

Paperback Traffic

Since I wasn't ready for bed yet, I went to the Giraffe, probably the best cruise bar in the Polk area, and since I had only been there once, I felt like I had been slighting it. The crowd was okay. I played Pac Man with a young guy named Craig who I think would have liked to pick me up. Why else would he keep feeling my leg? I guess he was okay, but I just wasn't really psyched. The bar closed and outside the door he was asking me what I had planned for the evening (evening? It was 2 AM.). Luckily, he

San Francisco, Part 2

ran into some old friends and they started gabbing, giving me a chance to discreetly leave.

Wednesday—June 24, 1981
San Francisco

Slept 'til noon today (again), had lunch at The Zims on Van Ness and Geary, then took the subway system here—clean, fast, and no graffiti. I walked in and out of The Balcony, another gay bar not very impressive, but I understand very hot on Sunday afternoons. Then I walked to the medical center on 17th near Noe, where if you tell them you're a resident you can get a free VD checkup. Although I have no symptoms, I thought might be a good idea.

Then on to Castro to buy t-shirts for Del, Scott, and Fred (and one for me). Back to Polk to do laundry. As you can see, not an exciting day. Oh yeah, while in Castro, I stopped in Elephant Walk, on the corner of Castro and 18th. They've been remodeling and today was the first day it's been open since I've been here. It's nice, kind of classy—reminds me of Park Place in San Diego (so that means it's very nice). At 4:30 PM it was very crowded.

Thursday—June 25, 1981
San Francisco

Well, last night the trio went to do the Castro bars again. CP, that slut, picked up a trick at the first one (Elephant Walk) and he must have been really horny, because I thought his trick was the pits. I think CP was more attracted to the guy's grass and coke. Bill and I split up and I went to Moby Dick. I found out yesterday that its owners are the same people who put out the Boys Town Gang album, *Cruising the Streets* (with "Remember Me / Ain't No Mountain" on it). Anyway, there was only one guy there I was interested in. He was real cute, and we carried on a little, but then he got wishy-washy and said he had to get up at 6 AM. That never stopped me.

So, I went back to The Elephant Walk, where I was supposed to meet Bill if he didn't pick up someone, but he wasn't there. Since the last subway train left at midnight, I hightailed it up there and just made it as the gate was starting to close.

I later saw Bill at The Giraffe back on Polk Street. Before he got there, I played pinball with these three guys, all very nice. One of them was in *News Boy*, which I saw last week (he played the jock roommate). So, it was an enjoyable evening.

San Francisco, Part 2

This afternoon Bill and I walked to Folsom to go shopping. We went to Worn Out West, a store I'd been wanting to get to. It's on Howard Street and sells mainly used clothing, a lot of

which would be great to wear to the bars—anything from leather to Western to military (sorry, no Lacoste...this *is* Folsom). They had lots of used 501s, worn out to different degrees, with tears and holes if you want 'em. I bought some 501 cutoffs for $2.50 and a denim jacket for $13. The jacket I love; it's worn to about the same degree as my jeans. I took Bill into A Taste of Leather and then we also just walked in and out of three of the bars, just to see them: The Watering Hole, The Eagle, and The Ramrod. Of course, at that time of day they were practically empty, but at least you can get an idea of what they're like, and all three seemed to be just ordinary Folsom bars.

Then we ate at Hamburger Mary's on Folsom street, which

I think is an institution. The food is really good and the atmosphere and decor are somewhere in that twilight area of camp, funk, punk, and junk. The waitpersons all look like the kind of people who would just love *The Rocky Horror Picture Show.* To say the least, it is a very interesting place.

Bill and CP rushed off to the financial district bars at 5 PM—Sutter's Mill and Trinity Place. Since I'd seen them, and it's a long walk, I passed. I took a nap, and then called Clark and then went out for dinner.

Later, I went to The Cinch for a while and then to Giraffe for about an hour and a half. I think I only saw one guy that appealed to me the whole time, and he was with someone. One thing I've noticed (and Bill thinks so too) is that when you're walking down Castro or Polk Streets, it doesn't matter whether it's day or night, you see just lots of good-looking men pass you as you're walking. But when you're in the bars, well, they're not there. The proportion of hot men *in* the bars isn't really any higher than in other cities. I don't know why that is, but it's too bad, cause how are you supposed to meet them on the street? Grab them as they walk by and say, *"Excuse me, but I noticed you walk by"*? Hit and run cruising is always much more difficult than the stationary bar tactics.

Saturday—June 27, 1981
San Francisco

I think I spent about nine hours yesterday in the Castro Street bars, just drinking and talking. I think the nicest guy I met all day wasn't in the bars, but on the subway. A guy named Jason Sanders—but he was on his way to work. So goes it. I did get his phone number.

This afternoon I went to Castro to buy some video tapes. I got *La Cage aux Folles* (dubbed in English, unfortunately), a Barbra Streisand collection, and I ordered *Liza with a "Z"*. I took the bus back to Market and Polk, close to the hotel.

Note: all this stuff I've mentioned buying, records, books, t-shirts, etc., I've been mailing back to Norfolk. It will feel like xmas when I get home.

At 4:30 PM, Jason met me at the hotel for drinks. He's a very nice guy, about 5'8", brown hair, mustache and beard, blue eyes and slender. MY type. It's a good thing I met him on the subway…in the bar he would probably have had on full leather and I never would have had the nerve to talk to him. He is going to be on the Moby Dick float tomorrow (in full leather). He is part of the recording team for their recordings.

He said it was really rare for him to give his number to someone on the subway. He told a couple friends about it and they couldn't believe he did that. It would have been really nice to spend the night with him, but since I'm leaving Monday early, and he has already made plans for Saturday and Sunday nights, I'll guess we'll be grateful for a Saturday afternoon. Oh yeah, he was runner-up in the San Francisco preliminary to the Mr. Leather International contest. The San Francisco winner went on to win the national title. And, also, another first for me—he was the first guy I've been to bed with that had a pierced nipple. Again, Jason is very hot.

Monday—June 29, 1981
San Francisco

Sunday started off with the four of us setting off to watch the parade (that's Bill, CP, Cory and I). Cory is a friend of CP's who flew up from LA for the parade. We staked out a place around 6th and Market and waited. The parade pretty much started on time and lasted two and a half hours. It attracted 250,000 people and was wonderful. I've got three rolls of film of it.

I can't list all the marchers, but here's a few that stood out to me: Dykes on Bikes, Gay Fathers, Rainbow Deaf Society, Foggy City Squares (a Western square dance club), Rainbow Cattle Co. (a Western bar), Gay Men's Chorus, Parents of Gays, I-Beam (a

bar, Candi Station sang on the float), San Francisco Tap Troupe, San Francisco Marching Band, Nancy's Little Pistols (pro gun control), Sisters of Perpetual Indulgence (Armistead Maupin rode in their car in priest drag), Castro Station (bar), Aloha Records, Moby Dick (a bar and record company), Lesbians for S&M, Great Outdoors Association, Gay Latino Alliance, and several church groups and just all kinds of political groups, etc. The official parade list has over 150 different groups. I got pictures of all the major floats and any group that had hot men in it; plus, I took some token lesbian shots, for balance. Yeah, sure.

    The weather was beautiful, couldn't be better, and as far as I could tell, things ran smoothly. There were these three guys next to Bill and me who we kidded around with a little. One started groping me and it must have taken five minutes before I could get him to stop (or maybe, it was five minutes before I stopped him, memory not clear). After the last float, we joined the parade back to the City Hall. There were many booths set up selling food, buttons, shirts, etc. and passing out literature.

    Two stages were set up and some of the big names on hand were Robin Tyler, Mel Boozer, Tom Robinson, Robin Flower, Chris Tanner, and Del Martin. There were at least 30 speakers and entertainers, but, other than the background music, few people really paid attention to the stages…the crowd was much more interesting. The same thing happened to some degree at the March on Washington in 1979. I took at least a dozen candid crowd shots, mostly of couples.

Around 4 PM, I started talking to a guy sitting on one of the building walls. I think his name was Joseph. Anyway, he gave me a ride to my hotel on his motorcycle, which I loved. I bet I haven't been on a motorcycle in 15 years. After stopping at the hotel to stow my camera, we went onto the Church Street Station for dinner, and then he dropped me off on Castro Street. Bill had left me a note that they'd be in the Castro, but I sure didn't find them. The bars were, as could be expected, *very* crowded after the parade.

All the Castro bars had lines outside to get in. I was in Moby Dick's, it turned out, the same time Bill was and missed him. As I said, the bars were very crowded. I guess it was around 7 or 8 PM when I finally decided to head back for Polk. I decided to walk in and out of Elephant Walk in case Bill was there. I go no further than five feet in the door and spotted just the *cutest* man, you know—all the clone requirements—and the nicest smile. He was in a Western outfit, which of course I complimented him on. We chatted for a while and hit it off and, like I hoped, off to his place.

His name is Tim Kane and what a find he was! He has dark good looks (he's part Italian), brown hair and mustache, 5'8" and slender, a very nice personality. It turns out he was one of the Western dancers in the Foggy City Squares. I may have a picture of him—I know I took some of several of the Western dancing groups—I hope I got his. He reminds me a little of Jader in Houston—he had something about him—some charm—that you just wanted to hug him (and then attack him!). He's a great cuddler and is also great to talk to. I guess it's fitting that fate saved the best for last—of all the guys I met in San Francisco (easy now, there were only eight), he was the only one who if given the chance would rate a second night.

But that wasn't to be, since I planned on leaving San Francisco early Monday morning. Well, I *almost* left early—I only got out of Castro at 10 AM. Tim has a very nice apartment on Noe Street. By the time I got back to the hotel, packed, got the car checked out and loaded the car, it was already noon. But it worked out okay, since I got to say goodbye to Bill at a more presentable hour. Can you imagine waking someone up at six or seven to say goodbye? Not gonna happen. Also, I ran into Bret at the hotel (he works there, remember, and stays at the guesthouse). He packed me a free lunch: a ham sandwich, pickles, oranges, and a bottle of pinot noir wine. It was all very nice of him—I needed some break after paying the $94 phone bill. Calls to Houston are expensive.

Anyway, I left San Francisco at noon and drove for nine hours to Elko, Nevada. California along Route 80 was beautiful. I stopped at a rest area near Donner Lake where they had a nature trail showing an area where a glacier had passed through. Shucks, I just missed it. The scenery was very rocky, with pine trees everywhere, very interesting landscape. It seems though that almost upon crossing the border into Nevada that the scenery got *b-o-r-i-n-g!* So the last half of the drive was very bland, very little vegetation and hardly any trees.

Elko is not exactly a wonderland. It has two "big" casinos, The Commercial and Stockmans. I went in both and decided to donate $5 worth of nickels to Stockmans. The $5 (in the nickel slots) lasted me a half hour… I should have gone to a movie, but you can do *that* anywhere. How many times do you get to be in Elko, Nevada? Once, I hope.

FOURTEEN

Salt Lake City / Denver

Tuesday—June 30, 1981
Salt Lake City

IT **WAS** about four hours from Elko to Salt Lake City. The drive was pretty bland except for the trek across the Salt Lake Desert. Despite being perfectly flat leading to mountains in the distance, I found the ground quite interesting. It is white with crystalized salt. Salt Lake itself is kind of just in the middle of a desert and has got to be the least picturesque lake I've ever seen.

I got to Salt Lake City around three and checked into The Travelodge. After dinner I went bar hopping. I started around 7 PM, just to see what bars might be good later. First, I went to the Sun Tavern; it was a private club, but they let me in. I was quite impressed with how large the space was. I wonder if the "private" aspect was for alcohol rules. It is split up into various rooms: a dance floor, a front bar, a game room, a large dining room, and a very nice tree-filled patio. The decor is really nice. The woman who let me in helped me update my bar list and told me, correctly, that The Sun would be the most popular bar that night.

Almost right next door is a dive called The Rail, and about eight blocks away was a new Western bar, The Deerhunter. It was small and the decor was nice (varnished wood slats) but looked like someone's den, rather than looking rustic. All the (six) bars are downtown, conveniently located near each other. The last new one I went to was Radio City, also called The RC. It seems to be an average downtown cruise bar, maybe a little nicer.

While I was there, I met a very cute clone named Curt P, brown hair and mustache, 22. His lover (whom he doesn't live with) was out of town, so Curt took me to his lover's apartment, because it was closer than his. That was kind of different. He was my third gay Mormon. After a quickie (during which the earth did not move) we went to the apartment of one of his friends, Demar, and we had some beer, and some pot. That was quite rare for me. I just agreed to be polite and had only a little. Afterwards we went next door to McDonald's, then they drove me up on the city mountain to show me a gorgeous view of the Capitol Building and the city lights. Curt looks a little like Teddy Neely, who played Jesus in *Jesus Christ Superstar*, but of course without the long hair. I am never attracted to long hair on a guy.

Finally, at about 11 PM, they dropped me off at The RC where I had left my car. From there I went back to The Sun Tavern, as I felt I should see the busiest bar. I owed it to myself while I was there. It was easier to get in this time—different doorperson, I guess. There was a nice sized crowd, good atmosphere, good quality of crowd. There were maybe four guys I thought were good looking.

By about 12:30 AM, I hadn't talked to anyone yet and the place seemed a little cliquish. I was thinking about leaving when this very hot blond named Bob H started a conversation. He is 25, has short blond hair and a mustache. Why didn't I just say, a blond clone. He is *really* cute, and a very nice guy. He is from Wisconsin and went to college here and decided to stay. He is not a Mormon. We went back to his apartment and amused ourselves until 3 AM. I guess he was impressed, too: He said he wanted to kidnap me so I couldn't leave. I think I could have put up with him as a kidnapper for at least a few days.

This was only the second time that I had had two tricks in the same day—the other time was in New Orleans. It is interesting that that should happen in two cities that really rate fairly low on the list of places I've been. It is also ironic that this should happen in Salt Lake City—a conservative city that one probably wouldn't expect to find a good time on a Tuesday night. And Bob showed me a good time.

Wednesday—July 1, 1981
Cheyenne

Drove across Wyoming today—Salt Lake to Cheyenne in seven *long* hours. There are probably a total of 25 scenic miles in those seven hours along Route 80 in Wyoming. It was really a hard drive, especially on four hours sleep.

At the hotel, I called the gay hotline. I was surprised that they even had one, as Cheyenne only has 45,000 people. The guy on the line told me that the three bars listed in gay yellow pages were now all closed, but there was still one place people would sometimes go called The Hitching Post, the bar of the Best Western hotel. However, he said it was a mixed bar—not mixed men and women, mixed gay and straight. I found my way over there (it's only a half block from my hotel) around 11 PM, and it sure wasn't mixed tonight. It was painfully straight, so I drank my Coke and left. So much for gay life in Cheyenne, at least on a Wednesday night.

I also called my parents and my roommates (Fred & Bill) last night. I've already told my parents that I liked Houston, and my dad said he wouldn't be surprised if I moved there. I think he was stationed in Texas during the war before he went overseas and he's always loved the climate there. I also told them that I would have company driving from Denver to Houston. My mom asked if I know the people, and I said, "Yeah, a guy I met in Houston." She then asked, "What is he doing in Denver?" "He's flying up to meet me," I said. She said, "Oh, I see." I'm not sure whether she really "sees," but it'll give them something to think about.

Thursday— July 2, 1981
Denver

Today, I left Cheyenne around 11 AM and took the long way to Denver—through the Rocky Mountain National Park, which is 50 or 60 miles west of Interstate 25, which runs south to Denver. It was a very scenic drive—the park is beautiful. The only trouble was that it was raining. Because of that, the roads were very foggy, and, in many places, you knew there had to be a great view out there somewhere, but you just couldn't see it. I still managed to shoot about a dozen pictures, but they probably won't be very good other than some close ups I took of the wildflowers. Along some of the hills there was also some snow that you could play in if you wanted—I certainly didn't. It's at least a 60-mile drive through the park and probably a 150-mile side trip. I guess it was worth it, but the weather sure sucked. Even so, there were lots of tourists. I'd hate to see it with weekend crowds.

Later: I only hit one bar tonight—The Triangle on Broadway. I had heard that it is one of the best bars in Denver, and I guess I believe it. It's a cruise bar and, from what I could tell, the crowd was better-looking than average. However, it *was* very dark. It's an all-purpose cruise bar—leather, Western, Levis and dash of Lacoste. I spent about three hours there, so I guess I have to say I liked it, even though I didn't talk to many people. I wasn't in a heavy cruising mood, but the crowd seemed friendly enough. One guy I talked to was there with his lover, both good looking, around 35. He said they'd been together 14 years. Kind of renews your faith, doesn't it?

I played a few games of Pac Man and bested my high score… now it's 30,510. (I know you're sick of hearing about this.) The bar played taped music, but it was a real mix of everything. I again heard a bar play Dan Hartman's "It Hurts to Be in Love." (The first time was in Salt Lake City.) I always liked the Gene Pitney original and, on a bar sound system, this one sounded

Salt Lake City / Denver

really good. I also heard another of those oldies medleys; I don't know if Stars on 45 does it or not. It included "Sherry," "Needles and Pins," "Runaway," "No Milk Today," "My Boyfriend's Back," "California Dreamin'," and at least 15 more, all over a disco beat. Not bad.

    The atmosphere of the Triangle was similar to that of the Arena in San Francisco—a definite cruise bar. The size of the crowd was about ideal for their space. I understand that the bar used to be packed every night, but about three months ago the police raided it. It seems they used to have a downstairs "anything goes" bar which got out of hand. The building the bar is in, incidentally, *is* shaped like a triangle.

Salt Lake City / Denver

Friday—July 3, 1981
Denver

Clark's plane arrived at 1:19 PM and you better believe I met him at the airport. As expected, he wore the MONTROSE 77 shirt I gave him (for being my seventy-seventh trick!). Also as expected, back at the hotel we "cuddled" for several hours. We went for a drive down Broadway to the edge of town and had dinner out there, stopping briefly at Cheesman Park on the way back. Around 10, we went to Charlie's, a Western dance bar way out east of Colfax. Although the decor wasn't really quite right for the place (more disco than anything else), it was a nice place and had a nice, friendly crowd. I hardly believe that Clark got me to dance the two-step, which I can probably do without causing too much of a disgrace. We had been talking to this really nice woman when they started to play "Cotton Eyed Joe." If they hadn't both dragged me out onto the floor, I never would have done it, and the next dance, a Schottische. Thankfully they weren't as hard as they looked and I guess I did okay. I still want to learn the Freeze, the line dance they do to "Kaw-Liga."

Saturday—July 4, 1981
Denver

This afternoon, we drove to the gay ghetto, which is not far from the hotel, and ate at the Denver Sandwich Company. The ghetto here is very nice, not run down at all. From there we went to Cheesman Park, which is in the ghetto and is apparently the gay park. There were just lots of people there sunning themselves, etc. The local Imperial Court (the drag organization) was giving out free hot dogs and beer as an effort to provide more of a social atmosphere. The park attracted many people, and the whole atmosphere and afternoon was very enjoyable. We talked for a while to a guy who is on the board of the gay community center. He is *very* political and an extreme feminist—he felt guilty about having his shirt off because the women couldn't. I gather that the community here is doing very well, with lots of organizations. We took a blanket and some wine and just enjoyed. Naturally I also took some random pictures...okay, pictures of hot men.

Sunday—July 5, 1981
Denver

We had dinner last night at BJ's Carousel, a bar on Broadway, which I really liked. It has a Western atmosphere and a large patio with a volleyball court. From there we stopped at Southtown Lumber Co., just to see it. It was only about 9 PM, so the place was almost empty. It's a nice place, though a little small.

From there we went to The Foxhole, which is further from everything else, in the middle of the train yards. It's a nice place, with a dance floor (disco) and a huge patio. Someone told us that we were there for one of the largest recent crowds. It was certainly a varied bunch—Levis, leather, preppy, queens, and women. I don't think it was a particularly hot crowd though, and have not really found any of the bar crowds here to be very impressive. There were only two or three guys at The Foxhole who I thought were interesting.

I'm very surprised I did this, but I just walked up to one and started a conversation. His name was John C. I think it was more that he looked nice, and I just felt like talking to him. I really wasn't cruising, but as we talked, I started to consider it, because he was obviously interested. And he said that he was before I even came over to talk.

I was a little concerned about the thought of tricking out with Clark being right there with me. We hadn't really talked about this part of our relationship and how we felt about it, although we both knew that we had been seeing other people while I was continuing my trip. From that experience I knew that that hadn't changed anything about my feelings for Clark, and I knew that it wouldn't now. But still, I wasn't sure how Clark would feel or

how I would feel. Clark and I talked a little bit about it at the bar before I left, and he, at least from outside appearances, had no problem with me leaving with someone. After all, he said, we had already had a threesome in Houston (but that was before our relationship had gotten heavy).

So, I ended up giving Clark the car keys and went home with John C, really good looking and a real nice smile. He has a nice house in the suburbs. I don't really think I'm going to have any problem with the concept of an open relationship. This is something that a year ago I don't think I could have dealt with at all. It was one of the problems with my relationship with Dick M last year. It was not a confrontation issue, but I knew he wanted to trick out while I had had absolutely no desire to do so.

By the way, John was my 100th trick. Yes, I keep a list. Would you expect a historian not to? I had figured from the beginning that this was information I might want someday and if not written down there would be no way to retrieve it. When I started

1981—MY GAY AMERICAN ROAD TRIP

this trip I was at number 67.

Anyway, I got back to the hotel around 9:30 AM and Clark, who looked terrible, had just got there around 6 AM He had gone to The Ballpark—Denver's famous bath—and apparently had a wonderful time (which somehow makes me feel better). I really am quite pleased with both our attitudes towards this and think this will work out.

This morning Clark dragged me to the Denver Metropolitan Community Church (MCC) services. I thought it was boring—very much like a regular church. They insist on singing every verse of every song. Clark didn't care for the service either, in comparison to what he's used to in Houston. There were about 60 or 70 people there. This afternoon we walked around Cheesman Park some more and then to the botanical gardens.

This evening we went to the Western bar Charlie's for their "steak out"—bring your own steak and they will grill it and provide the trimmings—salad, potato salad, and baked beans. Talk about a good deal. Then, at 6:30 PM, their dancing lessons started, which lasted an hour and concentrated mostly on the Schottische, Waltz, and the Freeze. I loved the Freeze—it's kind of a line dance, very neat. We stayed and danced for a while afterwards.

Later we went to what is presumably the main disco in town—Cherry Creek Mining Company. It is owned, or at least was started, by the same people that have the "Mining Companies" in Houston and Dallas. They all have the same design logo, but that's where the similarities begin and end. Those are cruise bars, while this is a disco with a large patio and game room area. I thought the decor and layout were okay but the bar in general was just average. It had a large enough crowd but not particularly hot or friendly. The music was just alright, and the dance floor was small. Also, all the bars here close on Sunday nights at midnight.

Monday—July 6, 1981
Denver

Today was a long day, but a very enjoyable one. We drove to Rocky Mountain National Park, which I had been to on Thursday, but then the weather was wet and foggy. The weather today was beautiful, and I took three more rolls of film of the park. We got to see some bighorn sheep, chipmunks, marmots (something like a beaver but without the tail), and an elk. And I got good pictures of them all. We saw the elk along a nature trail, and I was able to get within about 12 feet of it—unbelievable! All the animals didn't seem to be afraid of people. In retrospect, I was quite stupid getting that close to a huge elk.

The best part was when we stopped at one turnoff point and climbed way up a big hill. I got lots of photos of the wildflowers and the mountain peaks and pine trees. We kept climbing and found a snowbank, so naturally we had to take pictures of each other in it. The picture taking escalated to nude pictures in the snow, wrestling in the snow, and fooling around on a big rock next to the snowbank. We spent about two hours on that hill and the folks at Colt Studio would have been proud. Well, more proud of Clark than of me. It was beautiful—just the two of us, far from the road and all of civilization, alone on a mountaintop. I'll probably never forget it.

Tuesday—July 7, 1981
Denver

Today we went to several of the gay shops, which really were not very impressive. Then we saw the movie *History of the World, Part I*, which likewise wasn't very good. After that we spent about four hours at BJ's Carousel, including having dinner there. This evening we hit The Triangle again, so I could get a poster, and then went to the last major bar that we hadn't been to—David's. It's a disco and seemed a little better than Cherry Creek in atmosphere. I can't fairly comment any more than that since we were there kind of early on a weeknight. We got back to the hotel at 11:15 PM, since we plan to leave early tomorrow.

In comparing the seven main bars—Cherry Creek, David's, BJ's, Triangle, Foxhole, Charlie's, and Southtown—my recommendations would be to go to David's to disco, Charlie's to Western Dance, BJ's for neighborhood atmosphere, and The Foxhole to cruise. While the Triangle is a better cruise bar (and probably busier more nights a week), for my tastes it is way too dark. I didn't get any t-shirts from the bars here—wrong colors.

My main takeaway is that Denver was just *okay*. The bars are alright. There are five or six decent ones, and they are generally friendly, but they seem to have a small-town atmosphere. I think if I lived here that I would get tired of the place in about three weeks. I was not impressed by the bar crowds—hardly any good-looking men. The gay ghetto and Cheesman Park are pleasant, but nothing to write home about. I guess I think Denver is overrated for its gay life. Maybe that happens because there is just *nothing* else near it. Kind of like Atlanta, it's a gay island. Even if the climate was good, I would not want to live here.

FIFTEEN

Omaha / Kansas City / Oklahoma City

Wednesday—July 8, 1981
Omaha

CLARK and I spent 10 uneventful hours on the road today driving through Nebraska to Omaha. We had dinner at the Old Market Spaghetti Works, a very good place with very cheap prices. Its decor is like The Spaghetti Factory (Houston), and it is on a street of restored shops in an old warehouse district near downtown. They completely restored about a three-block area several years ago and it is very impressive. Any city would be proud to have it—who would have expected that city to be Omaha?

As for the bars…yuuuck! There are essentially two. The Diamond Bar is a trashy dive, and it attracts a crowd to match. The other bar is the Stage Door, a very large club divided into two large, long rooms. One is a John Travolta-type disco with light patterns in the floor—a bit much. The other room is a pool and pinball room that is just okay. It was not crowded. I know, it's Wednesday night in Omaha, and the few people there were not interesting.

Thursday—July 9, 1981
Kansas City

After about three hours of driving, we reached Kansas City that afternoon and went up in Liberty Memorial Tower for a terrific view of the city. We next stopped to see the cruise park nearby. After dinner, we went to Broadway Territory, a popular bar and restaurant, which was very nice but empty at that hour, and then to The Dover Fox, another good bar. While there, a drag performer named Claire Sheraton was practicing her act, which was very neat to watch. This city is Clark's old stomping grounds, as he grew up here.

Then to The Round Up, another dive. Finally, we got to Clark's parents' house, who he knew wouldn't be home until later, as they were still at work. I met two of his aunts (one of whom lives three doors down and reminds me of comedian/actress Fannie Flag). While waiting for his parents to return, we went to visit some of his friends—Bonnie and her clan, who all know

Clark is gay (his parents do not). These friends were quite colorful. Later, I met his parents, who seem very nice; and we stayed for two or three hours before returning to our hotel.

Saturday—July 11, 1981
Kansas City

Yesterday we had lunch with Bonnie, her daughter Connie, and Connie's two adult kids. We took them to restaurant/bar Broadway Territory, and it was very enjoyable—Bonnie is a real character.

Next, Clark and I went to see Crown Center, a very nice downtown mall in the Hallmark Complex. I think we spent most of the next 12 hours in bars and hit almost all of them. The afternoon we were back at Broadway Territory chatting the whole time with the bartenders.

We went in and out of Donald's, a piano bar, which just did not seem too appealing; and drove over to Kansas City, Kansas, to The View on The Hill, which is a private bar, and, in our opinion, a dive. It is about the only gay bar in Kansas City, Kansas—all the others are in Kansas City, Missouri, which is the big city and where all the action is.

We had dinner at the upstairs restaurant part of Arabian

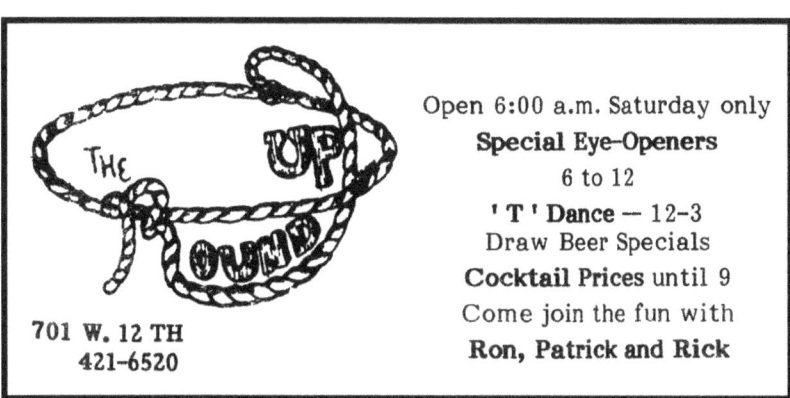

Nights, which had really good food but no atmosphere. Well, there was an atmosphere—all tacky. It is decorated like a Sheik's tent. The bar's nickname is "The Tent," and it's very gaudy. In the evening, we went to the Windjammer, which used to be one of Clark's favorite bars. It is a cruise-disco. The decor is okay, but the crowd was tiny for 11 PM on a Friday night. So, we went over to The Open Range, a bar with two separate parts—a Western cruise bar, and a disco. Both were very good, though the dance floor was a little small.

Then, on to The Cabaret, another disco—it left much to be desired. It had a good-sized crowd, but no air conditioning, and an awkwardly long and narrow layout. The disco also overused strobe lighting, which gets annoying. Next to the Cabaret is its other half—The Trading Post, a Western cruise bar with leather shop decorated like a barn. This city is one of the very few places where I've seen a cruise bar and a disco in the same building and

have it work for both.

At the Trading Post, I met two of Clark's friends—Bob, who I think brought Clark out, and Larry. I liked both of them a lot.

I guess if I had to generalize about the bars here so far, I would have to say that The Open Range and Trading Post are good, and the rest would occasionally be marginally enjoyable. I wouldn't want to live here (although I would still say the bars are better here than in Norfolk). I didn't think the men I saw in the bars were hot at all, even at the two best bars. Maybe a Saturday night would be better. I only saw one—Fred, a guy we also met at the park—that I thought would be worth taking to bed.

Clark and I could have gone home with two bartenders from The Open Range—one of them is one of Clark's (many) former tricks. He and his lover seemed interested in some sort of tryst, but I don't know whether it would have been a foursome or two twosomes. It didn't get any further than the offer, as I wasn't interested in either one of them.

Sunday—July 12, 1981
Kansas City

Yesterday afternoon we drove around a little—saw some of Clark's straight friends and stopped at a lake for a while. We had dinner at an (allegedly) internationally famous restaurant, The Golden Ox. It was good, but nothing special. Later, we went to Broadway Territory for cocktails and to The Windjammer after that.

The Windjammer had a decent crowd, and I danced a couple songs with a bartender from Broadway—David, a nice guy and cute. We had given him a ride over there from the restaurant and it was obvious he wanted a threesome—he asked for as much.

Omaha / Kansas City / Oklahoma City

Clark seemed to think that idea was fine, too, so we all agreed to go over to David's place after the bar closed. Just before we left, Clark started talking to this other guy—Ron, a cute guy with a very nice body but a thinning hairline…which is why he was wearing a cowboy hat. He brought Ron over to meet us and the threesome became a foursome. I guess Ron had noticed Clark and I together and was interested in both of us.

This turned out for me to be a very interesting experience. It was not fantastic sex, that's for sure—Ron was actually sort of a dud in bed. He certainly did not know much about oral sex and was not very responsive in either direction. No wonder he and his lover have an open relationship. I really could have spent more time with David; a threesome certainly would have been a better idea in this case.

As far as my reaction to Clark and I having sex with other people in front of each other—I didn't have any problem with that at all. The only thing about the whole affair I really didn't like was that Clark asked David and I if we minded if Ron joined us right in front of Ron, when it would have been very awkward to say no. Ron was cute—that wasn't the point. The point was that I really didn't (without making a scene) have any say in the matter of whether or not I wanted to go to bed with Ron. I hadn't even really talked to him.

Clark and I had talked about this kind of situation before and I thought, had agreed that a threesome had to feel right for both of us before we would do it. I know that I just cannot (and did not) get into such impersonal sex. I've got to be psyched or it isn't any good. So, we had a discussion (not an argument) about this in the car on the way home and Clark said he wouldn't do it again. I guess we'll see.

Another side note is that they were my 101st (and 102nd) trick, and I don't even know their last names (in Ron's case, I don't care). That means that I've been out for just under three years and have been to bed with a third of the people in the last three months. Isn't traveling wonderful?

The Windjammer

Omaha / Kansas City / Oklahoma City

Monday—July 13, 1981
Kansas City

Sunday afternoon and evening was spent at home with the relatives—a family gathering in the heartland of America, very wholesome. They are all nice people, but after four days I think I have OD'd on Clark's relatives. I think he has, too. Sunday dinner was great, steak cooked over charcoal and lots of fresh garden vegetables. Besides his parents, Clark's cousin Julie and her boyfriend Rusty joined us. I probably liked them about the best of his relatives.

Later, Clark and I made one last trek to the gay bars, this time just to Broadway Territory. Only two or three bars are open on Sunday: The Tent and Broadway Territory (restaurants) and Pete's, a private dyke bar. When we left, we got a royal goodbye from the owner (John, an old friend of Clark's), and David and Chuck, two of the bartenders. They really made you feel welcome there.

This morning, we left Kansas City early and made several stops along the way visiting relatives scattered over about a hundred miles of western Missouri. We finally got to Clark's parents' house near Lake of the Ozarks, a large, many-fingered lake at the center of the state. We were really out in the boonies. It's a very nice house, two floors, with a big yard and a large deck.

Tuesday—July 14, 1981
Oklahoma City

After about six long hours of driving, we just got to Oklahoma City. Before we left the Ozarks we went to one of the caverns in the state (a real tourist trap), Bridal Cave. Well, for $3.50 each, it sure wasn't very impressive, even though I had never seen a cavern before. It was a 50-minute tour that should have lasted about 15. Oh well.

On the way through Tulsa, we got off the interstate to check out its (allegedly) best bar, Tim's Playground, but not only did it look terrible, it appeared to be permanently closed, so we didn't even try the door. On to Oklahoma City.

Here, we went immediately to The Circa Club, supposedly this city's most popular bar. I guess for 9 PM on a Tuesday it was okay. We asked around for a nearby hotel and ended up at The Hotel Rio; kind of run down, but very cheap.

Later: Well, we hit four of the bars. Colorado's is a small, but seemingly popular, neighborhood bar, but the crowd was a bit young. Next, we went to TJ's Canal, a private club (with a Western motif), which was almost empty. Last, we went in and out of the Warehouse, a nice bar that is across the street, which had no customers at all.

We spent most of the time at The Circa Club, which is apparently the best (and only) cruise bar in town. I guess it was friendly enough. It was obvious that everyone knew we were the new faces that night. And we talked to several people, but I certainly would *not* call it a good-looking crowd—maybe not even an interesting looking crowd. No one really outstanding at all. One guy I talked to was very interested. I guess he was okay looking, but he had a lot to drink, not yet drunk but on his way there. He said he would probably be a rotten trick, so he gets points for honesty. I believed him and passed.

Images in this chapter courtesy Gay and Lesbian Archive of Mid-America, University of Missouri-Kansas City

SIXTEEN

Texas, Part 2

Wednesday—July 15, 1981
Dallas

TODAY we slept 'til noon and then left for Dallas, about a four-hour drive. We're staying at the apartment of Bob, an old friend of Clark's. We ate at The Bronx, a mostly gay restaurant, and then went to the bars: JR's, Throckmorton Mining Company, and The Village Station. I was not really in a bar mood tonight, so Clark went to the Station by himself. I figure the odds are probably about even that he picks up a trick.

Postscript: He didn't.

Thursday—July 16, 1981
Houston

It sure is good to be back in Houston and have a break from traveling for a while. We stayed at Clark's house last night, made dinner here, drank some wine, and went to bed early. It was a very lovely evening. I'll probably be here at least a week—I think it will give us a good chance to get used to each other under more *normal* conditions and not on vacation.

Monday—July 27, 1981
Houston

Well, it's been about a week and a half since the last entry. There are two main reasons for this gap—first, this has been, deliberately, a non-structured period. We both realize that if the only time we see each other is when we're on vacation or running around, then that would make it very hard to get a feeling of how the relationship would work on a daily basis. Secondly, an accounting of such activities would not make exactly fascinating reading.

Some things are worth mentioning, however. I've been to several new bars this week, the most notable is The Loading Dock, probably the hottest bar right now. It has opened since my visit in May. It is a converted warehouse and maintained the original look. We were there on a Saturday night and it was very hot in both definitions. It had essentially no air conditioning, and it was full of hot, sweaty bodies, half of which accordingly had their shirts off. This is part (all?) of the bar's appeal. It is dark, and there is disco dancing.

 I liked it, though I'm sure I would not always be in the mood for that kind of atmosphere. For sure, I have never sweat so much at a bar, my jeans were even damp. Many people made a big show out of wringing out their t-shirts. In total, it's the big bar of the moment. It's across the street from The Different Drum (more of a leather bar), which I'm sure helps the business of both places.

The other new bar I liked was Miss Charlotte's Dance Hall and Saloon (formerly The Saddle Club), a Western dance bar with good atmosphere and a good-sized dance floor. Other new bars I went to were the Grant Street Station (no good) and The Montrose Pub (formerly The Inside/Outside), which is I guess supposed to compete with Baja's as a preppy bar in atmosphere. It's fixed up very nicely and has an upstairs piano bar. Unlike The Loading Dock, when I call these place "new bars", I mean I had not visited them when I was in Houston in May, not that they just had opened.[1]

Last Monday night, I went with Clark as he subbed in the MSA (Montrose Sports Association) summer bowling league. I just watched, but I really enjoyed it. I know I would join if I lived here. For one thing, as a new face, it sure is great for your ego to get all the attention I got.

On the last two Sundays, I went to church (Metropolitan Community Church) with Clark. No, he didn't drag me; it obviously means a lot to him, so I want to find out about it too. They have here one of the largest MCC congregations in the world; with weekly attendance of at least 300. The service sometimes gets a little preachy (for me), but the minister (Rev. Chuck Larsen) is pretty interesting. This place has its shit together. I am most definitely not a religious person, so this is taking some real effort on my part.

Afterwards, a group of Clark's friends usually go somewhere for brunch, which is enjoyable, but does effectively kill the rest of the afternoon.

Also, this week I think I've met someone who I know would become a good friend if I lived here. Ron Groff joined us for brunch both Sundays, and for dinner twice, and he and I went swimming one day. He's really the first of Clark's friends I've really had a chance to get to know and I like him a lot. He's just moved here recently from Tampa, along with about eight of his friends. They just all decided to move here. And, oh yeah, we tricked during the first week we met.

I guess the other major event of the week was having a tooth pulled (back tooth, lower right), which had been giving me headaches, and still is, since the gums are healing really slowly. Wonderful to happen when you're traveling.

Now, back to some comments on how the relationship is going. I can't honestly give any glowing reports, for there are no pat answers. We've had several talks about various problem areas that we foresee but, lacking a crystal ball, I can't really do more than guess. I know that Clark is very afraid right now to commit himself. He is holding back emotionally—something that's been very hard on me. He'd held back some of the affection that I need especially right now when I'm insecure about what's going to happen. We've talked about this too, but I think things haven't changed because he is so afraid of being wrong in judging how he feels.

I know that emotionally I think I am ready to commit myself to a relationship, and to all the adjustments needed to accomplish it. Perhaps this is naïve. But since Clark isn't sure yet, I'm in limbo and just have to wait to see what happens. He has said that he won't be able to give me an answer until after I leave. I guess this is to see if he really misses me and to give a little time to think about his feelings. If pressed at this moment to give my guess on what he'll do, I would have to honestly say that he'll decide he isn't ready for a relationship. I feel he indeed does love me but isn't ready to deal with the commitment and all else that comes with having and being a lover.

Tuesday—July 28, 1981
Houston

I have decided that there's big possibility that I will move to Houston, with or without a relationship with Clark. So, therefore before I go back to Norfolk, I need to change my return trip plans. I want to visit my family in Ohio, friends in Rochester, and Philly, so, that's an extra long route. I have started to think of this trip, on the map, as being a big butterfly.

Endnotes

1   Charlotte was the bar owner of the Saddle Club, that got literally pulled into the mud wrestling match at the Brazos River Bottom; see entry for April 18.

SEVENTEEN

Memphis / Columbus

July 28, 1981
Memphis

I HAD SPENT 12 days in Houston, with Clark. And, well, on the road again, and in the ten hours it took to get to Memphis, I thought of little else but Clark and me. I guess I can't change anything I wrote on Monday—maybe amplify it a little. I think Clark is very afraid of taking a risk and making a commitment toward a relationship. I think that at least partially explains his holding back of emotions the last couple of weeks. It seems the closer we got to my time to leave, the more vague he got.

In Denver, he was talking about buying a house together (which would also scare me). However, as we got to the last goodbyes this morning, he could hardly even say he would miss me, much less even say that he loved me. While I don't doubt his love for me, I think he just isn't ready for a relationship. The nature of this is really hard to swallow. It would be easier if we had a fight or some major obstacle. Here it just seems like here I am in love and, all of the sudden, it ends and I just can't understand why.

I know this all sounds like supreme pessimism or the voice of doom when, after all, he said he needed a little time to think it over. I guess psychologically I'm trying to prepare myself for the worst. This is all complicated by the fact that we both know that I would probably end up living in Houston with or without a relationship. That's right, with or without—the city has plenty to offer on its own, and probably the most of anywhere I've been. My criteria of where to move would be that it have an organized gay community in the South, where it does not snow. Atlanta is a no (too much of an island), and LA is too big. San Francisco, mecca that it is, is too expensive, and also a bit too cold for me.

Of course, my deciding to move to Houston would make things easier on Clark, as he would not have to commit himself. After all, he'd have no responsibility in my moving to Houston. I can understand that he wouldn't want to have me move 1,500 miles only for it not to work out. However, what he doesn't see is that I wouldn't blame him if things didn't work. To move would be ultimately my decision.

I guess I can think of at least three scenarios for what might happen:

1. The idealistic one: He decides he really wants us to be lovers and to live together; we discuss it over the phone, I start packing before the phone has a chance to cool—with my state of mind as it is at this moment, that's probably what I'd do. It's just hard to be objective when you feel so strongly.

2. We talk about it and decide that I should move there but not live together. We would continue to date and see what happens. I don't know how I would feel about this one yet. There just isn't enough to go on right now to think much about it.

3. It's over. Then I'm back to deciding if I move anywhere; and do I like Houston well enough to move there despite Clark, or would it just make me miserable to be there. There are probably all sorts of other scenarios, but these are plenty to keep a worrier like me busy for a while.

Memphis / Columbus

Back to this morning: The alarm was set for seven and we went to bed at 10. We didn't have sex. I didn't want to. I just wanted to cuddle, and it seemed to me to be the best cuddling in two or three weeks. We talked a little too but, as usual, the talk ended up halfway between positive and negative with no strong leads either way. He said that he wasn't going to cry when we said goodbye this time because he had already got himself psychologically used to the idea. I chimed in that I thought he had got himself ready a week ago.

After we got ready—me to leave and he for work—we kind of cuddled and necked on the couch for a few minutes. Again, neither of us cried. I still haven't, although several times during the drive today I got a real hollow feeling in my stomach. I suppose I shouldn't have been listening to country music on the radio. Every third song must be about breaking up—one that almost got to me was Ray Price's "For the Good Times." You know:

"Don't look so sad, I know it's over"… "Hold your warm and tender body close to mine"… "and make believe you love me one more time…"

All I could think about was how good it felt to hold him last night and that I just couldn't imagine not holding him again. In the car, I even noticed that I missed not being able to reach over and rest my hand on his leg as I drove. I have really got it bad, and I better stop writing this before I drive myself crazy.

Back to the actual trip. I stopped in Little Rock at a gas station to ask for directions—good thing I stopped there. My car wouldn't start up—dead battery. The attendant readily charged the battery, but since it's probably the alternator, it won't keep a charge, meaning wherever I stop the car—it's really stopped. I decided I might as well try to make it to Memphis (another two hours) and deal with it there. So, once I got there my mission was to find a hotel next to a gas station.

Thankfully, that was pretty easy—I'm at the Admiral Benbow Inn across the street from a Goodyear Auto Service Center. I checked into the motel (leaving the car running) and then parked at the Goodyear place. Sure enough, when I stopped the car, I couldn't start it again. I hope when they open in the morning, they can fix it. At least they can charge the battery so I can get somewhere else.

As for going out tonight—that's out. I suppose I could take a taxi, but while I was looking for the hotel, I drove by the major bars. (I am ever painstakingly organized.) They don't look very inviting, and while one is only a few blocks from here, I wouldn't walk it even in broad daylight. They are in awful neighborhoods. While driving around just a few minutes I got solicited twice by prostitutes, one from a neighboring car, a convertible, at an intersection, and she followed me two blocks and honked several times. I yelled to them, "I'm gay." She replied, just that quickly, "We have a dildo!" Resourceful, and funny.

Friday—July 31, 1981
Memphis to Columbus

Thursday morning, I was able to get a new alternator and battery by 10 AM and start on the road again: 10 hours to Columbus. The real goal at this point is Northeast Ohio, and I really had no reason to stop in Nashville and Louisville, even though they were big cities of potentially gay interest. I was originally only going as far as Cincinnati, but I got there by 7 PM, looked at the bar guide, and decided Columbus (two hours farther) was a better bet. While this lines up with what I have heard, the Columbus bars are no sure thing either. My guide listed only three of the bars as being popular, so I went to all three.

First though, I checked in the YMCA downtown, which just happened to be within five blocks of all three bars. Okay, cue the Village People. It wasn't exactly nice, but at $10 it was fine. As it turned out, I wouldn't be sleeping there anyway.

To start the night off, I went to a piano bar called Trends, which was just alright. Then to Kismet (or Cha-Cha Palace), a

large, private disco. It had a very mixed crowd—lots of women, blacks, and queens, plus the crowd also tended to be younger. I asked one patron if it was the cruisiest bar in town. He said, "Well, it's the sleaziest." I said, "*This* is the sleaziest?!" Then I asked him about the third bar on my list, The Tradewinds. He said it was okay if you like a "rougher" crowd. I said, yes, thank you.

The Tradewinds didn't turn out to be very rough (not that I really wanted that) but at least the atmosphere was conducive to cruising. Part of it reminded me a little of Triangle in Denver, but not that heavy. The bar also had a back disco called Fort Dick's which, despite the great name, was merely okay. Not a great crowd for a Thursday night—I guess I'd give it a three or four. I wasn't really cruising but ended up going home with one guy named John, who turned out to be nothing to write home about. He was cute though. (I guess this *is* writing home about it.) The DJ played an interesting mix of Kano's "I'm Ready" and Soft Cell's "Tainted Love."

And that describes the first time in my life that I went to gay bars in Ohio, my home state. Somehow, it was what I expected.

Remember, I was years from coming out when I lived there. That didn't happen until the tail-end of Rochester, and with a bang in Norfolk.

Today, I drove the remaining three hours to Salem (population: 12,000) for my obligatory visit to the folks. I'll leave Monday for Rochester. I'm not going to badmouth Salem. In hindsight I had a good upbringing, a good education, and was well-prepared for college (25 miles away). I think growing up there in the closet with nothing to compare it to, I didn't realize how isolated the town was until many years later.

EIGHTEEN

Hometown and Rochester

Sunday—August 2, 1981
Salem, Ohio

WHY IS IT that any time spent at my parents' house always drives me crazy? Good thing I'm only spending three days here, I've already read every magazine in the house at least once, and they are real winners. *(Sarcasm.)* While here, I also visited my favorite aunt (Thelma) and my high school best friend (Kenny), which was good for a couple hours each. On the bright side, I got my laundry done, a button sewn on, and ate all my favorite meals. But still, three days is too much. There isn't even anything worthwhile on TV. I guess I was never all that close to my family.

Wednesday—August 5, 1981
Rochester

I got to Rochester Monday afternoon and mostly I've spent my time visiting old friends from living here 1970-78. I'm staying at Ron and Jackie's, straight friends I came out to a couple years ago. They now live smack in the middle of the gay ghetto, two blocks from one of the bars (The Avenue Pub)—talk about convenient! And they own a record store; how cool is that?

Tuesday night, my former secretary Sue and I went out to

dinner. I can't believe how close we are; we can talk about almost everything. I decided not to mention that I got nipple clamps, but I did tell her about the threesomes. And she was amazed that Clark was number 77—to her that seemed like a *very* high number. Aren't straight people naive?

Anyway, this evening I went to Jim's, a downtown disco that usually has a really good crowd, thanks to its 2-for-1 drink night on Wednesdays. However, this crowd was not good in quality; and I thought it was quite depressing. I only talked to three cute people, and two were from out of town. One blond was putting the make on me. I guess he was okay, but I just wasn't psyched. He didn't even have a mustache. So, I went home alone—after all, I'm not on a quota system. I'll insert that "drink specials" mean nothing to me, as I do not drink much, never have.

Anyway, Jim's was almost a Cha-Cha Palace. I say that because the décor was very dated, as was the vibe. There were lots of young *GQ* types, many queeny types, black people and women. *Not* a good bar (although the DJ was *very* good). Highlights of new songs were "Your Love," by Lime and "Try It Out," by Gino Soccio.

I'm glad I don't live here if this is supposed to be the best bar. Tomorrow night, supposedly the bar to go to is the Avenue Pub, when they have their 2-for-1 drink night. I was there briefly this afternoon. It doesn't seem too bad. It has almost a neighborhood bar feel to it.

I think I've told you that I've been listening to a lot of country music as I've been driving. Some of the songs I like best are: "Feel So Right" and "Old Flame"—Alabama, "Texas State of Mind" and "You're the Reason God Made Oklahoma"—Frizzell and West, "Am I Losing You"— Ronnie Milsap, "You Don't Know Me" and "A Headache Tomorrow or a Heartache Tonight"—Mickey Gilley, "Elvira"—Oak Ridge Boys, "Dixie on my Mind"—Hank Williams Jr., "Waltz Across Texas"—Ernest Tubb, and "All the Gold in California"—Gatlin Brothers. You should hear me sing along with Alabama to "Old Flame." Maybe not.

I talked to Clark just briefly this morning. I called him at work. His home phone has been out of order since Friday, which explains why I couldn't reach him all that time—it would sound like it was ringing but it wasn't, and sometimes there would be a lot of clicking noise. We could only talk for a few minutes, and naturally since he was at work it was limited to small talk.

Friday—August 7, 1981
Rochester

Well, this afternoon Clark and I finally had a chance to talk, and it went pretty much as I expected. I had to just about confront him to get him to talk about what his feelings are. He admits that he is probably holding back on his emotions because he is afraid the relationship won't work. He thinks there is a lot going for us, but this one area looms so large in his mind that he just won't let himself make a commitment. I personally think it's something we can work out. He *did* say that he wanted me to move to Houston and that he wanted to date and spend lots of time together there. And he said that he thought if we worked out the problems that we could have a beautiful relationship.

Is this the part in the soap opera where they play the ominous music in the background?

And, of course, we wouldn't live together until we were both sure. I guess that rationally I must agree with that. In a partial explanation of why he wasn't affectionate during the last two weeks, he said that subconsciously he started to just hold himself back because he was so afraid the relationship wouldn't work. I guess I don't know what's going to happen now. I've got a lot of thinking to do.

If I had to make an on-the-spot prediction right now, I'd say I will probably move to Houston. Both to see if the relationship will work and because I just want to move to Houston. It has so much to offer from the standpoints of jobs, climate, and gay community.

1981—MY GAY AMERICAN ROAD TRIP

I know, is this a journal or self-therapy?

Later: Tonight, I went to Rick Bell's wedding—he is one of my friends from the time I lived here, part of the "radio gang" that hung out when Ron Stein was doing his shows. It was just a lucky coincidence that I was here at the same time. The reception started around 8 PM and I lasted through the toasts, the meal, and the start of the dancing before it got to be too much for me (about 10:30 PM). When the typical wedding reception band (schmaltzy) started playing "I Left My Heart in San Francisco" and "New York, New York" I knew it was time to leave. It was a nice event, but things were just getting too heterosexual for me. Besides, it was time to go to the bars.

The Avenue Pub

522 Monroe Ave

244-4960

The #1 Sunday Spot

Naturally, I went to The Avenue Pub, and I quite like this bar. It managed to have a neighborhood feel while still being a little cruisy. I went home with a guy (David H) who has had a lover for the whole two years he's been out, and I was the first other person he's been with. He's blond, and very sexy. What was really flattering though is that we got to talk quite a bit about the trouble he's been having with his relationship. I think he really needed someone to share his thoughts with, and who better to talk with than a stranger? I think just by talking a little about it he felt much better and, in a way, I helped him start to sort it out. I'm glad I could be that someone to listen to him.

The Avenue Pub

NINETEEN

Philadelphia

Tuesday—August 11, 1981
Philly, with a dash of Rochester

WELL, I haven't written in several days. On Saturday night, I took Ron and Jackie out for pizza and a movie (*The Great Muppet Caper*) and then I hit the bars again. This time it was to Bachelor's Forum, the alleged leather bar—actually more like patent leather. It was surprisingly well-lit for a leather bar, which in this case was too bad since the crowd would have benefitted from dim lighting. I stayed until about 1 AM and then ended up back at The Avenue Pub 'til they closed around 2:30 AM. I saw David there again and he thanked me several times for being the shoulder to cry on the night before.

    I left Rochester around 11:30 AM on Sunday and got to Dennis Buckland's in Philly around six. I know Dennis from the Norfolk gay group, the Unitarian Universalist Gay Community. He lives in a very nice apartment on the corner of 12th and Spruce. Talk about a great location. It is right in the heart of the ghetto, within easy cruising distance of several bars and a block from Giovanni's Room, one of the country's best legit gay bookstores. We hit several bars that night: Woody's, Westbury, JP's, Venture Inn, and the 247 Club. The 247 was the cruisiest.

    On Monday, Dennis took the afternoon off, and we went to

Dennis Buckland

the park at Rittenhouse Square and just talked for hours. I had really needed to talk to someone about what I was going through with Clark, and Dennis was the perfect one for it. We've always been able to tell each other the most personal things, so it was good to get it off my chest. I only wish he would have been around at other times during the relationship when I needed to talk. Somehow, when you're explaining something like that to someone it forces you to crystalize your thoughts and the things you tell and the way you explain it help you to realize the perspective they have.

The next afternoon, he told me all about his long-overdue breakup with his ex-lover Daniel last May. I think Dennis is doing very well now. His self-confidence is much improved, and he's been tricking around quite a bit, which I think is great for him. He likes his new job, too, so he's doing better on just about all fronts. I had known Daniel a little in Norfolk and I don't think any of our friends thought he was a good match for Dennis.

Philadelphia

This afternoon, we just walked around. We went by the river to a park nicknamed "Judy Garland Park." You guessed it: It's a cruise park with lots of well-placed bushes. It seems that Dennis has just discovered the parks and the bookstores and has been really busy lately. At the park, I had sex in the bushes for the second time in my career—his name was Frank, and he was a nice-looking clone with red hair. As the cliché goes, the carpet matched the drapes.

Thursday—August 13, 1981
Philly

Tuesday night I went to Woody's, 247 and Equus, and Wednesday night just to 247. Equus is probably one of the more popular bars, with a disco upstairs. It's a half-block from Dennis' apartment. The crowd tended to be slightly younger and prettier than the other bars and more *GQ*. The two or three guys that I thought were really good looking appeared to be into S&M— Stand & Model. The music though I quite liked as the Equus DJ played a set of popular songs from a couple years ago that I really liked. These included "This Time Baby" (Jackie Moore), "Come to Me" (France Joli), "Ring My Bell," (Anita Ward), but he could have left out the over-tired "Celebration," by Kool & the Gang.

Wednesday afternoon, I diligently tracked down the eight or nine record stores near the ghetto and managed to buy only three albums and six singles. I didn't mail stuff home this time, as I'll be there in a few days.

Naturally, I've had some time since I talked to Clark on Friday to do some more thinking, plus talking about it with Dennis. I think part of me has decided that it is probably over, and it is unrealistic to think we could pick it up again. This is the part of me that is listening to my gut feeling about how Clark feels. I guess to me it seems like he has put his emotions on a shelf and that he'll bring them back down when/if we've worked things out. I can't quite understand how he can do this and still claim to love me.

There is just something missing in the quality of his voice when I talked to him, that feeling that he loves me and misses me. I felt it when we talked on the phone when I was in California, but I don't sense it now. The words are there, but I don't get the same vibrations. This is kind of hard on me. Yesterday I found myself thinking how much I missed just being able to hold him—my next thought was that he probably hasn't given it any thought at all.

Another thing I think about is that I probably can't expect Clark to react exactly the same way to a situation as I would. He could still honestly feel that he loves me, but that something inside him won't let him commit or risk any more of his emotions until he's sure it will work. This may be because he doesn't want to get hurt. Yes, my logic seems to be going in circles.

(Shit! I just paused in my writing for a few moments and my eyes started to tear. I've really got it bad.)

Anyway, I called Clark yesterday, mostly just to see if I would get any different feeling from the call. I guess I am slightly encouraged from talking to him. While there was no outpouring of emotion, he did again say that he wanted me to move there and spend a lot of time together. The tone of his words gave me the impression that it wasn't just something he thought he had to say; he really wanted it. This is really getting to be a soap opera, isn't it?

Saturday—August 15, 1981
Philly

Well, ta-da! This is the first anniversary of me being out of work, unemployed…I think that's kind of neat. A second anniversary, however, would not be a good plan!

My turmoil with Clark aside, my sex life has picked up considerably the last couple days. I was beginning to think I'd get through a whole week here and not pick up a trick. A whole week…what would the neighbors think? Anyway, Thursday night I went to Equus again and met a nice-looking man named Kevin R. He's 27 and has a studio apartment at 24th and Spruce. He was very interesting—for example, when we were talking at the bar, he asked me something to the effect of, "I'd like to take you home with me, but would it bother you if we didn't have sex?" I thought a second and asked, "Do you like to cuddle?" He said he did. A little later he said he routinely asks that to see if someone really wants to be with him or just wants to get their rocks off. Interesting approach, but a little risky if all you wanted were rocks.

A side comment is that both he and another guy I talked to earlier said they had noticed me sitting on the front steps of the apartment building Thursday afternoon. Sitting on the porch steps of Spruce Street seems to be a pastime here, and I certainly wasn't the only one. I sat there for about 45 minutes Thursday around 5 PM and I don't remember either of them passing me. I guess a new clone stands out. I did however remember having seen each of them before. Kevin I noticed on Spruce Street earlier, and the other guy was at 247 the night before. Likewise, Kevin said he also saw me at Equus earlier in the week. Isn't it marvelous how queers pay attention to these things?

Observation: One good thing about going home with lots of people is that you get to try all these different shampoos.

Friday night, I went to Woody's—my black sleeveless t-shirt didn't fit in there, so I headed over to 247, a different bar. Here, I talked again to Ron S, a fellow I was interested in Wednesday night at that bar. It *does* all run together after a while. I knew he wasn't really interested in me, but apparently, he liked me enough to offer to get me into The Cell Block with him. The Cell Block is a private cruise bar and disco on St. James and Camac that has strict membership rules. Most private clubs in the country I've found will let you in if you tell them that you're from out of town—not this one.

Anyway, at 2 AM we walked over there, and he went to the office (which is separate from The Block's entrance) and told them he left his membership at home and got a temporary slip

to give at the door, which he gave to me to use. This worked like a charm. The building also has a private disco called DCA that has a separate entrance; each have a separate cover charge. Total rip-off.

Between the two bars at DCA, it's the most popular place to be after 2 AM in the city, as it's open until 4 AM. The Cell Block is nice; it has a large dark bar next to a small dance floor, a side lounge with pinball machines, a pool table room and a back room. Yes, an actual back room—one of the few bars I have seen to have one on this trip. It had lots of nooks and crannies, one of which had the cab of a Mack truck in it (a rather large nook). That corner also had a row of storage closets that appeared to hold three people. The crowd milling around the back room indicated that there was 5% doing and 95% waiting. I did not consider participating, not my style.

I thought the bar's crowd in general was fairly good-looking. Among them was Mike H, 27, whom I met last February at the Oar House when he was on vacation in Norfolk. It was a pleasant surprise to see him again. And since he is really cute and I had very much enjoyed going to bed with him the last time, a repeat engagement was in order. He lives with his parents, so we came back to Dennis' apartment, and we made do with the couch. It was really nice—he's a great cuddler, too, and the couch certainly didn't cramp our style.

Oh, since I had originally tricked with Mike in February, when he was #56, he does not get a new number on the list. Only first time appearances count.

This sure has been a very interesting trip for me! I told Dennis yesterday that it would feel strange going back to Virginia because I didn't feel like the same person as when I left. And he said that I probably wasn't—five months is a long time. I think that with all that I've seen and done on this trip that I have changed a lot, probably more than for any other time span in my life. I definitely think it has been a change for the better.

In addition to providing a chance to see all those cities and gay communities, this trip has let me learn a lot about myself and how I would deal with new people/situations. It really forced me to be assertive about meeting people and has given me confidence in this area. I think I also feel better about how I look. For example, this trip was the first time I took off my shirt at a disco and didn't feel uptight about it. And now I feel okay wearing a tank top on the street or in a bar, which I'd *never* done before. And of course, going to bed with lots of people is good for the ego, too. Scratch that—not good...*great!*

Another thing I've been able to do the last few months is to really explore my sexuality. Without trying to sound like a psychologist, I feel that I have been able to approach some new areas that I've really been insecure about or even afraid to explore. My feelings about these things have changed remarkably for such a short time, and I'm really pleased about it. I feel more whole and more confident about my approach to sex. I've got a ways to go yet, but I think I'm learning. If I can deal almost matter-of-factly with situations like having my picture taken in the nude (in the snow in Colorado) or having sex in the bushes, then I think other new things will be less threatening or intimidating. I think I am better able now to deal with things I haven't done before, without just closing my mind from something. Okay, I guess that's enough patting myself on the back for one day.

Sunday—August 16, 1981
Philly

Well, it's Sunday night, 2:30 AM, and I've just got back from the bars on the last night of this epic trip. Tomorrow, it's back to the Never-Never Land of Norfolk. But first, back to last night. Would you believe I didn't go out on a Saturday night? I just didn't feel like it; probably something to do with the fact that I've hit the bars the last ten nights in a row.

Anyway, at my request, Dennis showed me how to make bread. It turned out very good, but then, since the dough had to rise twice, it took almost 3½ hours. For that much of an investment in time, it ought to be good. I've got the recipe and now know-how. So, anytime I feel like having a domestic fit I can go for it. I'm thinking this is unlikely.

Today, a friend of Dennis' came over, Bob, whom I kind of liked. Dennis has a pseudo relationship with him. They see each other often, but Bob is also firmly committed to going to the baths and the bushes...and his wife. So, Dennis is a sort of mistress, when convenient to Bob, which Dennis is not really comfortable with. Although, logically, he should be, since he says he's not ready for a relationship right now. But logic does not always rule, as I look in the mirror.

Anyway, the three of us packed a makeshift picnic lunch (quiche, tomatoes, cheese, bananas, iced tea and the bread) and drove out to Valley Forge National Park. Bob took us to the gay section, naturally. Note: it was *so* convenient for General Washington to have had his battle so close to the interstate.

Bob took us on a cook's tour of the appropriate paths, where I picked up a cute 20-year-old guy named Al. Who would have *ever* thought that I could travel the country and then get to Philly, and with Dennis—of all people—get trashy in the park twice in one week?

This is not the Dennis I knew in Norfolk. That Dennis didn't do the bookstores, the bushes, or the backrooms. At least I've got two of those "3 Bs" to go. As for me, that's not the JD I knew in Norfolk either—I can't really explain it. I know I wouldn't have gone there on my own. However, this cute guy was there (who was cruising very heavily) and it was *so* easy. As far as being satisfying, it wasn't very—certainly not worth a special trip to a park. I don't think I even felt an excitement of risk that I had imagined was part of the motive for sex in the bushes. Oh well, it was still an interesting experience.

This evening, we hit the bars again. Bob and Dennis (mostly Bob) talked me into wearing no shirt and my leather vest. I've never gone like this to a bar before and was kind of surprised I did it. I even wore my leather cock ring around my wrist—why not wear the whole costume? It was just for the hell of it. I certainly wasn't worried about who might see me. After all, I know almost no one in the city.

Well, we went first to a private club—Rainbows/The Left, which seemed okay in layout, but unfortunately (for us) they were having what they called a special dyke night. There certainly were a lot of them there. At least I got to see the place.

Then to The Cell Block. Bob is a member of both and got us in. The Block was where my outfit really looked good. Too bad I didn't feel like cruising. I'm sure I could have done very well, if not in picking up a trick, at least in the backroom. I didn't even go back to that part of the bar tonight; didn't feel like it (although Bob and Dennis did).

It's a private disco and part of the same complex. If you're a member you can get into both, but they have separate covers—again, a rip-off. Also, non-members can get in only with a member, and only if from out of town, and sometimes not even then. I guess they're real picky about letting people in. This is hard to understand, since memberships are only $25. It's really no big deal. Anyway—we got in okay, but since the disco was almost empty, we left immediately and hit The Venture Inn, Woody's, and 247. Accordingly, I've had more beer than usual so if this is a little scrambled, that's the reason. If you couldn't tell, then either I can write under the influence or the whole journal reads that way. Probably the latter.

TWENTY

Norfolk

Monday—August 17, 1981
Norfolk

IT'S NOW Monday night and I'm safely back in Norfolk. It took five hours to drive from Philly and I got here around 1 PM. I suppose some sort of statistical recap is in order:

- I drove 12,132 miles
- I was gone 140 days—or 4½ months
- I went to 180 gay bars in 24 states
- I picked up 43 tricks, and a bit telling of my tastes and the times, all but three had moustaches. Their average age was 28. I was 34 during the trip.
- I spent about $6,600 in total for everything—this includes gas, hotels, food, tolls, books, records, t-shirts, parking, film and developing, drinks, tires, videotapes, alternator + battery, gifts, medical, and lots of etc.

Also, while it is still relatively fresh in my mind, I should make mention of what I think are the best bars that I visited across the country. Admittedly, this is a difficult task since there are all kinds of ways of rating them…as a cruise bar, disco, Western, businessman's, etc. Furthermore, I saw many bars at off days or times so

JD's favorite photo from the trip, taken in LA on the grounds of Frank Lloyd Wright's Hollyhock House. Scott Swoveland was commissioned to create a drawing from it. He's famous for painting the window displays in the iconic bar Mary's, Naturally and his mural from those times, now seen in the Eagle club, Houston (see pp. 322-323).

it is hard to really fairly judge. Nevertheless, without getting too complicated, I'll just list the cities and the really good bars in each that I visited, roughly in order as I favor them. *(See the* **Notes** *section for a list of all the bars I visited.)*

Incidentally, I picked up 25% of my tricks at the bars. (Maybe I should have been a statistician?) I can't really fairly compare bars between cities, except that the Midwestern and Southwestern cities seemed to have the friendliest people, with Houston especially friendly and open. Atlanta had about the hottest men, though they are a little reserved. You have to make the first move there, but then it's worth it. The bars were particularly bad in New Orleans, Baton Rouge, Albuquerque, Columbus, and Salt Lake City. However, it is worth noting that it was in two of these cities (New Orleans and Salt Lake) that I picked up two tricks in the same day…

Other than Clark (who, of course, is no longer a trick), there were three people I spent more than one night with: Allen in Atlanta, Norman in Houston, and Michael in Los Angeles. There were, however, at least eight more that I would have had seconds with but didn't have time, considering my travel plans: John in Houston, Mike and Tim in Dallas, Dave S in Los Angeles, Leonard Matlovich in Russian River, Jason and Tim in San Francisco, and Bob in Salt Lake City. That is just about the same people I would mention if I had to list the best looking, which I guess is not surprising.

Sunday—August 16, 1981
Norfolk

Now that I have been home about four days, I am starting to feel like this is as good a time as any to end this journal. After all, in the last two or three entries, I did a lot of summing up of my feelings, both about Clark and about what the trip has meant to me. About the only thing left to own up to is the realization that I had made the decision to leave Norfolk a long time ago and just did not want to finalize it. I kept saying to myself that I would decide after I got back to Virginia. And, in a way, I think I almost wanted to prolong the trip so I wouldn't have to make a concrete decision.

If I'm being honest with myself, I think I had decided back in May or June. I knew that as soon as I got back here that there was no point in pretending any longer. On my first night back, I surprisingly found it rather easy to tell my roommates Fred and Bill about my plans. Once I had told them, it was easier still to tell John on Tuesday. After that, it became almost matter of fact with whomever I talked to, like Del or Ken. Of the people that know me, no one has been surprised—they are no dummies. It naturally occurred to them that I might move after such a trip.

I was talking to Ken at the Cue on Tuesday night, and he asked the seemingly obvious question, "So, where are you moving to?" I guess all that is left was for me to fill in the details about which city and when.

It will naturally be hard to leave these people, my first chosen family; but my being away has helped me put some emotional distance between us and has helped us get used to the idea of being apart.

As for my feelings about Norfolk—my decision to move has already seemed to emphasize the negative aspects of the city in my subconscious. For one, *Our Own* will likely fold in a few months.[1]

Also, the bar scene here seems as bad as when I left—the same old faces, more and more young guys, bar games. The job market for me here is awful. And, lastly, the gay community in general (outside of UUGC) is so apathetic. And, I've often joked, in such a small city I had already been to bed with everyone with whom I was likely to go to bed.

Of course, I also need to reflect on the positive. The gay community here welcomed me and helped me grow, emotionally, socially and as sort of an activist, with my work on the newspaper. I was able to make an incredibly large number of friends, more than I've ever had at one time in my life. Being part of this community was essential for my development.

So, Norfolk was good for me in the time I lived here, but now I need something more. It has become for me a "comfortable" place to live, but now, after having embarked on this trip, I know that comfort is not enough. On to Houston.

Endnotes

1   *Addendum, current info:* I was very wrong about *Our Own* folding in a few months; it lasted until 1998. I guess with a small-town paper that is always struggling, you always see the dark clouds.

EPILOGUE

Written August 2021

WELL, I officially moved to Houston on October 3, 1981. And an epilogue for this journal *has* to address the question of what happened to my relationship with Clark. We did not pick things up again, though we stayed good friends for many years. I built my own life in Houston, running around with some of the friends I made during my visit, like Ron. I joined the bowling league. Found an awful apartment on Garrott Street (apartments were hard to find then). And after six months moved into Montrose Gardens, which, as I always liked to say, was "148 steps from the Mining Company"—no one had to move their cars. The adventures continued.

That was 1981, and over the next forty years I had different jobs and relationships. I lost many close to me to AIDS in the 1980s and 1990s. I lost my partner of 12 years, Jeff Pierce, to cancer in 2007. He was my soulmate, and his parents still treat me like their son-in-law.

I moved several more times. I retired (as soon as I could) in 2010, but I continued volunteer work on the radio show *Queer Music Heritage*, begun in 2000, producing that for fifteen years. I moved on to two other huge projects, the websites Houston LGBT History and Texas Obituary Project—three sites that total more than 20,000 pages of content! I am now comfortably settled into the history niche I have created for myself, trying to capture as much of it as I can and make it accessible online.

Apparently, my websites are doing their job, as in 2019 the Library of Congress notified me that the sites were chosen for inclusion in their LGBTQ+ Studies Web Archive, quite an honor. This came out of the blue. I did not apply for it, or even know they were doing that until I got the email request. For me this is a very big deal. And I know especially for my *QMH* show many of the artists I played love that their music will be preserved long after us. They may have never been played on commercial radio, but they will be able to be found on my website.

Oh, another honor was being elected Male Grand Marshal of the Houston Pride Parade in 2014. I still cannot quite believe that happened. The Parade began electing folks as Grand Marshals in 1979, and it is indeed an honor. It feels good to be part of a group of those the community has honored, by public vote, over the years. Maybe my strongest memory of that was riding in the convertible, near the front of the parade as it wound down Westheimer Street. My friend Scott flew in from Norfolk to share the ride with me. You could almost feel the rush of emotions from the cheering crowd. In 2018, the Parade included a float for the 40th Anniversary, with as many former marshals as could make it. That was a very fun reunion.

But, back to the trip. I am very much an introvert, so this trip was a growth experience in a number of ways. It gave me the confidence that I could indeed navigate gay communities across the country by myself. I was able to make use of my experience editing the gay newspaper in Norfolk as a door opener. I used it to contact newspapers in a number of major cities, therefore finding out what was going on in those communities and what not to miss. That included what bars to be sure to visit and not visit.

Experiences to not miss were a nearby lesser-known National Park or a local play (Atlanta, San Diego, San Francisco), concerts (Diana Ross and Liza), a Vito Russo presentation in San Francisco, and meeting Armistead Maupin, Jim Kepner, Dan

Epilogue

Jeff & JD

Scott Wyatt & JD,
Houston Pride Parade 2014

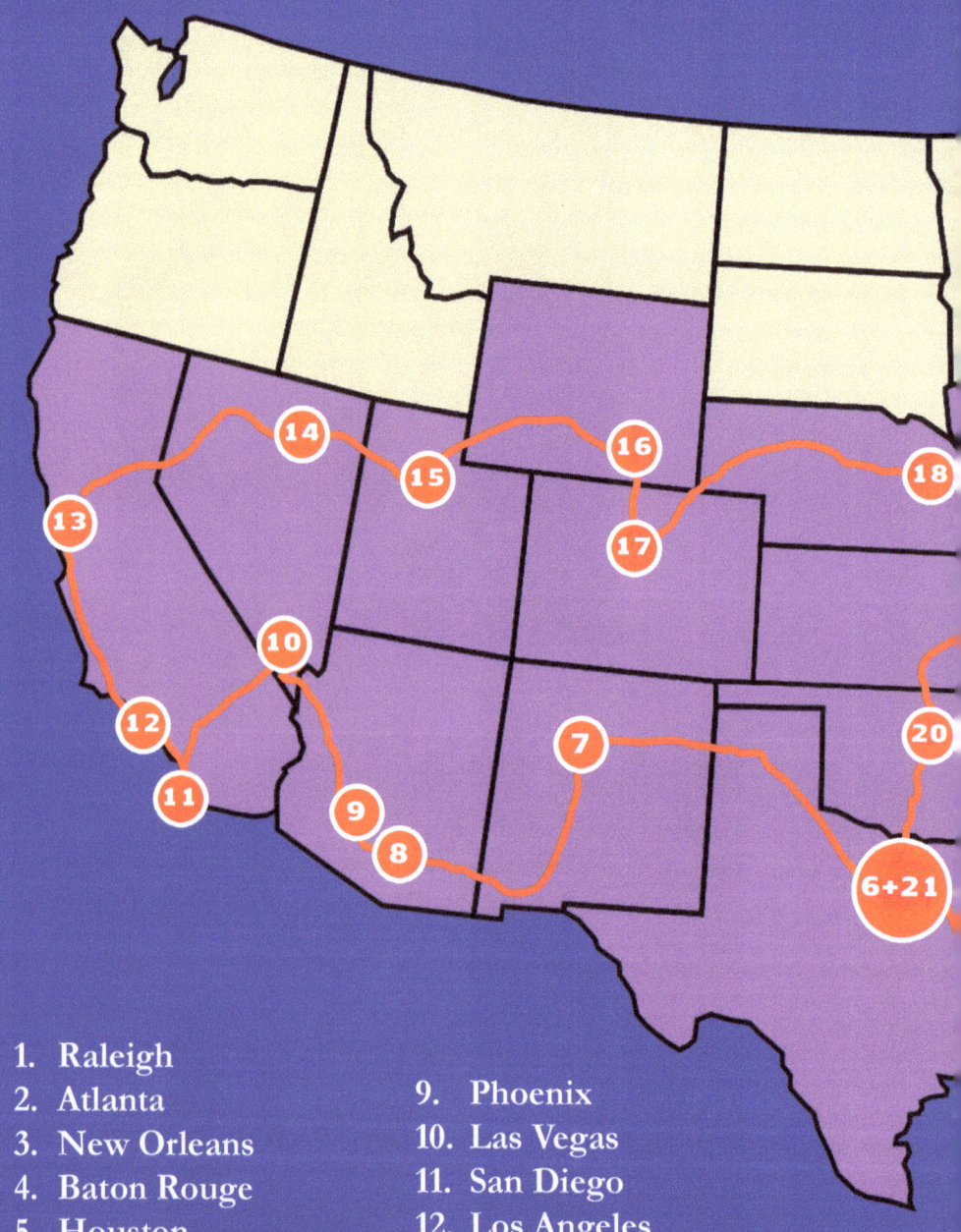

1. Raleigh
2. Atlanta
3. New Orleans
4. Baton Rouge
5. Houston
6. Dallas
7. Albuquerque
8. Tucson
9. Phoenix
10. Las Vegas
11. San Diego
12. Los Angeles
13. San Francisco
14. Elko
15. Salt Lake City

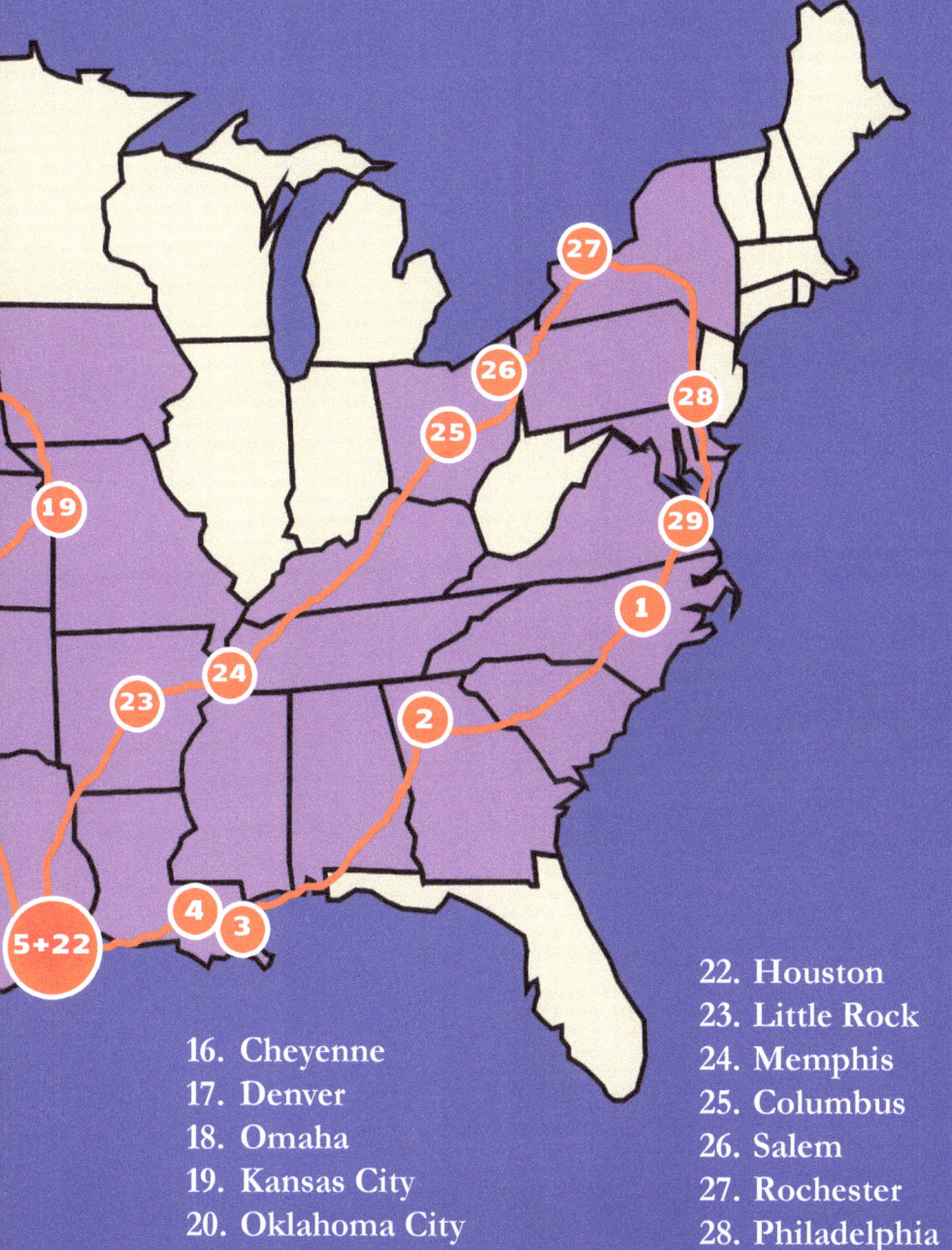

"This is the trip I took..."

16. Cheyenne
17. Denver
18. Omaha
19. Kansas City
20. Oklahoma City
21. Dallas
22. Houston
23. Little Rock
24. Memphis
25. Columbus
26. Salem
27. Rochester
28. Philadelphia
29. Norfolk

Curzon, Don Baker, Ray Hill, and of course Leonard Matlovich.

Naturally, I didn't expect the "love story." And that shaped a lot of the journey, and certainly changed the route back East. I had figured out that I wanted to move from Norfolk and that the destination was Houston. This trip was one of the best experiences of my life.

Reading this journal after so many decades was an interesting experience. I had literally just put it away, and not thought much about it for a long time. I had written it long-hand (no laptops in 1981), single-spaced, in ink on about 125 pages of a grid-paper tablet. I paid one of my millennial friends to transcribe it.

So, what did I think of the 1981 JD? Well, it was nice to remember my days working on *Our Own Community Press* and realize how much that experience meant. That was certainly a growth time for me. Naturally I had forgotten many of the details I had written down, but I was surprised how much I remember as I re-read them. I can still see images of many of the good-looking young men I encountered (though not all).

Now, let's not use the word promiscuous, but let's say re-reading this I was a bit surprised at how, er, *friendly* I was, forty-three times.

And, gosh, I sure did a lot of self-analysis over my relationship with Clark. I found it interesting to notice the progression of the emotions over a few months. Remember I was just writing this for myself. I was using the journal to try to figure things out. Maybe surprisingly I do not have any regrets that Clark and I did not become partners. There's way too much water under that bridge for that, and I have had several partners over the years since then. A few years after I moved here, he found a long-term relationship, with a man I like a lot. They are perfect together.

AIDS

This book's subtitle, *A Slice of Our Pre-AIDS Culture*, needs some discussion. Yes, the first cases of AIDS in America were uncovered mainly on the coasts in mid-1981, the same year as this trip. The first deaths in Texas began to be reported in March 1982 (Clint Moncrief in Houston), with six more that year. Decades after I kept this journal I realized the historical angle—I guess history had to actually pass to make that true. My trip involved observing gay culture in a number of cities just before AIDS hit us, thus radically changing our culture forever.

Again, I kept my journal without any intentions of it ever being read by anyone. It was just for me, as it certainly was not written the way someone from the world of academia would write. It was meant to capture my experiences as a somewhat introverted gay man exploring the culture and what I have jokingly called the "candy store." This was a time about twelve years after Stonewall when we were increasingly making ourselves known to the rest of the world. We had never before felt so sexually free to do so.

The AIDS years were devastating, in so many areas. The first person I actually knew who died of AIDS was Terry Grimes, on September 9, 1983. He was only 22, and I knew him through the gay bowling league, which I had joined immediately upon moving to Houston, in the Fall of 1981. In fact, we were on the same bowling team at one time. As it was a gay league, many of the teams had playful double entendre names. We were the Protein Supplements, and that was on our t-shirts. This death was so early it was shocking to all who knew him, and the reality of crisis was just beginning to hit home. If good-looking, fit Terry could die so quickly, what was our fate?

And then there was John Winn (1958–1986). John and I had a hot affair in late 1982, early 1983. We met at a house party, and I flirted like crazy, but discreetly enough to not do so around his lover. They lived in Dallas, and John got to Houston frequently for work. It became a habit for him to stay with me. I was living at the apartments called Montrose Gardens then, before they went condo. I fell in love, and he may have also, and I was told his relationship with his lover was not good and he may leave him "very soon"—a familiar song heard in affairs. I don't think he was being deceitful. He just didn't know what to do.

That was hard, and I used to joke that at least I got a good

Terry Grimes

Billie Holiday collection out of it, as I bought about a dozen of her albums. That's the only kind of music I felt like listening to. I could bury myself in the heartbreak of her voice. They weren't always sad times though. But after a few months we did break up, and I thought I had seen him for the last time.

I did see him again, two or so years later, around late 1985. I was, I think, at Charlie's Restaurant with a couple friends, and I looked across the room and spotted him in the middle of four or five friends I did not know, talking and laughing. I was pretty sure he spotted me as well.

What I also noticed, even from a distance of over 30 feet, were his KS lesions. I thought of going over to just say hello, but I didn't know what to say. I couldn't ask him how he was, as I could see how he was. So, caught in indecision, when my friends and I were finished I just left. He died in April, 1986. I am sorry, John, that I did not know how to handle that and give you a proper greeting.

The personal losses were profound and frequent. I lost a

Epilogue

John Winn

lover, Wes Gregson, in 1988, at age 29. We were together nine months, and he was only sick for six weeks. He went into the hospital and died six days later. He didn't even have time to show any visible signs of being sick. His quick death was numbing. I remember telling people that I felt like I had experienced the grief but not the attack of AIDS itself. It felt a little like the experience of that relationship was all a dream, like I had imagined it. It was over all too soon and too suddenly. I remember his mother and sisters came to the hospital to visit, but his dad originally did not come. None of them knew Wes was gay until this. I sternly told them that if his dad did not come visit, he would regret it for the rest of his life. Ultimately, his father visited on what would be the last day.

In the summer of 1988, a group of friends got together to help me make a Names Quilt panel for Wes at my condo. There was to be a showing of the entire Quilt in DC that October, and we wanted to meet the deadline for panel inclusion. Well, I just supervised, I was still too much of an emotional mess to actually help work on it. Two of his close friends, Jay Bacon and Clint McKay, who were lovers, were there that day helping. They died within three months of each other in 1991.

Wes Gregson

Jay Bacon & Clint McKay

Epilogue

Ron Groff

In addition to losing a lover, I was one of the few survivors of my gang of friends, taken between 1990 and 1993 (Ron, Buddy, Bill, Chester, Phil, Kim, and Dennis). Ron Groff passed away in August 1990—I was holding his hand in the hospital when he died. A bunch of our immediate group had set up a visiting schedule, so someone would always be with him. This was at Twelve Oaks Hospital. I remember starting my shift that night and the nurse telling me that this would likely be the last shift. He was correct. Ron had days earlier descended from the stage of being able to communicate with us. But I remember seeing a tear come down his cheek that last night. He was my best friend. People thought we were lovers because we would often bicker like an old married couple.

Less than a year later, in February 1991, Buddy Dreis died. I always described him as my rock. He was a realtor and it seemed like he knew everyone. I would joke that if you needed

Chester Wilson and Bill Glover

Buddy Dreis

a "left-handed Polish plumber," Buddy would know who to call. He had a small vacation cabin some miles outside of Luling. It was about 140 miles away and we would often go there. It was quite basic: living room, two bedrooms, bathroom, kitchen…nice, but still rustic enough to be fun. The shower was outside under a makeshift metal barrel, which we further jury-rigged to wedge a

Epilogue

Kim Spradling

heating plate under it to warm the water, after a fashion. Yes, that took a while, and didn't do a great job, but I remember thinking it neat to take a shower outside, with no shower curtain and no neighbors near at all. As were his wishes, Buddy died at home.

Next was Kim Spradling, only a week later. Kim and I met when we both lived at Richmont Square, and we lived together from around 1983-84. He was the first partner with whom I lived. After this we remained friends and years later, I was one of his care visitors. Due to my influence, he started collecting records and became obsessed with Connie Francis recordings, and in our short time together amassed an excellent collection, with many rarities. Her recording of "Among My Souvenirs" was played at his funeral service.

I remember meeting his mother only a couple of times. And those visits were awkward. Definitely *not* discussed were that we were gay, or that Kim and I may have been partners, so that entire situation was like there was an elephant in the room. Inside I wanted to be acknowledged as more than a friend, but the closet won that battle. His mother had always treated me with kindness, and as she would have no idea how to sell his record collection, I took over that responsibility and was able to raise a couple thousand dollars for her.[1]

I was always music oriented, and years later, on my radio show *Queer Music Heritage*, I covered many themes, and one show dealt with "Songs About AIDS." So, I got a chance to address the crisis that way.[2]

During the 1980s and 1990s, we all were barraged very frequently by the grief coupled with the loss, especially with fewer people around to support us emotionally. I well remember guys my age, survivors, saying they lost a couple hundred friends, cleaning out their address books. I always thought that had to be inflated, as I sure did not know anywhere near that number of people. And yet I have heard it way too many times to really question it.

I recently read a paragraph in a book by Charles Kaiser[3] that sums up the early years better than I could:

"If you are a sexually active gay man in America, being alive at the beginning of this epidemic feels like standing without a helmet at the front line of a shooting war. Friends are falling all around but no one even knows where the bullets are coming from. There are no weapons to defend yourself, no medicines for the wounded, and if you want to flee, when you start running you won't know when your own wounds are fatal—or nonexistent. Three years into this war, the battlefield is just as lethal, but now it feels like a huge tunnel filled with fire, strewn with bodies and booby traps. If you're still standing—one of the "lucky" ones—you keep running faster and faster, but you can never outpace the inferno. At the beginning there was nothing but terror and mystery."

After reading that I thought: yes, it was exactly like that, and I

Epilogue

wish people too young to have experienced it would know that it was exactly like that.

JD, during his time with Wes Gregson (1987).

On my trip I met a lot of guys, and I made an effort to see how many I could make contact with, even forty years later. This is a tough search. I had a list that included just a person's name, city, age, and where we had met. I was able to find some of them. Of course, many I could not find at all—gay people move around. And some I did find have died. That includes Leonard Matlovich in Russian River, Brad Truax in San Diego, Michael MacKay in Los Angeles, Norman Cousins in Houston, Tim Kane and

Jason Sanders in San Francisco, Alan Grimes in Atlanta, Helmuth Gosler in Sausalito, Richard Rogers in Dallas, Dale Williams in Phoenix, and on and on. And there were so many leaving just no trail at all.

Once one of my friends asked me to write about my impression of the AIDS Crisis, in just a few words. Here's what I wrote:

I feel like I am holding a camera that I must keep pulling back as to include more in the image. I've been through, during the late '80s and early '90s, the loss of a partner and all my close friends. However, this was not a unique experience, and so I pull back and think of all the personal losses that individuals faced. Then I pull the camera back even further, and immediately am faced with the absence of all those lost in the gay community and what they could have created for our culture: the writers, artists, political leaders, and of course many others. And then I pull back still further, and try to take in what the world has lost. It is an endless process of balancing the personal and the universal impacts, and of carrying with us the grief, anger, sympathy, activism, education, and hope.

Endnotes

1   Obituaries and candid photos for my friends can all be found at http://www.TexasObituaryProject.org

2   *Queer Music Heritage*, "Songs About AIDS," found at http://www.queermusicheritage.com/nov2007.html

3   *The Gay Metropolis: The Landmark History of Gay Life in America*, Charles Kaiser, 1997; pg. 279

NOTES

Chapter 1, Norfolk

I resigned as Editor of *Our Own Community Press* in March, 1980. I was getting little help and was going through severe burn-out. As a historical record and because it provides so much information, here is the resignation letter I wrote:

March 11, 1980

To the UUGC:

    This is my letter of resignation as Editor of *Our Own*. It is not a decision made easily or made in haste. It has been building for several months. I regret having to make the decision at all and the suddenness of its announcement, but "burn-out" has set in and my peace of mind demands it.

    The reasons are complex, and I expect only a handful of people close to the paper will understand. The main reason is basic. There is not enough help from the group for the writing and especially for the production of the paper. The burden of getting all the work done should not be placed on one person. But the group was apparently content with that, as evidenced by its lack of interest and involvement.

    Maybe I didn't communicate the need effectively, but every week I would announce the status of the work and make a plan for help—with the same predictable result. On the Tuesday before the last production week, I announced that there were already articles turned in and ready to be typed, and I passed around a sign-up clipboard. It went through 40 hands, but no one signed up. The next week, the Tuesday of production week, five people signed up and of those three showed up.

Both weeks I asked for comments on the movie *Cruising* for an article. I know at least ten people had seen it. I thought asking for two or three sentences from each was not asking a lot. I guess it was; no one verbally offered their impressions. For a while I had decided that, from that reaction, the group obviously did not want an article on *Cruising* and there wouldn't be one. But I broke down and wrote it anyway, although I would have rather it expressed many viewpoints and not just my own.

The paper however got finished on time again. Somehow everything was typed, proofed and ready for layout by the end of Thursday evening. As usual, I took off work the Friday and did the layout, leaving for Saturday the final proofing and last-minute odds and ends. I can pick out three reasons for the paper meeting its schedule this time. I was able to beg Jayr to come in and do some last-minute typing; I was able to get most of the headlines done by a friend on a varityping machine (saving 8 to 10 hours work); and John Chappell was always there when I needed him, doing whatever was needed. He's the first person in six months to show more than casual interest and willingness to act as a right-hand-man and relieve some of the burden. But he returns to school in mid-March.

Of these three reasons, I can count on none for routine help next month. John won't be there. I hate to ask Jayr because he does so much for the group already in other areas. And the headlines were done by someone outside the group. In other words, it appears that luck played a larger role in getting the paper done than the "group" in general.

I don't of course mean to imply that I've been doing the paper all by myself. There are a few other brave martyrs—Jim, Doug, Del and Dennis—who, already spread very thin, somehow find time and energy to provide extra help. Dennis, in particular, carries an enormous load with the advertising and distribution, with almost no help. I fear he is near burn-out also.

For some, my resignation should not be a surprise decision. I have been discussing my frustrations for several weeks now with a few close to the paper, Dennis, Jim, Del, Janelle and John. I think they understand, but no one seems to be able to figure out what to do about it. Jim suggested a program on the paper before the whole group to interest people in the paper. Perhaps I'm cynical, but I doubt that would work. After all, four programs on the gay information hot line did nothing to increase the number of people signing up for duty.

The people close to the paper have to some extent noticed my frustrations. My attitude is awful lately. I dread production week and resent the burdens and lack of help. And I'm afraid this attitude will result in a drop in quality in the paper. And I remember through all this that I didn't want to be Editor at all, and I would have been very content just doing the layout, which I loved. Now, I don't even want to do that.

This letter is not a threat or an ultimatum. My attitude has degenerated so far that even a big outpouring of renewed help and interest would not revive me. I need out. I *do* hope that there *will* be a big rally of interest, because I regret the burden, I know this will place on a very few people. I don't know who the Editor will be. No one has shown enough interest to learn what needs to be done. It would not be fair to expect Jim to do it. He has done more than his share and I hope he refuses. Otherwise, the group will not be forced to ask itself how badly it really wants a paper.

Also, I think the group will find that other people can do layout. There are many talented people in the group, and Jack or Jayr could certainly give someone enough help to get them going. I will be willing, on a *very* limited basis to spend a little time passing along what hints about layout or the flow of production if that is desired.

There are two or three other comments I want to make. I

want to thank those people who have helped on the paper. In just six months, what with the March on Washington, the harassment of the bars and effect on the paper, and the power struggle for the Lesbians Front & Center pages, there have been some interesting times. And I want to apologize to those friends I've neglected during this time. One of the unhappy parts of being Editor for me was that I was getting to the point where I wasn't enjoying other UUGC activities. Everything I did was always accompanied by the burden of the paper.

Everything I attended I felt I was "covering" it for the paper. I was not able to simply enjoy an activity. Even during the breaks on Tuesday meeting night, instead of being able to visit with my friends, I instead had to run around cornering people for articles, imposing on friendships and asking favors. I resented not having the time to enjoy my friends.

Another point is to mention that there are other demands on my time. I am currently involved in a relationship, though this has not been a factor in my quitting. I have not let the paper interfere with it, although it does make me value my spare time and resent more the lack of help on the paper. And spare time is something I now have less of, since my job requires me to work on one or two weekends a month. One or two weekends at work and two production weekends a month leaves little time for me.

Finally, I don't know how the group is going to react to all of this. There are some, probably not close to the paper, who will be ready to lay a guilt trip on me for quitting. I ask them to remember that, after all, this is a "volunteer group," and if a person's involvement ceases to be enjoyable, then that involvement should be questioned. The paper was taking 60 to 80 hours a month of my time. With the dwindling amount of help, it just wasn't worth it. It is supposed to be a group project and it should be up to the group, not a few, to decide how badly it wants it.

—JD

Notes

Gay/Lesbian Books coming on the market in the late 1970s

It took several years for the market to appear, and in the late 1970s, the books themselves showed up. For a lot of LGBT people, this was the first time the literature was even available. Like my friends, I had spent my life not being to read about my gay world, to learn my culture's history. I felt like I had to read everything I could, in all categories. I could not get enough.

Some of the books coming on the market in those years were:

Loving Someone Gay — Don Clark
Skinflick — Joseph Hansen
Dancer From the Dance — Andrew Holleran
The Gay Report — Karla Jay & Allen Young
Lavender Culture — Karla Jay & Allen Young
Faggots — Larry Kramer
Metropolitan Life — Fran Liebowitz
Tales of the City — Armistead Maupin
The Lord Won't Mind — Gordon Merrick
Taking Care of Mrs Carroll — Paul Monette
Gold Diggers — Paul Monette
The Lure — Felice Picano
Rushes — John Rechy
Best Little Boy in the World — John Reid
The Front Runner — Patricia Nell Warren
Joy of Gay Sex — Charles Silverstein and Edmund White
States of Desire — Edmund White
Word Is Out (book and documentary)

Chapter 7, Dallas (May 3)

Notes on the other representatives to the Gay Press Association meeting. This goes into too much detail for the flow of the book, but I believe it contains too much history on an important time in our culture to not preserve it.

More on the elections and attendees:

Four regional caucus directors were elected, none of whom I really had a chance to talk to. They are:
    Northeast—Mike Rutherford (*Out*, DC), seemed nice (by far the cutest member there).
    South—(Which includes Virginia) Bob Swinden (*Cruise*, Atlanta). Seemed very competent. Cruise is a major and historic publication. It began in 1976 and covers the entire Southeastern region, and often into Texas.
    West—Pat Burke (*Update*, San Diego/LA). Seemed competent, didn't get a chance to talk to him at all. He is the managing editor. I did meet their executive editor, Don Hanck, who invited me to stop by their offices. I sat with him at lunch on Sunday.
    Midwest—Chuck Renslow (*Gaylife*, Chicago) seemed very dynamic. I heard he wanted to be elected GPA president. He was very business-like. He chaired the meeting Saturday and very competently guided the discussions on the bylaws. Things never really got too far out of order—amazing, considering the diverse types of publications and personalities.
    National—Henry Mach (*First Hand*). I liked him and thought he has a lot of good ideas. I voted for him for secretary (though he lost) and was glad that he got on the board anyway.
    Director at Large—Richard Rogers (*TWT*, Dallas office). I liked him a lot. He reminded me very much of Michael Collins (who I met in NYC last year) in his personality and even facial features. I thought he was cute, even though he is about 6'3". I also think he has a lot on the ball and was about the most im-

pressive member of the *TWT* staff I met, and probably also the friendliest.

That takes care of the board. Other people there were:

Chuck Patrick (*TWT* publisher)—I met him in Houston. He is civil, but not friendly. I never got the impression that he gave a shit whether he talked to you or not. At the meetings he just about talked only to his own staff. I didn't see him really mingle at all, or exchange views with anyone else—which I would have thought he, as coming from a major publication, should be doing. He wore a baseball cap all day Saturday, which looked ridiculous. (I guess he's bald or balding). He wasn't at Sunday's sessions). Other *TWT* staffers present were Blase DiStefano, and Rob Clark.

Roy Hall (*Metro Times*, Dallas). Although he coordinated all the accommodations and hosting functions for the convention, to meet him you wonder how he did it (and did it well). He is not at all impressive, and he also has kind of a whiny voice. He was nominated for VP, which I could hardly believe. He is the one-man band at his newspaper, a publication which I don't like at all, by the way. I think it is very amateur.

Henry McClurg (*Montrose Voice*, Houston)—I did not meet him in Houston, which was probably a shame. He seemed very nice and I wish now I had called him, although he did say he is almost impossible to reach at the office.

There were two people from *Austin Connections* that I didn't meet at all. They stayed in the back of the room and kept to themselves. And that takes care of Texas, which had nine members at the meeting.

From Atlanta were Mike Jameson and David Jones from *Gazette*, Bob Swinden and one other from *Cruise Weekly*.

On Sunday I sat beside Don Beavers, associate publisher of *In Touch*, who invited me to stop by their offices in LA (I think he had more than a tour in mind). Also at that table were Bob Ross (*BAR*, SF), Scott Anderson (*Advocate*), and Bob Beachamp (*NATF*). Bob complained a lot about the apathy in SF and the high cost of living and how "intense" life is there. Scott, you may remember, is the *Advocate*'s associate editor, who I met briefly in Houston. We chatted a little at various times during the weekend and I was kind of surprised when he invited me to visit their offices in California. It, of course, had come up in conversation that I would be out there on my trip in May or June.

His publisher at *The Advocate*, Peter Frish was also at the convention. He reeks of attitude. I never saw him go out of his way to talk to anyone. I don't even remember him smiling! He was very aloof and had kind of a *GQ*-air about him. Although he wasn't dressed the part, he acted it. His whole demeanor said, "Don't talk to me." I didn't. During the meetings he gave one of the committee reports on ad format and as expected, did a good job, but it was a very business-like report.

I was however interested to notice that neither he nor Scott said much during the discussions—I guess I thought because they represented such influential publications, that they would try to influence overall decisions of the meetings, but they didn't at all. Whenever they did comment, it was completely appropriate and professional. Maybe they were making a conscious effort *not* to throw their weight around.

One more from California newspapers (making a total of six)—Chuck Morris of *The Sentinel* (SF). I only talked to him a little, but I liked him. He gave me his card and an invitation to visit his offices.

Oh yeah, one more from California, but not a publication—Mike Smith of *BWMT (Black & White Men Together)*, which has ads in *Our Own*. A nice guy and real nice looking. I think it is his pictures in their display ads that I've seen in other publications.

From *GAZE*, Memphis, I met their editor Bill Johnson, and artist, Ken Hagenback—they were both at the Baton Rouge conference, but we didn't meet there. They had two other staff members with them. I guess it is only an eight-hour drive from there to Dallas. Bill shared my concern about the dues being too high and about some of the big papers being a little insensitive to the position of the small ones.

I already mentioned that Harry Losleben from *TWN* (Miami) was there. Rico came late Saturday night, although I don't know why he bothered. He didn't attend all of Sunday's sessions and didn't pay attention when he did. I don't think I could get along with him; he seems very moody and quick tempered.

Steve Kulicke is *Gaylife* (Chicago's) city hall reporter. He seemed nice and to have a lot on the ball.

Roy Lindberg from a paper in Staten Island sat in front of me, and I also had breakfast with him on Sunday. He is, I guess, around 50, and nice and, although not dynamic, very conscientious.

Other papers represented (of whom I didn't meet their representatives) were *Cruise Weekly* (Detroit), *Buck Rogers Happening* (an LA bar mag), *Akron Gold,* and *No Bad News* (St. Louis).

By quick count, all this adds up to 44 people and 25 publications. I think there were at least three or four more people that I remember but didn't meet or notice who they represented.

The Trip

180 Bars Visited

The bars I favored the most in the large cities are listed first.

Raleigh
Mousetrap
Rathskeller (Chapel Hill)

Atlanta
Backstreet
The Armory
Crazy Rayz
Numbers
Bulldog
Jocks
Texas Drilling Co.
Sweet Gum Head
Pharr's Library

New Orleans
Jewel's Tavern
Café Lafitte in Exile / Corral
Bourbon Pub / Parade
The Refuge

Baton Rouge
George's Place
Cock & Bull
The Emporium

Houston
Montrose Mining Company
Venture'N
Galleon
Wildwood Saloon
Brazos River Bottom
Baja Sam's
Mary's
Dirty Sally's
The Hole
Parade
Midnight Sun
Bunkhouse
Copa
Briar Patch
Different Drum
The Barn
Babylon
Mary's II (Galveston)

Houston (second visit)
The Loading Dock
Grant Street Station
Miss Charlotte's Dance Hall & Saloon
Montrose Pub
Badlands

Dallas
Round-Up Saloon
JR's
Throckmorton Mining Company
Village Station
Studio 69
Crews Inn
Fraternity House
Eighth Day
No Name
Wild Crowd Saloon
Dallas Crude
Alcatraz
Sassies

Albuquerque
Foxes Booze & Cruise

Tucson
Dale's Graduate
Back Pocket
Hair Tiz

Phoenix
Connection
Sammy's Steakhouse & Saloon
Tommy & Clyde's
Taylor's
Hot Bods
Farrah's
NuTowne Saloon
Trax

Las Vegas
Red Room
Gipsy
The Garage

San Diego
Park Place
Iron Spurs
The Hole
WCPC
Mr Dillons
The Caliph
Nickelodeon

Los Angeles
Motherlode
Blue Parrot
Rusty Nail
Spike
Eagle
Jungle
Greg's Blue Dot
Griff's
Nutowne Saloon
Four Star Saloon
Pure Trash
Detour
Saddle Tramp
Studio One
Garden District
Mike's Corral (Long Beach)
The Mineshaft (Long Beach)

San Francisco
Church Street Station
The PS
Badlands
Midnight Sun
Castro Station
Phoenix
The Village
Moby Dick
Bear Hollow
Le Disque
DeLuxe
Stud
Febe's
Brig
Arena
Cinch Saloon
Kimo's
New Bell Saloon
Giraffe
Polk Gulch Saloon
The Stallion
Pendulum
Wild Goose Saloon
Buzzby's
'N Touch
QT
Sutter's Mill
White Swallow
Sausalito Inn
Trinity Place
Cafe St. Marcus
Patsy's
Balcony
Elephant Walk

Watering Hole
Ramrod
Eagle

Russian River
Rainbow Cattle Company
Fife's
The Woods
Sundog Saloon
Rusty Nail

Salt Lake City
Sun Tavern
Crazy Pete's Rail
The Deerhunter
Radio City

Denver
Triangle
Charlie's
BJ's Carousel
Southtown Lumber Co.
Foxhole
Cherry Creek Mining Co.
David's

Omaha:
Diamond Bar
Stage Door

Kansas City
Broadway Territory
Dover Fox
Round Up
Cabaret/Trading Post
Open Range
Windjammer
View on the Hill
Arabian Nights (Oasis)
Donald's

Oklahoma City
Circa Club
Colorado's
TJ's Corral
The Warehouse

Columbus
Trends
Kismet
Tradewinds

Rochester
Avenue Pub
Jim's
Bachelor's Forum

Philly
Woody's
JP's
247 Club
Equus
Westbury
Venture Inn
Post
Cell Block
Rainbows/Loft

Norfolk
And, for historical sake, the bars I left behind in Norfolk
Nickelodeon
Oar House
The Cue
The Late Show
The Paddock
The Nutcracker
Shirley's

Trip Playlist
The Music I Connected With During My Journey

Image courtesy of Moby Dick Bar/Corporation

"And I will say that I proclaimed the song "Remember Me / Ain't No Mountain High Enough" by Boys Town Gang as my song of the trip."

My Introduction—Pre-Norfolk

"No More Tears (Enough Is Enough)"
                         Donna Summer & Barbra Streisand
"Relight My Fire"   Dan Hartman
"Heaven Must Have Sent You"   Bonnie Pointer
"I Can't Help Myself"   Bonnie Pointer
"At Midnight"   T-Connection
"The Boss"   Diana Ross
"If You Could Read My Mind"   Viola Wills
"Gonna Get Along Without You Now"   Viola Wills
"If My Friends Could See Me Now"   Linda Clifford

Beginning the Trip

"Heaven's Just a Sin Away"   Kendalls (C&W)

Atlanta

"Sound of the City"   David London
"Touch Me in the Morning" (disco version)   Marlena Shaw
"Turn the Beat Around"   Vicki Sue Robinson

Houston

"You Ain't Woman Enough to Take My Man"
                                        Loretta Lynn (C&W)
"Remember Me/Ain't No Mountain High Enough"
                                        Boys Town Gang
"Superman"   Celi Bee
"It Feels Like I'm in Love"   Kelly Marie
"It's Not What You Got, It's How You Use It"   Carrie Lucas
"On and On and On"   ABBA
"Lay Your Love on Me"   ABBA
"Rain"   Goombay Dance Band
"I Can Hear Music" (disco Beach Boys cover)   California

Houston…and there's a love story

"Love is the Drug"   Grace Jones
"The Hunter Gets Captured by the Game"   Grace Jones
"La Vie En Rose"   Grace Jones
"I Need a Man / Breakdown / Bullshit"   Grace Jones

Dallas

"My Shoes Keep Walking Back to You"   Ray Price (C&W)
"Old Flames (Can't Hold a Candle to You)"
                                        Dolly Parton (C&W)

1981—My Gay American Road Trip

Albuquerque

"Tonight the Bottle Let Me Down"   Merle Haggard (C&W)
"You're The Reason God Made Oklahoma"
                              Dave Frizzell and Shelley West (C&W)
"I'm Coming Out / Upside Down"
"Theme from *Mahogany*"   Diana Ross
"Reach Out and Touch"   Diana Ross
"Ain't No Mountain High Enough"   Diana Ross
"The Boss / My Man"   Diana Ross
"Touch Me in the Morning"   Diana Ross
"It's My House / Remember Me"   Diana Ross
"Baby Love / Stop in the Name of Love"   Diana Ross
"Love Is Like An Itching in My Heart"   Diana Ross

Los Angeles

"Cry to Me"   Precious Wilson (Eruption)
"All That Jazz / Yes / New York, New York"   Liza Minnelli
"The Man That Got Away"   Liza Minnelli
"City Lights / My Man / Bewitched"   Liza Minnelli
"Cabaret / Welcome / Money"   Liza Minnelli & Joel Grey

San Francisco

"Step by Step"   Peter Griffin

Salt Lake City

"Cotton Eyed Joe"   Johnny Gimble (C&W)
"Kaw-Liga"   Charley Pride (C&W)

Memphis / Columbus

"For the Good Times"   Ray Price (C&W)
"I'm Ready"   Kano
"Tainted Love"   Soft Cell

Notes

Hometown and Rochester

"Your Love"   Lime
"Try It Out"   Gino Soccio
"Feels So Right"   Alabama (C&W)
"Old Flame"   Alabama (C&W)
"Texas State of Mind"   Dave Frizzell and Shelley West (C&W)
"Am I Losing You"   Ronnie Milsap (C&W)
"You Don't Know Me"   Mickey Gilley (C&W)
"A Headache Tomorrow/Heartbreak Tonight"
                                    Mickey Gilley (C&W)
"Elvira"   Oak Ridge Boys (C&W)
"Dixie on My Mind"   Hank Williams, Jr. (C&W)
"Waltz Across Texas"   Ernest Tubb (C&W)
"All the Gold in California"   Gatlin Brothers (C&W)

Philadelphia

"This Time Baby"   Jackie Moore
"Come To Me"   France Joli
"Ring My Bell"   Anita Ward
"Celebration"   Kool & the Gang

If you have a Spotify account, you can hear the dance songs from this list, as I set up a Spotify Playlist; only a few tracks were not available. Search for **JD Doyle** *and* **Playlist #1**.

Driving across country, you mostly find country music on the radio, and for those songs that seeped into my head, look for **Playlist #2**.

Notes

The iconic Mary's Naturally bar in Houston for many years had painted on an outside wall this mural capturing its essence. The original artist, **Scott Swoveland** (who also did this book's cover portrait), recreated the mural for the Eagle Bar in 2017, where it is prominent in an upstairs area called the Phoenix Room, devoted to Houston history. *Courtesy Scott Swoveland.*

Acknowledgements

Many have helped and encouraged me over the years it took to bring this to publication. Special thanks to Barrett White, who I conned into transcribing my handwritten journal, and Jay Arora for initial editing. To Hugh Ryan for the wonderful Forward, and Dr Brian Riedel for early support and editorial advice. On the image side I owe thanks to Scott Swoveland for the cover art, and for his permission to include his mural of Mary's bar in Houston. Other image help came from Sara Fernandez and Robert Young.

I also want to shout out to those who had to listen to me talk about the book for years, and for some who were just there for me in general: Wyatt Doyle, Norman Gholson von Holtzendorff, Kent Parks, Mister McKinney, Fred Osgood, Scott Wyatt, Cathleen Rhodes, Steve Brown, Ron & Jackie Stein, Bob O'Boyle, Kelly N, James Spear, Austin Davis Ruiz, Stephen Miranda, Blake Mudd, Judson Dunn, Donn Mumma, William Richards, Louis Niebur, Dr George Chauncey, Eric Cervini, Gerard Koskovich, Lucas Hilderbrand, Jonathan Ned Katz, David K Johnson, Allen Young, Michael Flanagan, Jim Baxter, Todd Camp, Mark Donahue, Joshua Burford, Maigen Sullivan, Matthew J Jones, Ross Hancock, Jack Valinski, Eric Liston, Ken Dunn, Brandon Wolf, Andrew Edmonson, Brett Buffalo, Ryan Wilson, Arden Eversmeyer, Bryan Hlavinka, Dr. Laura E McMorris, Chris Wilson, Alex Rosa, Jim & Alyne Pierce, and Mike Doyle.

And thanks to my parents for raising me without religion.

JD Doyle (born 1947) is an American LGBT music/history archivist and radio producer. In addition to his engineering job, he did volunteer work as the Editor of *Our Own Community Press*, a gay newspaper based out of Norfolk, Virginia. In 1981, Doyle moved to Houston, Texas, where he later produced the radio programs *Queer Music Heritage* on the station KPFT, and *OutRadio*, heard on the internet. His currently active works include the Texas Obituary Project and the Houston LGBT History website, all part of his 501(c)(3) non-profit, the JD Doyle Archives. Those archives also contain one of the largest collections of queer music in the country. In 2019, the United States Library of Congress selected the archives for digital inclusion in a collection of LGBT history. He believes that history exists to be shared, not hoarded, and strives to make his collection accessible to all.

Doyle's work has been honored by numerous awards, such as the Legacy Award from the Greater Houston LGBT Chamber of Commerce (2023); Trailblazer Award from Texas Conference on Digital Libraries (2021); a Proclamation from Houston Mayor Sylvester Turner during LGBT History Month (October 2022) naming it "JD Doyle Day;" from the Houston LGBTQ Political Caucus, given the Lifetime Achievement Award (2019) and Kristen Capps Social Conscience Award (2021); Legacy Community Health Mint Julep Award (2023); Male Grand Marshal for the 2014 Houston Pride Parade; and the Alan Bérubé Prize, from the Committee on LGBT History (2012).

1981—My Gay American Road Trip is his first book.

Photo: Alex Rosa

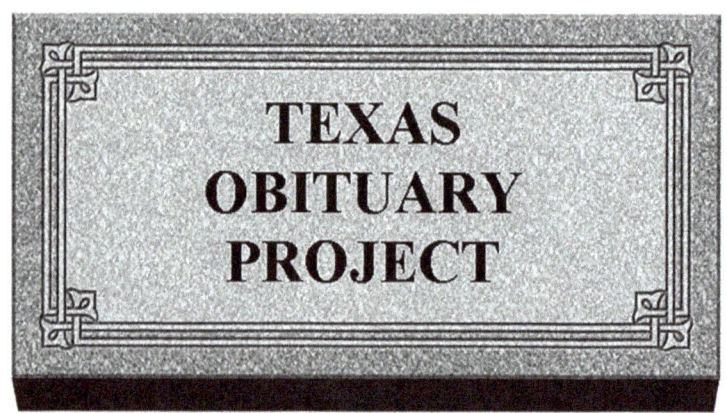

JDDoyleArchives.org

Also from # new texture

By Jimmy Angelina & Wyatt Doyle

 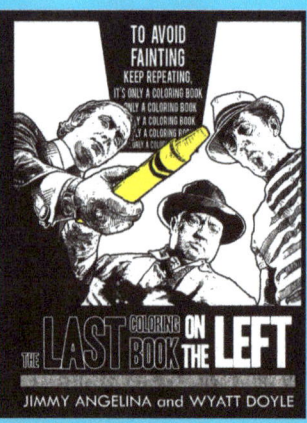

The Last Coloring Book
The Last Coloring Book on the Left

"Images of great movie icons, groundbreakers, and cult movie weirdos…in a pair of VERY unusual works of cinephilia. These are 'anti-coloring books' populated by cult heroes and heroines…"
—Ed Grant, *Media Funhouse*

"Truly inspired!" —Steven Puchalski, *Shock Cinema*

"Perfect gifts for the cult movie fan. Crayons not included."
—Laura Wagner, *Classic Images*

Be Italian

People pretending to be Italian and Italians pretending not to be. A one-of-a-kind visual history exploring Italian identity in motion pictures from the silent era 'til now. Featured on *Gilbert Gottfried's Amazing Colossal Podcast*.

Black Cracker, *an autobiographical novel by* Josh Alan Friedman

1962, flashpoint of the civil rights struggle. And young Josh is the lone white boy in a segregated grade school. An unflinching funhouse tour of a Long Island boyhood, and its now-forgotten poor Black shantytowns. Hilarious and heartbreaking.

Tell the Truth Until They Bleed, *by* Josh Alan Friedman

Up close and personal with important and unsung figures in blues and rock 'n' roll: the self-made, the self-serving, and the self-destructive. Illuminating parts of the music industry most don't talk about, this is show business without the showbiz.

Stop Requested, *stories by* Wyatt Doyle; *illus.* Stanley J. Zappa

"A series of rueful, witty and occasionally heartwrenching stories about riding the bus in LA. Doyle finds consequence in the inconsequential. He's Bukowski without the nasty streak. And he's real good. Highly recommended." —Marc Campbell, *Dangerous Minds*

---

nu luna, *a novel by* Andrew Biscontini

After 400 years of colonization, the moon is home to nearly a billion people, living in a crowded industrial police state on the verge of collapse. *nu luna* is a deeply personal matinee space adventure, spun through an improbably plausible future history. The future is beautiful and dangerous.

PHOTOS BY WYATT DOYLE

AVAILABLE IN SOFTCOVER AND DELUXE HARDCOVER WITH ADDITIONAL CONTENT

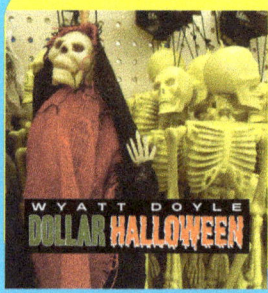

Dollar Halloween

Documenting off-brand junk and sparkly death totems, made to be thrown away. Where there's a need, or even a mild desire, a dollar store stands ready to fill it for whatever you've got in your pocket.

I Need Real Tuxedo and a Top Hat!

On the buses, on the corners, in the city streets. Portraits and lives of the forgotten, the avoided, the ignored. Street people and street life in raw, poignant photographs and stories.

Buty-Wave Is Now Closed Forever

Things that are gone, and things that remain. Includes portraits of Rev. Raymond Branch, Georgina Spelvin, Ray Bradbury, George Clayton Johnson, Tura Satana, Ernest Borgnine, and Carl Ballantine.

Jorge Amaya Doesn't Live Here Anymore

Abandoned places, empty spaces, forgotten faces. Indelible images from across the United States, documenting the wreckage and remnants of the American experience after the parade has passed.

 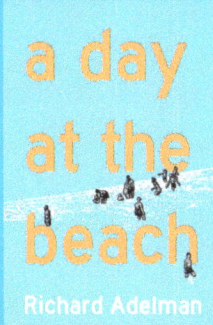 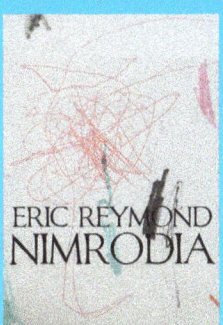 

Teacher Tales, *a novel by* Richard Adelman

For 40 years, Mr. Kessler has kept his head down and not made waves. But new acquaintances and bad decisions in his final year before retirement bring his ordered world crashing down around him—tragically and hysterically. A smart and darkly comic novel.

A Day at the Beach, *a novel by* Richard Adelman

Atlantic City, summer of '63. A boy. A girl. And the other boy, who reluctantly pretends to date her to help his pal. A funny, nostalgic novel of young love, best friends, and poetry, capturing one 12-year-old's last great summer as a kid down the shore.

Nimrodia, *poems by* Eric Reymond

Visual art and ancient history are the starting point for most of the poems in this collection, as the modern world intersects with these domains again and again. Though language, culture, and time may divide us, these are also the forces that link us together.

Sub-Sub Librarian, Extracts on a, *poems by* Eric Reymond

The title poem imagines *Moby Dick*'s Sub-Sub Librarian experiencing transcendence and illumination through his wide readings. Additional poems find inspiration in texts as diverse as contemporary poetry, vocabulary quizzes, and course syllabi.

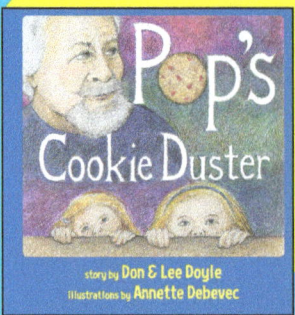

Pop's Cookie Duster
by Don & Lee Doyle; *illus.* Annette Debevec

Rainy afternoons aren't much fun for two lively little girls who love to play outside. But a hands-on kitchen activity with their visiting Pop might just save the day!

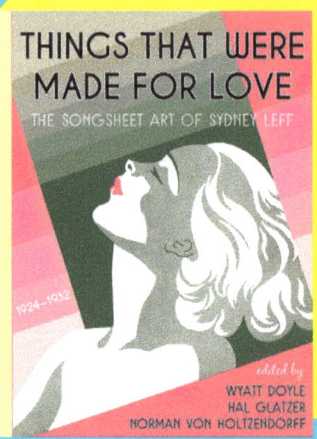

Things That Were Made for Love: The Songsheet Art of Sydney Leff
Wyatt Doyle, Hal Glatzer, Norman von Holtzendorff, *editors*

The first-ever songsheet art collection presenting the cream of the Jazz Age illustration artist's work on songsheet covers from 1924–1932. A gorgeous visual feast that playfully captures the moods, elegance, and style of an era.

new texture Music

CD / DOWNLOAD

I've Got Heaven on My Mind
Reverend Raymond Branch

Sixty Goddammit Josh Alan

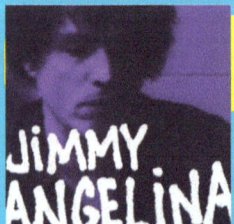

Jimmy Angelina s/t

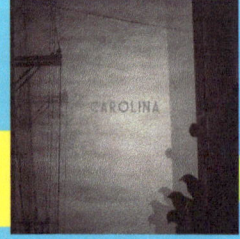

Cursed Carolina

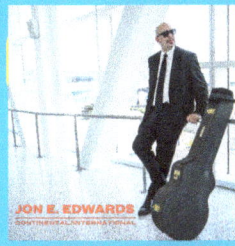

Continental / International
Jon E. Edwards

Map of the Moon s/t

Sing-Song Songs
Stanley J. Zappa

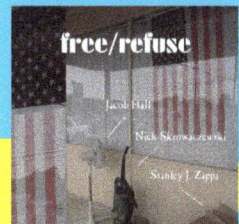

Free / Refuse
Hall, Skrowaczewski, Zappa

Live a Little
Manzappaczewski

The Stanley J. Zappa Quartet
**Plays for The Society
of Women Engineers**

Crossing Guards
Carter, Leffue, Sikora, Zappa

Turkey Bacon Donuts Bitches
MANZAP REBORN

Balloons

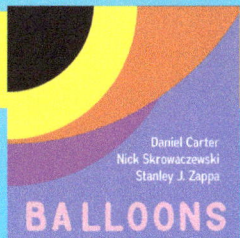

Daniel Carter,
Nick Skrowaczewski,
Stanley J. Zappa

---

new texture   Words and Pictures and Music

THE MEN'S ADVENTURE LIBRARY

MANY TITLES AVAILABLE IN SOFTCOVER, EBOOK, AND DELUXE EXPANDED HARDCOVER EDITIONS

ROBERT DEIS AND WYATT DOYLE, SERIES EDITORS

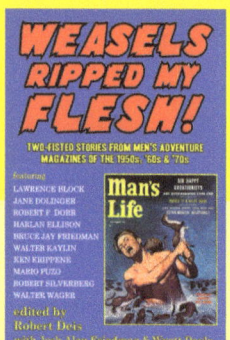

Weasels Ripped My Flesh!
With guest editor Josh Alan Friedman
Featuring Lawrence Block, Robert F. Dorr, Harlan Ellison, Bruce Jay Friedman, Walter Kaylin, Mario Puzo, Robert Silverberg *and more.*

From the jungles to the deserts to the mean city streets, the men's adventure magazines of the 1950s, '60s and '70s left no male fantasy or interest unexplored. War stories, exotic adventure yarns, (allegedly) true, first-hand accounts of white-knuckle clashes between man and beast, and spicy tales of sadistic frauleins and tropical queens hungry for companionship…plus salacious exposés of then-shocking subjects like free love, the Beat Generation, LSD, homosexuality, and the secret horniness hidden in calypso lyrics. This definitive guide to MAM fiction is your passport to a gonzo world where manly men fought small mammals bare-handed!

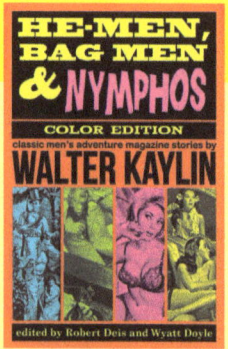

He-Men, Bag Men, & Nymphos
Stories by Walter Kaylin

Leaving an indelible mark on three decades of sweat-soaked pulp fiction, Walter Kaylin tackled testosterone-fueled subjects from Westerns to war, secret agents to sex sirens, Nazis to noir. His frequently over-the-top plots and characters scaled new heights of ingenuity and invention, while setting the standard for the kind of unapologetic savagery and excess that made men's adventure magazines notorious, then and now. Includes reminiscences by Kaylin, his family, and his former editor, writer Bruce Jay Friedman.

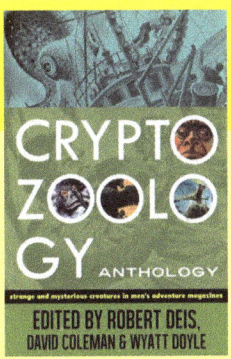

Cryptozoology Anthology
With guest editor David Coleman
Featuring Arthur C. Clarke, John Keel *and others*

When American men had questions about the Yeti, the Loch Ness Monster, Bigfoot, and other weird beasts from the strange world of cryptozoology, they found answers in the hard-hitting pages of men's adventure magazines. Here are samples of sensational period reporting and wild, "true" accounts of savage, fist-to-claw duels between man and Sasquatch, man and fishman, man and monster! Plus full-color vintage pulp artwork that accompanied the stories' original publication, rare archival discoveries, men's pulp history, expert analysis by crypto authority **David Coleman**, cryptid-by-cryptid commentary, and much, much more. Don't leave civilization without it!

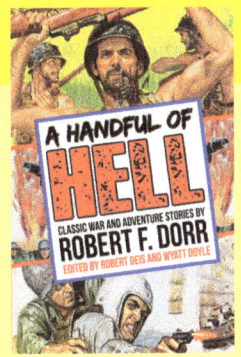

A Handful of Hell
Stories by Robert F. Dorr

Aviator, diplomat, and historian, Robert F. Dorr was uniquely qualified to write for men's adventure magazines, bringing sweat-and-blood, nuts-and-bolts authenticity to his stories of risk, combat, and sacrifice. Vivid, gripping tales of aerial conflict, battlefield heroism and action—some fact, some fiction, all adrenaline-fueled, white-knuckle adventure from one of the genre's greatest voices.

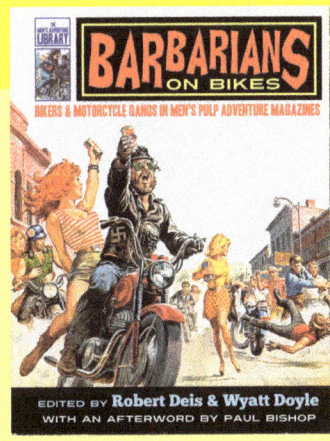

Barbarians on Bikes
Afterword by Paul Bishop

An oversized color collection compiling three decades of motorcycle-themed magazine covers and interior spreads from the 1950s through the 1970s, most unseen since their original publication. Biker illustration art at its most savage. A biker movie between covers, **Barbarians on Bikes** is big, bad, and untamed… Think you can handle the ride?

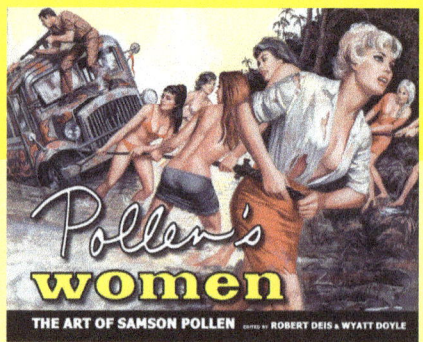
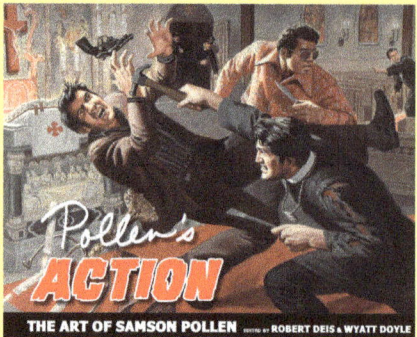

The Art of Samson Pollen
Pollen's Women
Pollen's Action
Pollen in Print 1955–1959

A series of lush visual archives collecting some of artist Samson Pollen's most memorable pieces, selected from the hundreds of jaw-dropping illustrations he provided for men's adventure magazines (MAMs) from the 1950s through the 1970s. Pollen was equally celebrated for his abilities to effectively render action and movement, as well as his gift for painting beautiful and dangerous women. Illustrating work from authors like Mario Puzo, Martin Cruz Smith, Richard Stark (Donald Westlake), Norman Mailer, Ed McBain, Richard Wright, Don Pendleton, Erskine Caldwell, Walter Kaylin, and Robert F. Dorr, Pollen's immersive illustrations transported adventure-hungry readers from tropical jungles to brutal battlefields to raging seas and mean city streets. Samson Pollen painted it all—spectacularly. Yet almost none of these stunning illustrations have seen print since their original publication. Until now.

Both **Pollen's Women** and **Pollen's Action** are drawn from the artist's own exhaustive archives of his original artwork for MAMs, while **Pollen in Print 1955–1959** is the inaugural volume of a projected series presenting his artwork chronologically as it appeared in the magazines, allowing us to fill gaps in Pollen's archive and definitively chart the trajectory of a remarkable career.

All three big 11" x 8.5" horizontal volumes include the late artist's reminiscences and autobiographical comments.

Eva: Men's Adventure Supermodel
by Eva Lynd

Blonde Swedish countess Eva Lynd's multi-faceted career touches every aspect of 20th century popular culture. A model for leading illustration artists and top glamour and pin-up photographers of the era, she also appeared with some of the biggest names in entertainment on both the big and small screens. Eva shares her story in her own words and pictures. Includes artwork from pulp masters such as Norm Eastman, Al Rossi, Mike Ludlow, and James Bama.

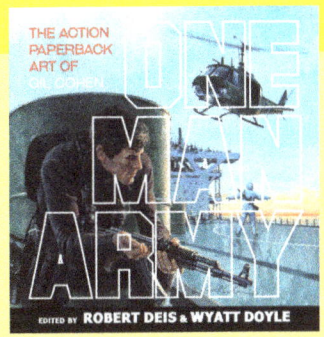

One Man Army *by* Gil Cohen

Exploring the incomparable talent of Gil Cohen via the unique perspective he brought to the Mack Bolan universe as one of **The Executioner** series' most celebrated cover artists. **One Man Army** showcases Cohen's spectacular and original paintings for the bestselling action paperbacks, chronicling his seminal role in establishing the Bolan mythos for millions of dedicated readers worldwide.

Mort Künstler: The Godfather of Pulp Fiction Illustrators

Celebrated for his ability to present large-scale action while never losing sight of essential details, **Mort Künstler** is a master of capturing conflict in paint—both its spectacle, and human cost. At last, here is a stunning selection of his finest pieces from the MAM era in this long awaited collection. A close study of an unequaled career, every page explodes with action, color, and artistry.

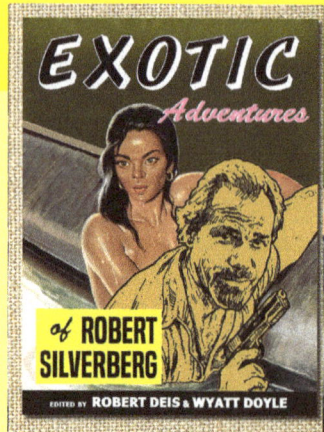

Exotic Adventures of Robert Silverberg

From safari to bordello, from smugglers' cove to opium den, Robert Silverberg's lost pulp exotica returns to print for the first time since its original 1950s publication, presented in bold new facsimile re-creations that look fresh off the newsstand, circa 1958. Strap in for fully illustrated globe-trotting adventures from the vivid imagination of one of speculative fiction's most honored talents, working incognito.

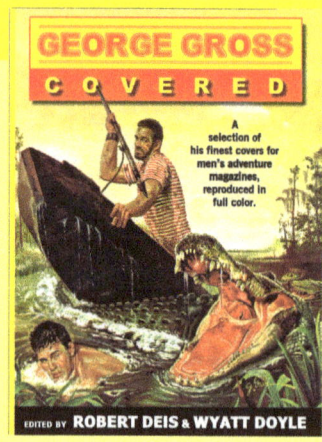

George Gross: Covered

A top artist for pulps, men's adventure magazines, and paperback covers, George Gross's artwork spans decades, and helped establish a visual vocabulary for action/adventure and hard-boiled fiction. A unique talent who led the way for generations of artists, his imagery continues to inspire and influence. Spotlighting dozens of his memorable covers, this full-color collection includes contributions by historian David Saunders and artist Mort Künstler.

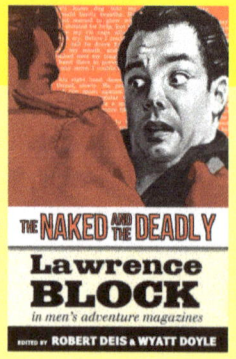

The Naked and the Deadly
Stories by Lawrence Block

Spicy detective stories, international intrigue, and bedroom secrets… Before the bestsellers, Block cut his teeth on MAM fiction and nonfiction articles, collected here in their complete and uncut versions for the first time since their original publication. Includes a new introduction by the author.

SOFTCOVER AND EXPANDED HARDCOVER EDITIONS AVAILABLE

ROBERT DEIS AND WYATT DOYLE, SERIES EDITORS

I Watched Them Eat Me Alive
Killer Creatures in Men's Adventure Magazines

Cuba: Sugar, Sez, and Slaughter
Cuba and Castro in Men's Adventure Magazines

Maneaters
Killer Sharks in Men's Adventure Magazines

The Men's Adventure Library Journal is a bold and explosive annex of The Men's Adventure Library, devoted to deep dives into some of MAMs' most popular and potent subjects. Titles include **I Watched Them Eat Me Alive**, a hot appetizer sampler of killer creature survival stories; **Cuba: Sugar, Sex, and Slaughter**, presenting MAM fact and fiction centered on Castro and the Cuba in the 1960s; and **Maneaters**, a savage collection of terrifying shark fiction and illustration art paired with mythbusting by contemporary shark experts, including contributions by **Shark Week** creator **Steve Cheskin** and sharkfilm director **Ace Hannah**. All are available in softcover and expanded hardcover editions featuring additional content.

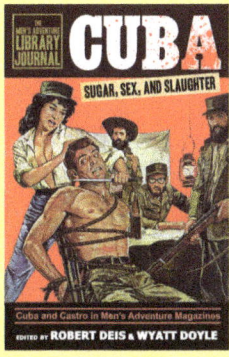
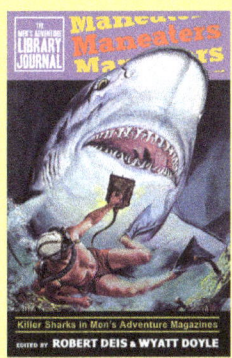

www.ingramcontent.com/pod-product-compliance
Lightning Source LLC
Chambersburg PA
CBHW041323110526
44592CB00021B/2798